INNOVATIVE PLANNING FOR
ELECTRONIC COMMERCE AND ENTERPRISES:
A Reference Model

INNOVATIVE PLANNING FOR
ELECTRONIC COMMERCE AND ENTERPRISES:
A Reference Model

by

Cheng Hsu
Rensselaer Polytechnic Institute
Troy, New York 12180-3590

and

Somendra Pant
Clarkson University
Potsdam, New York 13676

Kluwer Academic Publishers
Boston/Dordrecht/London

Distributors for North, Central and South America:
Kluwer Academic Publishers
101 Philip Drive
Assinippi Park
Norwell, Massachusetts 02061 USA
Telephone (781) 871-6600
Fax (781) 871-6528
E-Mail <kluwer@wkap.com>

Distributors for all other countries:
Kluwer Academic Publishers Group
Distribution Centre
Post Office Box 322
3300 AH Dordrecht, THE NETHERLANDS
Telephone 31 78 6392 392
Fax 31 78 6546 474
E-Mail <orderdept@wkap.nl>

 Electronic Services <http://www.wkap.nl>

Library of Congress Cataloging-in-Publication

Hsu, Cheng, 1951-
    Innovative planning for electronic commerce and enterprises : a reference model
    / by Cheng Hsu and Somendra Pant.
        p. cm.
    Includes bibliographical references and index.
    ISBN 0-7923-8437-7
    1. Electronic commerce--Case studies. 2. Electronic commerce--Planning. I.
Pant, Somendra. II. Title.

HF5548.32.H78 2000
658.8'4--dc21

                                        99-049947

Printed on acid-free paper.

Printed in the United States of America

To Diana and Shilpa

CONTENTS

PREFACE

We learned about the Industrial Revolution from textbooks. We saw documentaries about Andrew Carnegie, Alexander Bell, and Henry Ford on the History Channel. Now, we find the boy next door, Bill Gates, climbing to the same historical stature right under our noses. Emerging industrial giants of the same caliber are all over the map. We are eyewitnesses of the Information Revolution. We were unbelievers when the Mainframes and Minis came about. We were skeptical when the acronym PC became a household word. We cried foul when industries poured all kinds of money into any kind of "the information thing" - where is the payoff? We (including Bill Gates) thought we had everything figured out just when the World Wide Web was knocking on our doors. Then, we are sure that e-commerce - or e-business, or e-service, or e-economy, or e-corporate, or e-city, or e-society, or e-warfare - is just about doing business on the Internet; or are we? We might as well wonder a little more - why did the computer come to the U.S. first? Why the PC did not go to the rivalries in late 1970's and early 1980's? Why the Internet and the Web community in 1990's followed a similar path of diffusion? Why is e-commerce emerging from the grass roots, again, in the same manner as the string of inventions that changed the world in past decades? Is there any inherent relationship between the democratization of a people and an information revolution - and is the relationship causal in both directions?

We are interested in e-commerce. We are interested in its ability to create wealth, to improve the institution of capitalism, and to renew the democracy of the global village. However, the authors wrote this book only to humbly propose a planning model for developing strategic goals for e-commerce enterprises. We might sometimes be provocative in the book, but we have the sense to opinionate that no one really knows how to plan an innovative e-commerce enterprise that definitely works and makes money. We just try to provide a framework of a structured search for such plans. Therefore, the book has three parts. The first part is the planning model and a methodology to use the model. The planning model is based on principles derived from the literature and the authors' past projects. The methodology also uses Value Chain Analysis to connect e-commerce goals with business processes. The second part evaluates the model and calibrates it to industrial cases as well as the established scholarly results in the field. The last part consists of three exploratory plans for some industrial applications, including supply chain integration, Internet banking, and customer service (ordering) for heavy industry. About fifty cases are discussed in the book at various degrees of depth. The three industrial cases illustrate how to apply the planning model using the methodology. They also supplement the model in the sense that they provide some generic plans for a few classes of common processes. Between the planning model (and methodology) and the industrial benchmarks, a reference model for e-commerce is obtained. We hope that the calibration with the literature has given the reference model some accountability.

The authors are indebted to many people who made the book possible. Dr. Hyun Taek Sim and Mr. Kwangsik Kim collaborated with the authors on two industrial cases; we owe them our sincere gratitude. We are also grateful to Mr. Gary Folven, editor of Kluwer Academic Publishers, for his patience and encouragement. Cheng Hsu would like to thank Dr. Daniel Berg, Dr. Gregory Hughes and Dr. James Tien of Rensselaer Polytechnic Institute; their support has been instrumental to his research on e-commerce. Somendra Pant would like to acknowledge the constant encouragement, love, and support of parents: Kiran and Harish, sister, Mini, brother-in-law, Jacob, brother, Pankaj, and friends: Betty, Harsh, Rajesh, Rishi, Lalit, Pradeep, and Suman who have been with him every step of the way, all the way. We also wish to express our gratitude to our colleagues at Rensselaer and Clarkson, including Drs. Boleslaw Szymanski, Faye Duchin, Jeffery Durgee, William A, Wallace and many others with whom the authors discussed their ideas. We regret that we cannot include all people who assisted the project in this brief acknowledgement. Ms. Michelle Wallace proofread the manuscript and, along with Ms. Barbara Clause, helped format the book; to Michelle and Barbara, we express many thanks.

Cheng Hsu
Somendra Pant

ELECTRONIC COMMERCE AND ENTERPRISES

Information technology did not generate the hypes of the new millennium. However, information technology has provided creditability to some of the hypes about the new millennium. A sensible question to ask is how solid is this creditability. Is the talk about the new economy (and the new society) of information revolution a reality or myth? The reality check seems dubious, many say. Most "dot com" companies are still losing money. Virtually all business Web sites still operate outside the core production functions of their businesses. For instance, the industrial leader Amazon.com still relies on the traditional mode of business to acquire its books and manage its inventory. So, what is so magic about the Internet and the Web or, for that matter, about the new information technology? How could any one possibly know that electronic commerce is the future? How could any economist justify the market's religious faith in Internet companies, running unabatedly through 1999? In 1998, the combined market capitalization of the top 25 standard-bearer Internet companies is 60 times their combined *revenue* of $5 billion (with a loss of $1 billion). In comparison, IBM has total revenue of $80 billion and market capitalization at 30 times its 1998 *profit*. Overall, the Internet industry in 1999 has accumulated in five years a value that is higher than what the automobile industry took a century to build. Is this not a classical case of over-evaluation? In fact, this big question is not new. Economists have been questioning the payoff for all the investment in information technology since 1970's. This is the famous Productivity Paradox question. There is still no conclusive answer to the question. However, we would like to provide a reasonable analysis to identify the promises and opportunities of the new information technology. We start with the information power in an attempt to examine the promises and limits of current practice of electronic commerce. We will then go beyond, to consider the whole enterprise and the promises of information technology for creating innovative enterprises.

1.   The Information Revolution: reduction of societal transaction cost.

Common sense tells us that information technology, in general, and Internet, in particular, is changing the way we go about our businesses. The schools, stores, companies, governments, and even our own households are embracing not only the computer but also the way of life that the computer affects. As the world enters the new millennium, a new information infrastructure is also emerging. In the U.S., 40% of households own a Personal Computer, a third of the population routinely use the Internet, and 75 million people use cellular telephone that eventually could be connected to the computer. The statistics are getting more staggering every day. It is hard to deny that a silent revolution is going on in our society. There is a simple explanation for the revolution. That is, information technology makes our life easier.

The driving force of this sea change is the power of information technology to reduce transaction cost in all aspects of our society. It reduces transaction cost for institutions (businesses and non-business organizations) to reach customers and to acquire materials or services from other institutions. It also reduces transaction cost for an enterprise to simplify its business processes and speed up its production cycles. More profoundly, it reduces transaction cost for we the people to live our own lives.

The best example of transaction cost and how it shapes productivity in one's life and the economy is the Dollar. The Dollar is a currency. It is also a currency that virtually all countries accept at its face value. People take the first statement for granted and hardly appreciate its "convenience" - i.e., its magic power to reduce transaction cost. However, let us remind ourselves of the barter system and see what an inhibiting transaction cost there would be. Imagine someone trying to trade 10 (empty) bottles for a copy of New York Times that is worth 50 cents. Although each bottle has a deposit of 5 cents on it and, hence, 10 bottles can claim a value of 50 cents, no news stand owner would accept this trade. The problem is obvious: the owner cannot give these bottles as change to another buyer who hands over a dollar bill. No one could use these bottles as s/he can with two quarters. Besides the obvious "inconvenience" of carrying bottles (another part of the transaction cost), someone must first transact to turn them in at a store that accepts bottle returning before anyone can claim the value of 50 cents. There is a real transaction cost involved in terms of effort in trading these bottles. The currency reduces the cost to nil. Try to imagine a society or an economy where every one must transact by using bottles, clothes, wooden chairs, dental works, mechanical labor and so on. Transaction cost is the difference between exchanging with currency and bartering. Transaction cost is, therefore, the basic reason why all civilizations use currency and is also the reason why a currency-based economy is more productive than a bartering economy. It follows easily that any economy that reduces transaction cost improves productivity, and any society that reduces transaction cost improves its quality of life. The second statement about Dollar that it is universally accepted is also often overlooked. Dollar's status as the global currency gives important direct advantage to U.S. companies doing international trading. They do not need to convert their accounting, pricing, costing, and a number of other business matters into another currency in order to transact, benchmark, and compete. Companies in other countries need to do that. How important is this saving on transaction cost for the U.S. economy? Just ask European countries that are converting to a single currency Euro. The European Community moved mountains of obstacle so that its member countries can reap the benefit of a pan-EC currency to boost their economies. The Dollar is already pan-world for businesses.

Anyone who has tried to search for information without using the Web knows the meaning - and value - of transaction cost, too. People can now easily and quickly find out application details about many boarding schools, summer programs, and local activities almost anywhere in the U.S., all in the comfort of their own home or workplace, using the Web. Try to imagine how much time, effort, and money they must otherwise spend to achieve the same results. Similarly, consider how difficult it is for individuals and small vendors to find buyers for their commodities without using any Internet marketplace (e.g., eBay), or to locate the best providers of the goods and services they want. In this sense, every user of Yahoo! and other portal sites is a living testimony to the significance of transaction cost and transaction cost reduction. All these examples illustrate transaction cost and its essential role in modern economy. All these examples also show how information technology improves productivity and effects a new economy, through reducing transaction cost. Therefore, we could infer that any new information technology must **reduce transaction cost, in the acquisition of pertinent information and/or the conduct of the actual businesses (internal and external)**, to become relevant. This overarching principle should guide the development, employment, and deployment of any new information products and systems. From an enterprise's perspective, Mr. Bill Gates' notion of a digital nervous system, which avails executive level information to all members of the enterprise, pushes for the former (information). Many various enterprise integration technologies such as supply chain integration, concurrent engineering, and virtual manufacturing focus on the latter (enterprise transaction). In the latter case, information technology enables the enterprise to share its information resources and shorten its sequential transaction cycles. Together, the enterprise will be capable of tightening up all its strategic planning, product development, production, and delivery functions to achieve optimal performance. The integration can extend to including the enterprise's external constituencies, such as customer, supplier, vender, and dealer. The integration can also reach the whole industry, forming an industrial information infrastructure of operation. The immediate result of integration is the improvement on productivity and quality, made possible by the reduction of the transaction cost involved. These practices and visions put the enterprises at the center of inspiration and control. An interesting thing to observe for the new society in the new millennium is how soon the enterprise information technology will find its way into developing personal information products and systems for the personal well being of we the people. This new perspective promises to open up innovative ideas and opportunities.

The previous Productivity Paradox that questions the payoff of investment on technology has shown signs of resolution lately. The annual productivity growth of the U.S. economy has reached 2% since the early 1990's. This level is a 100% jump from the prevailing level in the preceding two to three decades. Mr. Alan Greenspan, Chairperson of the Federal Reserve Board, has prominently cited this new reality in his congressional testimonies in 1999 as a piece of evidence that perhaps the economy has indeed entered a new age driven by information technology. The productivity of capital is another dimension of the possible resolution that information technology might have ushered in a new economy. A 1996 McKinsey Global Institute's report (in collaboration with the World Bank) has discovered an important, previously under-noticed facet of the U.S. economy in comparison with those of Germany and Japan. The study used a new measure to compare the economical effect of capital investment in three countries, the U.S., Germany, and Japan. Its finding is shocking. The capital productivity in the U.S. is roughly 50% higher than the other two countries whose figures are similar. That is, money works harder for the U.S. Although this conclusion helps explain the puzzle of how the low savings rate of the U.S. can sustain her high economical growth, it raises more questions. Economists attribute the result to macro-economical policies such as de-regulation, pro-business tax code and the like that the U.S. has enacted relative to Germany and Japan. Others credited institutional factors including welfare-to-work and organizational mobility. We, however, would like to recognize a single factor of transaction cost reduction through investment on information technology. The 1996 report is the first study of its kind. Thus, we can neither prove nor disprove this assertion. Our logic, however, is quite simple. Other factors, policy and institutional, seem to be stable - i.e., the relative position of the U.S. with respect to Germany and Japan on these factors have been largely consistent during these countries' industrialization, at least in this century. The U.S. has always been freer - or less socialized - than Germany and Japan (some Japanese scholars consider the Japanese style of organization a special form of socialism). Have the three countries' relative positions of capital productivity stayed the same throughout the period, until the advent of the modern computer? Has the U.S. improved its position since she invented - and pervasively adopted - information technology? The "information" gap or, more precisely, the "transaction cost gap" between the U.S. and Germany and Japan seems to be widening all the time since early 1980's. If this observation is not entirely wrong, then we would submit that the relative capital productivity in the U.S. was higher in 1996 than in the preceding decades, and it is getting even higher today. It follows that the situation will change only when Germany and Japan catch up with the U.S. in the information revolution. Catching up is, of course, entirely possible as the Internet leads the wave of change sweeping through the global village.

How profound is the change? Does the Internet - and more broadly, the information technology - truly deserve the laureate of the agent of change? The jury is in. There are at least 200 million Web sites that are usable by the global village (reachable through search engines) in 1999. All kinds of dictators, large and small, in all corners of the world are scrambling to try to hold on to their control and monopoly of information. From the perspective of change, the real story is not how many businesses are buying or selling on the Internet now. The real story is how quickly the World Wide Web has come into being as a global virtual community and how effortlessly the community has integrated with the global economy. It all started in 1993-1994 when Mosaic took off at the National Center for Supercomputer Applications, Urbana-Champaign, Illinois. People all over the world immediately embraced the open and public domain Mosaic system and used the home page as *the* universal, common user interface to share information. (This easy, common user interface for processing and retrieving all documents is itself a reduction of transaction cost, which previously was very significant thanking the difficulty to inter-operate among heterogeneous interfaces.) Nearly a million Web sites popped up in just a year, cutting across all stripes of life. All this happened strictly on a volunteer basis without any planning or control from any authority or industry. People who jumped into this ever-growing community are primarily ordinary folks and not the usual nerds. (Again, transaction cost in the form of learning new knowledge and acquiring new skills had kept ordinary people from using new information technology.) Then, Mosaic became Netscape and WWW became e-commerce. The rest is history. This infant history of only a handful of years has possibly turned up over 800 million Web sites worldwide and is expected to induct up to 400 million citizens of the global Cyber-community by 2002. The spontaneous and instantaneous expansion is nothing short of a big bang. One could say that after decades of the increasing use of computers, the society is finally primed for the pervasive adoption of information technology in life. Perhaps more accurately is to observe that after decades of development, the new information technology has finally ripened to tackle the problem of reducing transaction cost at a personal and societal level, as well as for enterprises.

The compelling question to ask now is where this revolution is leading the economy (and society) and what is in it for the citizens. A review of the power behind the revolution would help us better appreciate the scale of changes and the nature of these changes. We might then be able to answer the question more intelligently.

2. The Power of Information Technology and Systems

We might agree that the power of information technology stems from its ability to reduce transaction cost. However, then, what is this ability? Many scholars have studied transaction cost from the perspective of economics. Foremost of them include Professor Ronald H. Coase and Professor Oliver E. Williamson. What we intend to do here is to take a common sense approach and review the impact of information technology on transaction cost. We use the term transaction cost in a broad sense and interpret the concept intuitively.

To say that the computer saves transaction cost because it stores, retrieves, and processes vast amounts of data with ease is to state the obvious. However, the obvious sheds new light on the promises of information technology if we consider the implications at a *personal* level, not from the perspective of an enterprise as has always been the case. This personal perspective is actually more enlightening to illuminate the past, present, and future of the information revolution. The person is both a part and not a part of organization. The person has many roles beyond any formal organizations for which the previous economical studies of information technology or transaction cost have conducted. The person is a customer and a seller. The person is a parent and a child. The person is a teacher and a student. The person is a socialite and a loner. The person is an information consumer and provider. The person is public and private. The person is business and leisure. The person has unlimited roles as a constituent of the society. The information power is the added capacity that information technology affords the person to play *all these roles* better - to facilitate the person's acquisition of pertinent information and his/her actual conduct of the roles in the play. The work-related roles of a person are just a small part of the big picture; although, they have always been the focus. The big promise of information technology for reducing societal transaction cost goes beyond the organizational roles and reaches the rest that information technology has never before belonged. The person's other roles are the main drivers why people are attracted to the Internet. Business use then followed the person.

Modern information technology brings two basic capabilities to a person: extending his/her indigenous information processing capacity and physically connecting him/her to other persons and organizations. Again, this person could have many facets of which business is only one. The business aspects collectively give rise to enterprise information systems and previous business use of the Internet. However, the many other aspects represent the new opportunities for developing information technology to reduce the societal transaction cost.

Information technology extends our indigenous information processing capacity (for business or otherwise) in three basic ways. It first puts massive memory and computing power to the disposal of a person. It then couples this raw power with extensive decision and other information processing models. Finally, it makes both capabilities accessible to the person through ubiquitous interfaces at pervasive points of contact. A ready example is the notebook computer. The person can carry and use it anywhere and can also plug it into the network of many servers supporting transactions at many points. It is used in many aspects of a person's life. There are other examples, too. The ones that are emerging include personal digital assistants or palm-top computers, mobile phones combined with the Internet, and information appliances. We would also add to the list the future biological chips that perform the functions of today's Personal Computers. We might emphasize that the model of extension to a person's capacity identified above is *not* based on a stand-alone system such as a PC. In fact, the new information technology of the continuing information revolution has two salient characteristics. First, it is attached to a person (or, even, embedded to the person) in a mobile way; second, the embedded power can be joined across systems on the fly. Today's concept of networking computing or distributed computing already supports this model. When a person literally carries her/his (information processing) chips on her/his shoulder, the notion of extending human's indigenous capacity will reach a new height. With these extended capabilities, it is possible to integrate data and knowledge for a person as opposed to integrating them for organizations only. Currently, personal data that manifest people's existence in the society do not belong to the persons, nor are they integrated. The personal data are scattered in all kinds of organizations and in all kinds of format. A person has to move from system to system to obtain his/her data and to go from place to place to use them. This piece meal manner of handling one's life incurs significant transaction cost for one to live a holistic life. In addition, the new capabilities could also include decision aids to facilitate the person processing the data and knowledge for the person's best utility. The processing can take place at almost any point of contact the need arises. We can consider a number of scenarios how these capabilities might manifest themselves for a person on the job or at leisure. The basic fact that matters is that the new capabilities facilitate any situation where a person needs to acquire or process information that is not readily available. The savings on transaction cost are, therefore, the time, effort, and resources a person must consume to do the same without these added capabilities. To name a few specific examples, the integration of scattered files into database systems saves mainly the transaction cost on the searching and sharing of information, not the cost of paper. In a similar way, application systems save transaction cost through simplifying or empowering business processes, to which saving labor is only secondary. This is how information technology reduces transaction cost. The story does not stop here, however.

Information technology also connects a person to other persons and organizations. In other words, it joins the above extension to a person's indigenous power to the power of other persons and organizations through, presently, third party connection providers. The connection technology traditionally includes networking and telecommunications but is rapidly merging with computing and other technologies. Telecommunication companies such as AT&T has offered personal networks and personal telephone numbers that a person can carry anywhere s/he goes. Coupling this personal connection system with wireless palmtop computers and mobile or Internet telephones, the person has virtually unlimited access to all kinds of computing and information systems, personal and organizational alike. The significance of this connection is more than psychological. It is the basis on which persons conduct their business in life. The physical connection provides the means for persons to conduct transactions in some context, such as getting our workflow through, obtaining services, taking courses, or dating. Without connection through information technology, people need to travel some distance for a face to face meeting, talk over the telephone, collocate at the work place, or send hardcopies via some carriers. All these connecting activities are forms of transaction cost involved in the conduct of actual business. Therefore, information technology also enables a person to conduct actual business (physical transactions) via the extended network and, thereby, reduces transaction cost not only in the acquisition of information but also in the physical transactions. There are many contexts of the connection. When we consider a person as a worker, then the connection of persons (with added capabilities) gives rise to an integrated enterprise. The connection would, for instance, cover both digital nervous systems and enterprise resources planning. In a similar way, the connection of persons who belong to different organizations amounts to some integrated extended enterprise, such as supply chain integration and business-to-business e-commerce. There are many more types of connection for many more roles of a person's life. The connection of a person to organizations with which s/he does business is an integration of the person's information across these organizations (perhaps in certain domains). Each organization has its own (integrated) customer information, but the customer's own information that different organizations own deserves integration, too. The latter is a view for a whole person rather than the traditional view of a customer. The personal information is the whole of the many pieces of scattered customer information pertaining to the same person. Furthermore, the connection of persons outside work or business contributes directly to the democracy of the society. The connection of persons outside any organizations is the realm of family, friendship and all kinds of personal relationships. When information technology reduces transaction cost in the connection of persons and organizations for business, it is capable of the same for personal life, too. Just like telephone improves our relationship and, hence, our quality of life, the connected "chips" of our information processing capacity links persons closer throughout the global village. The ubiquitous and scalable networking technology available today already made this prospect close to reality. The continuing progress would certainly imbue new fundamental models. In this sense, the present Web community is but a harbinger for the upcoming all-dimensional connection.

The supply always follows the demand. Thus, a number of possible categories of e-commerce - or more generally, Internet enterprises (including government and non-profit enterprises) become apparent from the above analysis. Each type of connection will breed certain categories of business opportunities. There will also be opportunities for the providers of technology or solutions required by the connections and opportunities for the services of these connections. Some of the connection types have already produced particular classes of e-commerce or Internet enterprises. Others are bound to emerge as we enter the new millennium. The logic is, again, simple: the connections are always what the people want, but deprived of us due to inhibiting transaction cost. Now that the new information technology has lowered the threshold and put them within our reach, they will happen.

3. Electronic Commerce.

E-commerce accounts for 6.5% of the Gross Domestic Product of the U.S. in 1998-99. It should reach 15% within a couple of years. Coupled with the information technology (manufacturing) industry itself, the information sector will become the largest of the GDP. Its anti-inflation nature will certainly add to the overall strength of the economy keeping inflation at bay. This sector is full of misconceptions, however. To many people, e-commerce is Internet-based commerce, or the business use of the Internet. This view is correct but incomplete. Although Internet and its successors probably will remain a key element of any kind of e-commerce, other elements of personal extension and connection that we discussed above will play a key role, too. In some cases, the Internet might even be secondary to other elements, such as when there are other ways to connect persons and organizations, in addition to broadband connection. The deciding factor is only the particular technology's ability to reduce transaction cost. (We really cannot over-emphasize this point.) E-commerce is the best and fullest use of information technology to date to reduce the transaction cost that is inherent in the traditional way of doing commerce/business. This is the reason why e-commerce has exploded so quickly, and there can be no turning back down the road. E-commerce might fade away in its own success as better and more powerful applications of information technology emerged from its achievements, but it would be its expansion and not its demise. We submit that there are two pairs of concepts helpful for analyzing the paths of e-commerce: acquisition of *information* vs. conduct of actual (business/production) *transactions*. The second pair is connection of *persons* vs. connection of *organizations*. We might also mention that we interpret e-commerce broadly, to include such notions as e-business, e-enterprise, and Internet enterprises. The other notions usually highlight more activities than the narrowly defined commerce *per se*. In a broad sense, however, they all belong in the same family.

3.1 Business-to-Customer E-Commerce.

The most visible class of e-commerce is business-to-customer e-commerce, which is essentially retailing on the Internet. There are three types of Web sites involved. The first is company retailing sites, such as Charles Schwab, Barnes &. Nobel, and Dell Computer, which conduct direct sales using the Web (comparable to the retailing channel of factory outlets or branches/franchises). The second is domain portal sites such as WebMD, Expedia, and Amazon.com, doing retailing in a certain industry (comparable to the channel of dealers, retailing stores, and department stores). Then, there are general portal sites such as Yahoo!, AOL, and Go.com, providing retailing contacts for companies and sellers (comparable to marketplaces, shopping malls, and business districts). This class excels on the connection of organizations to persons from the businesses' perspective. Many sites focus on providing information - or facilitating the acquisition of information for persons. Those that cover transactions tend to focus on facilitating selling *per se* - or customers' purchasing transactions and do not extend to their internal business processes. Thus, this class of e-commerce does not necessarily represent the full use of the promises of information technology for reducing transaction cost. Because it focuses on direct sale, there is clearly a threshold of users (or buyers) below which business-to-customer e-commerce would not fly. No one really knows what this threshold is in terms of patronage on the Internet, but in the U.S., 1997 seems to be the year e-commerce took off. The Internet statistics of that year could offer good insights. Then, there is the factor of anticipation. Enterprises in other countries would have all the reasons in the world to believe that what happened in the U.S. will also happen soon in their countries, in the age of the Internet. Thus, companies might be willing to pioneer and, hence, push the threshold lower.

Internet retailing has established itself within just a few years. Economic statistics in the U.S. in 1999 shows buying on the Internet is already a part of people's daily life. For example, one in five persons have purchased something over the

Internet, and 50% of travelers have used e-tickets. Charles Schwab does more than 60% of its trading through its Web site, with a volume exceeding $10 billion a week. Stanford University has established a virtual university that delivers higher education over the Internet - using distance learning. Tens of thousands of small businesses have used eBay to sell their commodities. The combined revenue of Internet retailing is estimated to reach $20 billion by the end of 1999, rising from $8 billion in 1998, and nearly zero a couple of years before that. However, we need to look beyond. Would this growth mean that Internet retailing (or all forms of distance retailing for that matter) is poised to overtake the traditional face to face retailing and make the latter out of business some day? What is the impact of this class of e-commerce on traditional companies and, hence, on our economy and society?

We will try to contemplate the second question first since it follows naturally from our previous analysis about transaction cost. The first question involves human nature and hence is not that clean to ponder. The magic of the Internet is really its power to function as a marketing and distribution channel for *everyone*. Distribution typically accounts for about 40% of total operating cost for a traditional company such as General Electric and Citigroup. Traditional companies invest heavily on their distribution channels, consisting typically of a myriad of wholesalers and retailers. These channels are not easy to establish over a short time period. They need to be nurtured, developed, and accumulated over time. This is the reason why distribution channels are a major competitive advantage that established companies enjoy over their upstart competitors. Just imagine some one having invented the best mousetrap in the world and trying to reach its potential customers all over the world. It is extremely costly to advertise for the global market, let alone to put the products where the customers can see and buy. The person needs either to set up the global channel or to hire someone else who owns or has access to the channel. Virtually all the cost incurred in this effort is attributable to transaction cost. Now, all of a sudden the Internet came like a gift from the heavens. The seller no longer needs to worry about the distribution channel. The Web site can put the product at every cyber citizen's fingertip to view and purchase. The common carriers such as postal services will do the rest. So, between the Internet and the carriers, every person has the *global* distribution channel at his/her disposal while only the global companies were able to do so in the past. In fact, any person could develop a Web site that looks and feels like the Web sites of industrial giants - and practically works like one. The mousetrap inventor could rival General Electric when it comes to Web site design, functionality, and professionalism. The open and public Web community that imposes only negligible transaction cost to all citizens to use is, in this sense, an equalizer of businesses, large and small. It allows everyone who is willing to do it become a competitor to any companies in the global marketplace. New ventures, especially those providing (information) services, become more feasible for entrepreneurs to set up and operate. Small companies have unprecedented opportunity to compete and grow. Established big corporations face healthy competition as well as new incentive to innovate and leverage their resources for improvement. Coupling this low transaction cost global distribution channel with the low transaction cost information availability over the Internet, what emerges from e-commerce is an economy where Adam Smith's perfect competition gets closer to being a reality. Recent human history has proven vividly that a free economy based on competition gives flexibility and mobility to the society. The impact of the Internet and its successors is nothing short of effecting a highly democratized economy and society. We will discuss more of this point in the last section of the chapter.

The question of whether or not traditional face to face retailing will disappear in the face of Internet and other distance retailing is hard to answer objectively. We might, however, consider a telling case; i.e., distance learning. Is our society ready to accept a virtual university for educating our next generation? How many parents are willing to send their kids to a virtual university? Many might say that the thought of having your children living with you for the rest of their adult life is enough to kill this idea. Just consider the significance of summer camps for parents who want a little bit of their own lives during the summer. However, the matter deserves some serious thinking. Why do we have the institution of universities in the first place? Is learning advanced knowledge the sole purpose of going to college? If the answer is positive, then it follows that who are we to prejudge that the student cannot learn as well remotely from a virtual university - or, for that matter, from a home college? The question suddenly becomes one that can be analyzed objectively, comparing pedagogy, courseware, educational psychology, and so on. However, learning knowledge most likely is not the only main purpose for going to college. There is the purpose of socialization, to know one's peers, to make friends with them, and to network professionally. Growing and maturing are critical aspects of schooling, one that many might consider more important than the aspect of taking courses itself. When this aspect is introduced into the pondering, then the picture is no longer finite. One could argue reasonably that distance learning would be good for mature students who either come back to school after many years of working experiences or are working full time while taking courses in a school. In this case, the same argument for e-commerce works fully for virtual universities. The savings on transaction cost for mature students could be enormous; it could spell the difference between being able to attend school or not. It follows that one, therefore, would argue for adopting Internet-based learning as the mode of education for graduate schools. Yet, one could also counter many more arguments showing the need of social networking even for mature students. Every one knows the value of social networking in professional life. There are many professional programs designed expressly for mature working students to network. In science, the sense of peers is also crucial to one's career. Is Internet learning really up to the job of learning teamwork, group dynamics, and a sense of community? The only safe answer for now seems to be the usual compromise: yes, both modes are important for what they do best. Likely, the virtual universities will, at best, co-exist with the traditional universities at all levels of learning. Some programs might favor one over the other, but we do not expect the traditional campus to disappear any time soon, if ever. Does this case shed any light on Internet retailing in general? Do we also have a "social" dimension in retailing? This question may be subtle, but deadly real. We submit that the answer is yes. Perhaps no one can prove it, but the trust and craving for personal touch in transactions seems to be a part of human nature. Just consider the prediction a few decades ago that paper money would disappear in the face of check, debit or credit card, and electronic versions of fund. Paper money is still well and alive today, as robust as it has ever been, amid the increasing use of other forms of money. People have also predicted the demise of paper books, pad papers, paper notes and reports, paper newspapers and magazines, and much more. In the end of the day, we see computer files and Web sites co-exist with hardcopies. Television and VCR did not wipe out movie theaters, or Broadway. Word processors did not make a pencil a thing of past, even for professional writers. Are these harbingers enough to foretell a co-existent world for both Internet retailing and traditional retailing? Consequently, the million-dollar question seems to be how to sort out the mixed bag and how to tell which classes of retailing will go Internet and which will not? Perhaps people have learned to be humble before a question like this.

The next question, however, would be possible to figure out. Why do many business-to-customer Web sites lose money? A simple version of the answer is because they focus on information and do not conduct enough business transactions. As we mentioned before, the culture of the cyber community is volunteerism. Its life is the value that Web community provides in the form of information sharing. There is little tolerance for charging user fees for information. In fact, the irony is if this free flow and provision of information is taken away, the vitality of the Web community might go with it and, hence, greatly reduce its value for e-commerce. We will discuss this point more in the next chapter. Therefore, a Web site cannot rely on information services to earn its bread and butter. A business-to-customer e-commerce enterprise that does not facilitate users conducting some business transactions would have difficulty developing enough revenue-generating business for itself. To be sure, there are two basic types of lynchpin for an information-focused Web site to generate revenue: selling customer base and value-added information services. The viewer database can make money in more than one way, including advisement and database marketing for other companies who want to tap into the customer base. However, experiences show that this form of business is dubious. The free, public domain information could pave the way to proprietary information or related information services. The challenge is the reliability and scale of market might be tenuous because of competition. Besides, the value of information to customers is not easy to justify or predict in many cases. The real opportunity still would come primarily from offering value to facilitate the customer's actual transactions, such as purchasing and after-sale services. This practice might have to be expanded to include as many types of transactions as possible in order to turn a profit. Therefore, we must examine the other side of the profit problem, that is, the cost. The e-commerce enterprise needs to generate enough revenue, but it also needs to lower its operating cost. In other words, the enterprise ought to apply e-commerce to re-engineer its own business (including production) processes and reduce its transaction cost. Many retailing sites still operate internally in the traditional mode of business. When the revenue generation of an e-commerce is stalling, yet its cost side enjoys no advantages, losing money is not a wonder but inevitable. This point, applying e-commerce to an enterprise itself, leads its way into the next class of e-commerce.

3.2 Business-to-Business E-Commerce.

Business to business trading over the Internet is actually the majority of e-commerce practice; although, it is less glorious in terms of popularity. This class of e-commerce focuses on actual business transactions and the connection of organizations. It includes two basic types of Web sites: company sites for a company's particular group of business partners and marketplace sites for companies to conduct their business-to-business e-commerce. The first type, in essence, is a continuation of the decades-long trend of enterprise integration, except that its current practices concentrate on the procurement and supply processes. In this sense, these business sites are similar to Internet retailing sites other than the fact that their customers are other businesses, not individual consumers. The second type, which is comparable to portal sites in Internet retailing, aims at the business community at large (e.g., CommerceOne). They consist of industrial clearing houses, cyber trade shows, and various service providers. The current concentration on procurement and supply is natural and makes perfect sense since the Internet offers ready connection for businesses at minimal transaction cost. The Internet, in fact, represents a heaven-sent gift to many businesses that were using more costly alternatives for the same purpose at the time the business use of Internet emerged. The standing challenge for many companies using this simple model is how to continue expanding the practice. Otherwise, the business-to-business e-commerce model would still face many of the same limitations that make many Internet retailing enterprises lose money. By the same token that the Internet is not just for free information mining, the Internet is not just for cheap electronic data/document flows either. It, when joined with other enterprise information technology, is a potent productivity tool for the whole enterprise to achieve information-enabled integration of its business transaction cycles.

The predecessors of business-to-business class of e-commerce include the venerable models of Electronic Data Interchange (EDI) using proprietary third party Value Added Network (VAN) for paperless business procurement. Many incompatible, proprietary protocols are involved in these systems. Thus, it is costly to develop and run the systems required. It is a small wonder then that the EDI/VAN practice has been a profit generator for big businesses and prime companies, as opposed to being a service tool for contractors and suppliers. These proprietary systems soon melt away like snow under the sun when the universal Web interface technology and the Internet came about. A telling example is the joint venture between Wal-Mart and Warner-Lambert, which in late 1990's developed a Web-based supply chain to link the two companies (retailer and manufacturer) and their respective retailers and manufactures. However, the incompatibility of EDI protocols still requires significant technical solutions for the integration of systems and information objects at the application software level. The joint venture had to provide a solution library to its participants. In general, lacking an open protocol has been a major factor inhibiting companies from freely joining and leaving an otherwise truly open market of electronic procurement. This is an illustration for the kind of new technologies that business-to-business e-commerce entails, in the way of enterprise integration. CommerceOne, for example, is devoted to developing integration technology to inter-operate among protocols and replace the previous EDI practice. IBM, Oracle, Hewlett-Packard and many other information technology vendors are also racing to develop required technologies based on their established results for enterprise integration. Another forerunner of the use of the Internet for businesses is the practice of Intranet and extranet. Both models represent company Web sites designed for internal employee use. The difference is that while Intranet is for use within the company's own boundaries, extranet is for the use of an extended enterprise (still internal to the extended enterprise defined). Both tend to focus on information for their intended employees and usually do not emphasize workflow and other enterprise transactions. EDI/VAN and internal Web sites were soon merged to become the backbone of the majority of today's business-to-business e-commerce after the business use of the Internet took off in late 1990's.

Business-to-business e-commerce raked in $43 billion in 1998 and is expected to reach $1.3 trillion by the end of 2003. Therefore, its scale is many times larger than Internet retailing. This is not surprising since most of the commercial activities take place in the stages of the production stream that precede the final stage of retailing. However, it has other fundamental differences from business-to-customer e-commerce, too. From the perspective of its impact on the economy and the society, replacing EDI/VAN with the Web and Internet is not as revolutionary. The reason is that businesses tend to do business with a limited number of other businesses, on a highly selective basis, while businesses want to do business with an unlimited number of customers on a random basis. Therefore, the sea change in this field is more a controlled process than a spontaneous explosion that took place in business-to-customer e-commerce. Its impact is predictable, is evolutionary, is yet another phase in the never-ending process of enterprises' striving for ever-bettering performance. However, its impact is still growing and promises to continue to grow until sweeping the whole economy. The driving force is the collaboration among organizations, or extended enterprises, to reduce transaction cost and create innovative information products. Just consider a vision that Banc One and several other banking institutions developed in early 1990's to assist their customers integrating their financial information and some transactions, but did not implement. The will to overcome inter-organizational barriers was, of course, a pivotal factor in a vision like this one. Yet, technically speaking, a major problem facing these companies at the time was clearly the fact that they lacked an easy, scalable, and most of all, inexpensive means to connect organizations and customers. They had to require the customers to go to the banks to use the system. The same idea would be more feasible today given the Internet. We expect the practice of business-to-business e-commerce to become standard for all enterprises before it moves ahead to the next milestone. We also expect that the previous Intranet and extranet practices to get deepened and broadened to become the standard enterprise workflow management system. This system will be further integrated with other enterprise systems such as enterprise resources planning, concurrent engineering and computer-integrated manufacturing to improve the enterprise's basic core production processes. This extended model will couple with Internet procurement and supply chain management to result in an integrated environment for the entire extended enterprise from customers to vendors. This is the natural way and the only way the cost side of the profit equation can continue to improve. The basic business-to-business e-commerce in this broad sense might not generate huge revenues by itself, but it will create what it counts most, that is, competitive advantage in cost and productivity. Some enterprises might create core competence in this field as they excel in the practice. The basic practice can lead to more advanced ideas promising new businesses, though. The key here is to develop innovative opportunities that do not exist without extended enterprising.

Both classes, business-to-customer and business-to-business, currently face a bottleneck in their way of turning their e-commerce practice into new profit. As we discussed above, the bottleneck is due to two limits in their practices; namely, the bias towards information (i.e., lack of functions for conducting business transactions) and the bias towards setting up separate e-commerce entities. Both limits stem from the same root cause: the e-commerce enterprises alienated their e-commerce plans and processes from the traditional plans and processes. Many e-commerce companies created a dual system: one is for e-commerce based on the Internet, the other for the "regular" commerce. The e-commerce entities are kind of a profit center external to the regular, traditional enterprises and even being kept at an arm's distance from the latter. Relatively few companies have adopted a holistic approach to integrating e-commerce models and technologies into their enterprises as a whole. We expect the holistic approach to e-commerce - one enterprise covering both information and transactions - to become the norm in the next few years. Chapter 2 discusses a planning model for this holistic approach. However, we first discuss some additional possibilities for e-commerce beyond the above two models.

3.3 Industrial E-Commerce.

The above analysis of e-commerce considers only individual enterprises reaching to their respective customers, clients, or business partners. Even the marketplace sites we discussed above tend to concentrate on the "retailing" of some information products (e.g., procurement services). The scale is still very much catering to individual companies by themselves. There is, however, a much larger scale of practice emerging, comparable to the wholesale of information products. This practice aims at developing e-commerce for a whole industry or a major region. An example is the logistic center. Major organizations that involve significant flow of materials and products usually have their own logistic centers. These centers tend to be a part of their distribution channels. Federal Express, Wal-Mart, and the latest move by Amazon.com all have this practice. Other organizations would rely on third party providers, including trucking, shipping, and warehousing companies, to handle their logistics. These providers might operate their own logistic centers or use yet other providers' facilities. When the operation is international, then governments and other institutions are also involved. What would e-commerce mean to these logistic centers? For company-owned centers, the logistic e-commerce would be just a part of the company's own system, perhaps a part of the integrated enterprise. It would represent an application of e-commerce to the enterprise itself. A third party logistic center, however, would mean something much more intriguing. An industrial logistic center or a government-owned regional logistic center would be an infrastructure supporting all types of organizations. Thus, an e-commerce system in this case would actually be a combination of the physical infrastructure and the information infrastructure, to which the client companies could plug their systems and conduct logistic e-commerce throughout. This integrated e-commerce infrastructure might even be connected with the government and other related systems to form a seamless connection supporting the client companies' own e-commerce. For instance, a shipping company would be able to offer the same information services (tracking the cargo and parcels) to its clients that Federal Express is famous for, say a trading firm. The firm, in turn, would be able to offer its clients the same kind of information services. Both would be conducting e-commerce but using the third party infrastructure, which is the wholesaler of e-commerce information product.

The industrial e-commerce is conspicuous by its scale and the requirement of infrastructure. It is both capital intensive and organization intensive. This nature distinguishes itself from the typical marketplace sites of business-to-business e-commerce. The intrigue comes from the new potential that the wholesaler could make possible for its retailers to come up their own custom e-commerce, without having to own the heavy infrastructure required of the company (logistic) e-commerce. This is a form of equalization, too. It would allow many smaller companies and perhaps innovative entrepreneurs to enter the transportation business as long as the third party wholesalers exist and, thereby, could transform the industries into a more distributed landscape. The possibilities are not limited to logistics or transportation industries, of course. This model shows the same trend of "mass customization" - customizing for the client companies at a cost of mass

14

production, similar to the general portal sites providing free personal home pages. The profit potential is, of course, different. We continue this trend and zero in on *personalization*, not just customization (either for clients or for customers) in the next section. We might stress that the Industrial e-commerce model is an extension of the prevailing business-to-business e-commerce practice. It emphasizes extended enterprises and directs the focus of e-commerce unambiguously to the core production processes of the user enterprises. The new focus is the reason that new basic opportunities emerged. The focus on personalization is at least as promising.

4. Person-Centered Commerce: a new e-commerce model.

Business-to-customer e-commerce has capitalized on the new connection of one organization reaching many persons that the Internet brings about. Business-to-business e-commerce has capitalized on another new connection of many organizations linking to many other organizations. They left some additional new connections unutilized, which spell new opportunities for e-commerce. First, one person is connected to many organizations, and second, many persons are connected to many other persons. Furthermore, present e-commerce practices ignored the fundamental new condition that persons are empowered by the new information technology. We the people not only have unprecedented new capabilities for information processing and computing; we, because of the new capabilities, also expect more control of our information and transactions for own lives. This new person-centered awareness is evident in the Web community and is particularly visible through the burgeoning sites offering personalized homepages and services. Therefore, we propose a new model of e-commerce (broadly interpreted) devoted to this new person-centered worldview. New information technologies (including, e.g., palmtop computers and embedded chips, pervasive telecommunications, ubiquitous computing, scalable global integration, and distributed knowledge) will focus their application on reducing transaction cost for a person in work, leisure, relationship, or anything else. More control of one's own life and better quality of life will result.

We could take a broad view of this idea. Human society always struggles between the conflicting needs for centralization and decentralization. Even for a democracy, our inability as a person to manage our societal context beyond our immediate reach has resulted in a power structure that puts government and businesses at the center of control. However, the new information technology, for the first time in human history, has changed the premise. It extended our natural capacity and, through this extension, availed a direct connection for all people everywhere. As discussed in Section 2, this extension could grow to allow a person associating remotely with others and, thereby, enable a large society to function on a decentralization basis. This decentralization could permeate a person-centered economy leading to a highly democratized society. From this perspective, there is another reason to believe that today's e-commerce is but a harbinger. The current practice is still company-centered. Its architecture, processes, and systems are all oriented toward businesses, government agencies, and other organizations. The person-centered economy would, instead, recognize that the new information technology puts potentially the whole world at each person's disposal and, therefore, seeks rewards in the creation of new architecture, processes, and systems that realize this potential. These new personalized capabilities could start with integrating personal information and transactions with all organizations and providers in all

15

aspects of life. Examples include a person's financial dealings, healthcare activities, and leisure arrangements. They could then extend to enhancing inter-personal relationships, all the way to the society's mode of production and public affairs. A group of researchers at Rensselaer Polytechnic Institute, including Drs. Cheng Hsu, Gregory Hughes, Boleslow Szymanski, Daniel Berg, Faye Duchin and Jeffrey Durgee, has started to work on the first level of the person-centered economy.

They envision a new system of Personal Wizard to help bring about the new model of e-commerce. We describe below the new system in the context of Person-Centered Commerce, focusing on its overall reference model. There are four layers of the system: the personal mobile device (the physical level Personal Wizard), the interface clients (points of contact), the integration servers, and the service and product providers. The personal mobile device is the direct extension of the person and is wholly owned by the person. It is also the agent of integration and decision in the system for the person. The interface clients are contact points located at home, offices, stores, agencies, stations, airports, streets or any other locality that a person can use to obtain services or access to the rest of the system. The integration servers work in the background and may belong to some third-party integration providers. These servers handle the many-to-many complexity in the system and connect the many persons with the many providers. They include the Web, Internet and other necessary provisions. The providers are companies, organizations, government agencies, and individual vendors. They transact with persons. They own their proprietary systems and integrate their businesses for their own purposes. The Personal Wizard system can be specialized for a particular domain, such as a Personal Healthcare Wizard, a Personal Finance Wizard, a Personal Leisure Wizard, a Personal Education Wizard, and even a form for military endeavors.

The personal mobile device could be a next-generation smart card, palmtop computer, or notebook computer at present. Capabilities such as telecommunications and geographical positioning should also be included. As technology progresses, embedded (bio) chips could become the medium of extension to the person's natural capacity. In any case, the device contains three basic categories of data and knowledge. The first is the personal repository of information, including (1) the appropriate archive of records required for integration at the integration servers and (2) the personal repository that can be stored on the device. A personal repository on the device simplifies the complexity of integration, enhances scalability, reduces real-time distributed processing, and provides reliability and system-wide backup. However, its greatest value might be the sense of personal control that it embodies. An alternative is to put (some of) the personal database at the integration servers. The second category is personal metadata, describing and personalizing the person's interaction with the rest of the system. They affect security and serve as the personal key to the whole system, through which the user obtains personalized services from all providers and conducts integrated transactions for a holistic life. Finally, the personal decision tools constitute the third category. These tools include metadata that personalize the public assets provided at the other layers, as well as indigenous personal models, knowledge and agents stored on the device. The particular technology for the device and the person's choices of usage will dictate the contents of the personal mobile device. However, some common protocols are required.

The interface clients (contact points) should be ubiquitous and include devices that are non-intrusive (such as optical scanning from a distance) as well as contact-based (e.g., inserting a card into an input-output instrument). An interface client minimally has the ability to interact with the personal mobile device and interconnect it to the appropriate integration servers. In addition to the protocols, the interface client could include the ability to autonomously perform local processing and update the personal database or metadata. It could also contain models and knowledge bases to assist the personal mobile device, to optimize the requests for integration servers, or even to execute some classes of these requests (such as queries and Internet search). In all cases, the interface clients provide intelligent agents to facilitate distributed computing for the Personal Wizard system.

The integration servers inter-operate the Personal Wizard with the provider systems. They, at present, could compare to a Web server providing general portal services and personalized portal services, where the personalization is accomplished through the real time data that the personal mobile device generates. The personal portal conducts transactions as well as assembling information. The actual design will be open to available technologies and applications. In general, the servers offer three categories of functionality. The most basic is distributed computing. These servers, on the one hand, integrate all Personal Wizards' requests for individual provider systems and, on the other, integrate necessary pieces from all provider systems involved for the individual Personal Wizards. This basic category includes all necessary middleware, integration engines, and telecommunications processing. Second, the integration servers offer consolidated knowledge bases for the Personal Wizard's use. Evaluation of providers and products (e.g., rating and reports), progress on concerned topics (e.g., medicine and politics), and reference materials (e.g., economical trends and consumption patterns) are but some examples. Tools for personal collaboration and cooperation in all domains (from work to public affairs) are yet more examples. Resources such as general models and other decision tools that the Personal Wizard can tap in and use are also included in this category. Finally, as mentioned above, the personal databases could also be stored and managed here at this layer. In this case, the integration servers join the personal mobile device by providing the latter some personal vaults to construct the personal repository. The user still controls his/her storage vaults through the personal mobile device or other direct access, using the personal metadata. The servers add value in terms of security control and streamlined overhead, as well as performing the key role of real-time distributed computing for transactions.

The provider systems are company systems that we have presently (or in the future). They continue to serve their host organizations and perform their indigenous functions. We do not envision many changes that would be required at this layer, at least not changes that will significantly alter their normal state of design and operation. The other three layers characterize the new system. Therefore, the entire Personal Wizard system could build up from adding new modules and new capabilities to existing systems. It does not impose sweeping restructuring on company systems. Only the new opportunities are sweeping. Although the new model can be implemented using today's technology for many powerful applications, the full vision of Person-Centered Commerce using Personal Wizard entails new basic results in certain disciplines.

The Personal Wizard itself consists of the personal mobile device and the possible personal portal. It requires powerful chip, computing, and telecommunication technology. The interface clients and the integration servers constitute a new challenge to distributed computing and scalable integration. The universal connection itself represents a major step forward from the current networking and telecommunications technology. The architecture and the accompanying protocols can result only from a large-scale investigation engaging both industry and research community. Then, there are the basic research tasks concerning personal decision support via data and knowledge systems at all four layers. There are also tremendous challenges in systems engineering areas for the design and construction of the Personal Wizard system. Finally, we face some pivotal social issues. We must understand, for instance, the privacy issues, the personal responsibility issues that accompany opportunities, and the fundamental challenges of understanding what people will, in the future, value in the way of personal services.

To conclude, we expect the current e-commerce practices to grow larger and more sweeping. There will be more services to support persons and organizations conducting their actual business transactions. There will be more integration of e-commerce with traditional business processes for new and better enterprises. Most of all, there will be more practices focusing on improving the quality of life of persons. There are certain lessons and principles for new e-commerce planning that one can derive from the existing practices and promises of the technology. We discuss some of these principles in the next chapter.

2

PLANNING FOR ELECTRONIC COMMERCE

"Where one stands depends on where one sits" (George Washington). The question of how should an enterprise approach the new business model called e-commerce has many different answers. However, there are some common themes in e-commerce, as Chapter 1 indicates. These common themes could shed some light on the question. For instance, initially, entrepreneurs and small businesses might find the Internet's reach to customers particularly attractive. Entrepreneurs, therefore, might focus on creating new innovative information products for the customer. Small businesses, on the other hand, might emphasize its promises as the marketing and distribution channel for them. Still other start-ups might seek to capitalize on the new power for creating a new industry such as e-commerce marketplace. Big corporations and other established enterprises are in a different situation. They could justifiably perceive the Internet's "equalizing" power as a threat, as well as an opportunity. Yet, they must follow suit. They are in an advantaged position to exploit e-commerce for procurement and supply chain management. However, deeper thinking would lead all enterprises, large or small, to the same realization that all forms of e-commerce are inter-related and can multiply each other's promises when combined. Every business has to provide value-added information services in order to attract customers, needs new information products to generate significant revenue, and must integrate the enterprise to increase productivity and reduce cost. Therefore, a holistic approach to planning for e-commerce is valuable. We first review briefly the basic elements of e-commerce development. Then, we present a planning model for e-commerce enterprises from three perspectives: providing information services and products to customers, joining e-commerce with internal business processes, and linking with other partners. This is a high-level reference model.

1. The Basic Strategy and Technology.

Many companies start their e-commerce with a Web site that shows the company logo, pictures, performance, products, and so on. The site would contain only static information and serve as an electronic mirror image of the company brochures. Such a propaganda site might be good enough for traditional public relation practice since it has clear advantages over hardcopy brochures: easy to develop, easy to update, and easy to deliver. In reality, however, the site does nothing for the company other than making some people feel good. The problem is simple: the Internet allows everyone to reach the company site, but it does not promise to bring anyone there. Why should the cyber citizenry visit the propaganda sites? They have not even discovered the companies' existence, let alone been thrilled by company logos. Thus, many company sites soon added more dynamic and useful information to the propaganda, especially the human resources and directory functions, to attract viewers. Online application, contact by e-mail, and other interactions start to do something for the company, except for bringing the green back. A chief executive officer of an entertainment-news conglomerate was once quoted to say that the Internet business was a black hole sucking in money with no benefit coming out. That was 1996ish. Soon after that, bone fide Internet marketing would start and new functions would allow customers to order stuff online through the site as well as getting customer services. Procurement and EDI functions would come, too. The e-commerce finally comes to the company in earnest. Many companies followed this path. Many other companies still stop at some early stages while the next waves are already sweeping the field.

The next three sections will review, comprehensively, some basic principles for e-commerce planning. To prepare for the discussion, however, in this section, we quickly look into a simple and yet telling question: how to identify appropriate e-commerce applications? There are a few halfway decent rules of thumb to use before embarking on a serious analysis. The basic point to keep in mind is the promises of the new information technology, in particular the Internet (see Chapter 1). That is, in a nutshell, the new technology helps its user to reach customers, businesses, and co-workers at low transaction cost. So, the right planning question for a user to ask is: do I face any bottlenecks in my business that the Internet could help remove? To get more specific, ask a few questions:

- What promotion mechanism would I invest if I had the money? If the answer is advertisement, direct mail, catalog sale, telephone sale, referrals, and so on to find, contact, and connect with the right persons or organizations, then e-commerce is for you. The Internet could be used either to complement or to substitute for some of the business mechanisms such as distribution channels.

- Where do I have the most paper work that takes too much time through too many stops to process? E-commerce has promises for simplifying these processes. The Internet could either replace the traditional connection or bypass some intermediaries.

- Would the customer (or client, employee, partner, etc.) enjoy doing business with me in the comfort of his/her home or office? A "yes" answer would suggest profitable e-commerce opportunities for conducting reservation, ordering, payment, after sale service, communication, workflow, and many other transactions. The U.S. Postal Services has finally asked this question and answered it with a conscience. Internet stamp is one of the most telling examples about reducing societal transaction cost through e-commerce.

- Finally, since I am investing on e-commerce, should not I plan to make the best out of it from the start? You bet. The beauty of information technology is the fact that it is scalable. As long as the system architecture is designed and done right, the e-commerce site could start small but grow rapidly and smoothly. One would like to start with the most visible and easiest e-commerce practice, but there is nothing to stop the planning from being comprehensive and forward looking. In fact, at the speed with which e-commerce is moving, any planning short of forward looking is unconscionable.

There are a few categories of system architecture for e-commerce. Each gives a different class of e-commerce capabilities. At this point, we do not consider the sizing issues of a system; in other words, these categories are transparent to configuration and distribution concerns.

- *Document Connectivity*. This class represents stand-alone Web sites that offer static home pages. It is capable of file transfers and presentation of documents written in different formats and systems. Its basic technology includes (1) HTTPD and HTML for the common user interface, (2) TCP/IP for the common communications protocols, (3) e-mail protocols and tools for global communication, and (4) word-processing and other document-oriented software for application development. All Web sites use this class of technology as at least a component. Most Web sites use probably only this class of technology. E-commerce sites are moving beyond this class. However, it is apt for simple online ordering systems, online job application, and the like and, hence, can support business-to-customer e-commerce that requires only these functions.

- *Application Connectivity*. Application software is also connected to the common user interface (i.e., the home page) in addition to documents. Thus, dynamic home pages become possible, and Web sites do not have to be stand-alone any more. They can connect to regular business processes and systems. This class of technology adds CGI and XML (extended HTML) to the line-up to serve as adapters among applications (i.e., API-application protocols interchange) and between the home page and the applications. Active-X, PERL, and JAVA are some of the general purpose scripting systems available for developing applications amid many Web-oriented software engineering tools and products. Its best capability is to support heavy-duty document processing (including forms and files) with light-duty computing. Examples are plentiful, ranging from ordering to EDI and procurement. Virtually all business-to-business e-commerce sites and significant business-to-customer sites have this class of technology. When stopped here, the e-commerce sites would tend to lack the capability to integrate with traditional enterprise information systems because the latter tend to involve heavy-duty computing. The next two classes of technology become necessary when enterprises want to integrate e-commerce with their traditional business processes.

- *Database Connectivity*. Databases are the engine of enterprise information systems. They integrate enterprise data resources and make them available to distributed and heterogeneous user groups to share through the users' own application software. Without connection to enterprise databases, the e-commerce sites would have difficulty providing real time and online information or transactions with the customers and other outside users. A familiar case of non-real time applications is Internet stock quotes available from free information sites. They often have a 10 minute or so delay because they are only periodic snap shops of the real databases. The application connectivity class of technology is sufficient for supporting periodical refreshment on a batch processing basis, but is inept for real time interactive processing that online

21

trading requires. The added technology includes ODBC and JDBC, which connect certain application programming languages (e.g., C++ and Visual Basic) with certain database management systems (e.g., Oracle, Sybase, DB2, and Access). CASE tools and other data engineering systems also are available. With this class of technology, Web home pages have the ability to become *the* universal user interface for all database applications and, hence, the whole enterprise information system. This is a pivotal tool for integrating e-commerce with traditional enterprise processes. Many portal sites, online traveling reservation sites, auction sites, and marketplace sites are all good examples of e-commerce using this class of technology.

- *Enterprise Connectivity.* A significant enterprise usually has multiple databases distributed at various places over local area networks, campus networks, wide area networks, or even global networks. Thus, to integrate e-commerce into these kind of enterprises, one must integrate the multiple databases first. It turns out that multiple (heterogeneous) database systems integration has been the central topic of research for enterprise integration since late 1970's. The research is continuing to-date. Although a great number of results have come out, a great deal more are still required. JAVA-CORBA is a recent example that bridges the gaps for connecting multiple databases in e-commerce. CORBA is a traditional integration technology; thus, its coupling with JAVA fills in the role of presenting distributed databases to Web applications. Other distributed computing techniques are needed, too. The emerging information technology mentioned in Chapter 1 promises to play important roles in the continuing progress of this class of technology. In turn, the progress promises to breed the continuing deepening and broadening of e-commerce into the next waves of new models. Many significant e-commerce sites, especially business-to-business, have used this class of technology. It is even more critical when companies start to join e-commerce sites and link their transactions in an extended enterprise manner. We expect this class to become the dominating class of technology for the future e-commerce models.

System architecture involves configuration and distribution. There are five basic technical elements of an e-commerce system: Web server, application server, database server, internal network, and Internet connection. For small businesses with a low volume of transactions (e.g., hits), all the first four elements could be combined into a single high end PC. For big corporations, each element itself might actually be a collection of many distributed parallel elements. There could be, for instance, a collection of hundreds of parallel processors to comprise the database server. There could also be a myriad of networks to play the role of "local or company network." Notwithstanding, there are some basic lessons the field has learned for the design of system architecture. On top of the list is reliability. System backup is of primary priority. The backup could include mirror sites, duplicate systems, and standard database backups. Design for reliability is important for a number of reasons; among them are security, integrity, and performance. Next, each server type (Web, application, and database) is better to have its own physical system, self-contained and fully separated from each within a site. If necessary, their connection to other (internal) enterprise systems could deliberately include some manual intervention or intermediary management process, either in lieu of or in addition to the usual automated procedure. This design sometimes is a low cost alternative to full integration; but more interestingly, it adds a physical firewall to the software-based security control for the site. Internet hackers are a fact in life with which e-commerce must learn to cope and beat. Physical separation often is the easiest and most trustworthy means to combat hackers. Finally, the database engine is the key of the whole system. Thus, adequate investment must go to this element and assure that the adopted technology has a suitable path for growth or migration when the practice evolves.

How to start e-commerce? One needs to implement the above ideas. Consider the Internet connection first. Internet is an invention in the U.S.; thus, IP addresses and domain names reflect their historical roots. There are six original categories including com, net, org, edu (educational institutions), gov (government), and mil (military) designated for the Internet when it was still a U.S.-only community. The first three categories are generic and are open to all persons and organizations to use (anyone can register a domain name within any of these categories). The last three, however, are usable only by the qualified organizations. When other countries later joined the Internet, each country is considered an additional category and assigned a particular country code. Some examples are: ca for Canada, de for Germany, fr for France, uk for Britain, tw for Taiwan, kr for Korea, jn for Japan, hk for Hong Kong, in for India, au for Australia, at for Austria, and cn for China. The country code appears at the end of all domain names registered with the country. A council, the Internet Corporation for Assigned Names and Numbers, regulates all Internet registrations in the world and is the only authority on the Internet. The ICANN controls the registration database, but it has authorized a number of companies to operate with the database. These companies (e.g., networksolutions.com), in turn, provide Internet registration business to anyone wishing to register. The traffic on the Internet used to be U.S.-centric (90% of them went through the U.S. in 1998), reflecting both the history and the fact that most high capacity bandwidth exists in the U.S. Thus, a message sent from India to Pakistan would most likely go to the U.S. first and then to Pakistan. In a way, the Internet used to look like a star configuration with the U.S. being the central hub. The situation is changing rapidly with new high capacity bandwidth networks. Europe is changing first. Asia is picking up the pace, too, since 1999. The future e-commerce will most likely be using three global hubs in Spain, Singapore, and the U.S. As for the other four elements, there are package solutions available from many vendors for all kinds of budget. Document connectivity is practically bundled into Microsoft's operating environments for PC and small workstations. Application connectivity is available from a large number of third party vendors as well as from Microsoft, IBM, Sun Microsystems, Oracle and other primary producers. The database connectivity and enterprise connectivity vendors are more limited, especially for significant e-commerce systems. They tend to concentrate in large consulting firms providing allegedly custom solutions, plus large database vendors. Finally, many portal sites offer "e-commerce for lease" - i.e., a slot in their e-commerce shopping malls. This one stop solution should be an attractive alternative feasible to companies operating limited-scale e-commerce.

We now turn to developing a more comprehensive analysis for e-commerce planning. The next three sections describe respectively three main principles of planning, each of which consists of three detailed principles. These nine principles comprise a model for e-commerce planning. Thus, the nest three sections are three parts of the same cohesive model.

23

2. The Information Service and Product Principle (Principle 1).

Internet retailing, or business-to-customer e-commerce, needs to develop information services and products in order to promote the company and generate revenues. Even business-to-business e-commerce could use the same principle, not only for marketplace sites but also for companies that want to recruit partners. The term information service is interpreted broadly. It recognizes the gathering and provision of information per se, but also includes assistance for transactions and products and offerings of software.

2.1 Marketing: Providing Free Information Services to Customers (Principle 1.1).

How to advertise on the Internet? All companies doing business-to-customer e-commerce understand the pivotal importance of advertisement on the Internet. After all, there are over 200 million searchable Web sites on the Internet. The Internet technically allows any Web site to reach any user, but the odds that any user would go to the site by chance (or keyword search) are not much better than lottery. Would Internet advertisement change the odds fundamentally? The answer is, of course, yes but with a severe qualification. Companies can register with any number of portal sites; however, how many companies can a portal site publicize effectively? There are two very fundamental differences between portal site advertisement and advertisement on traditional media. One is the limit of the screen - the advertisement must be incorporated into the regular pages and, therefore, competing for the precious "real estate" of the screen. This situation is comparable to television commercials that must show during regular programming. In this case, the commercials always take only the form of captions, which is ineffective and hence seldom used. The other difference is transaction cost. The viewer of an advertisement must put up with some extra effort (e.g., to click and leave the regular page and then come back again). This problem is related to the first one of limited screen space. Other forms of advertisement exist, including Internet direct mail (e-mail alert) and cookies. They have their own problems and are even less effective. These inherent limits have made Internet advertisement less than sufficient. There does not seem to have any major breakthrough any time soon to change the situation. This is the reason why significant e-commerce businesses rely on the costly traditional media to advertise their non-traditional Web sites. This is also the reason why Yahoo! and other popular sites on which businesses advertise charge very moderate fees. Try to compare their fees with the prices of traditional media that have the same level of viewers. In this sense, advertisement presents a bottleneck to new e-commerce ventures. The bottleneck does not have to exist since Internet advertisement ought to take a totally different form - i.e., free information services.

We need to keep in mind how the Web community has come into being. It came because the World Wide Web provides mind-boggling value in information services - all free and all available on the basis of volunteerism. The information services are always of the cybercitizen, by the cybercitizen, and for the cybercitizen. This awareness is the key to Internet advertisement. A business site (especially a new one) that wants to attract cybercitizens to patronize with it must first prove its worthiness as a cybercitizen in the community. That is, it must first provide good value to the viewers. The Web community is like a treasure hunting ground. People

24

respond to treasures, to valuable information, better than any advertisement in any portal sites. In fact, all successful portal sites build their livelihood (the viewer base) on provisions of free information services. Just recall how Yahoo!, Lycos, and Excite got started as the free search engines for cybercitizens. They still generate patronage using these services. Their growth is always fueled with more and better services to the cybercitizens. Other examples are all over the places. Many free news sites, free email sites, free personal relationship sites and similarly mass-market oriented services have been acquired and become the killer application for their parent portal sites. Many software manufacturers offer free downloads and trial products to attract visitors. Almost all producers provide free online services in the form of product information, maintenance, and after sale services. Even retailers that excelled because of their pioneering transactional services to customers have an integral component of free information services in their business. Amazon.com distinguished itself, for instance, through its library and literary critique style information services about books. Charles Schwab is famous for its provisions of free online information including trading data, portfolio, and research reports. We would content to say that all successful e-commerce sites have a major component of free (information) services that are critical to their success (marketing). We would also mention that these services are uniquely belonging to the Internet - traditional means can hardly achieve the same functions.

The principle of free information services is not new. It has been characteristic of companies that successfully employed and deployed information technology since 1970's (see Chapter 4). However, for e-commerce, this principle is the cardinal rule for marketing. This is the only way an e-commerce company can reliably promote itself on the Internet - and the beauty is the company has full control of this means. It determines its own destiny this way. To be sure, free information service is not a one-size-fits-all solution. Different types of e-commerce sites have different choices of strategy. The general portal sites must offer general-purpose services and tools applicable to the maximum possible viewers. The domain portal sites and marketplace sites should choose to specialize in services tailored for the target products and industries. The direct sale sites could emphasize information services designed for some particular groups of customers or niche market. The successful services will combine industry-standard provisions with the company's own innovation. The objective is to create unique (information) value for the cybercitizens and lure these treasure hunters to the site. The name of the game is electronic word of mouth and momentum. On the Internet, both can be swift and decisive. We review some particular ideas below.

The industrial standards for general portal sites are easy to find out from the industrial leaders. Current practices include information search and directory, personal home page and e-mail, and news and other informational provisions. The array of provisions is nothing short of impressive, already. However, the quality and depth of many these standard services seem to be lacking at present. Better and more innovative services could easily turn into a competitive weapon. Some of the analyses in Chapter 1 could lead to a few new possibilities.

- *Personalization.* More and better support for personal information (tools, repository, and processing) will come from integration, as opposed to relying exclusively on new items. The integration could be simple linking of certain content items (e.g., financial portfolio) with particular transaction sites (e.g.,

25

E*Trade) to create real time online information. It could also be edited summaries or reports (e.g., pertinent healthcare information), according to personal interest using information from the regular content providers. The basic point is that the level of service needs to go up a notch to add more value to the plain search and other basic Internet tools and provisions.

- *Transactional Support.* Information leads to transactions. A person searches for information because there is certain need for the information. Therefore, the next level of information services should be the addition of decision support capabilities to process the information provided. The decision support could take the form of linkage to actual business transactions, parametric decision tools, and embedded knowledge or agents.

- *Evaluation.* The current industrial standard practices for informational provision (e.g., search or directory) are not far from being "garbage-in-garbage-out." There has been little monitoring or digesting provided by the general portal sites. In contrast, there are a few successful domain portal sites featuring evaluation of software, books, movie, and other products. Again, adding new value to raw information will be an important direction for creating new services. A basic value here is trust. Good evaluation not only creates value for the users, it also creates an invaluable asset for the business: trust and loyalty, commodities hard to come by on the Internet.

The above three possibilities apply to portal sites specialized for certain niche market (domain) and to company-owned direct sale sites, as well. In fact, these sites tend to do a better job in these areas than general portal sites. Quite a few successful companies have already established good practices along these lines. Examples are found in book retailing, music, healthcare, software, computer, investment, hospitality, and entertainment, just to name a few. However, they have only begun to explore the possibilities. In addition to deepening and broadening the existing practices in these areas, we add three new categories to the list of possibilities.

- *Enthusiasts services.* Most domain portal sites and company retailing sites tend to ignore the kind of "community" information services practiced by general portal sites. This would be a mistake. A customer of fishing goods will go to a generic fishing information site for, e.g., chatting, local fishing news, and professional improvement. An e-journal for young women discussing diet and relationship, as well as make-up, will be a sensible addition to a cosmetic retailing site. Fashion design, domestic issues, or even exotic topics are related to a retailing site selling high-end silk bedding products. The point is whatever worked for general portal sites to attract viewers will be promising for niche market sites, too, albeit needing customization. The power of the indirect approach to marketing cannot be over-emphasized.

- *Single-Window Customer Services.* Online ordering, Web-based helpdesk, and product service have been powerful practices that e-commerce sites embrace. The same idea should extend to other activities that customers must conduct in relation to their use or possession of the particular products or services they buy. These activities could be different stages of the "life cycle" of the buyer's transaction (e.g., planning to buy, analyzing the alternatives, financing the purchase, and so on), but could also be other components of the same "package," such as vacationing. This "alliance" idea is commonplace to airlines, which sell the travelers car rentals, hotels, and other things a traveler might need. Similarly, a realtor offers financing and legal connections. For the Internet, this idea lends itself naturally to the notion of extended enterprises that we will discuss in Section 4. Thus, a fishing retailing site can join force not only with fishing information sites but also with travel and hospitality sites. The notion of being an agent for the customer promises to renew the conventional thinking of customer service.

- *Internet Products and Services.* Comparable to free information services, another unique practice the Internet business model has brought about is free information products. Companies offer trial versions of their software product free of charge or even give away some products (e.g., Web browser) in order to lure customers for their core profit-generating business (e.g., Web server). We expect this practice to become even more profound as the cost of current Internet technology continues to decrease. Among the first to give away will be the Internet service (connection) itself. Then, all tools that help increase the customer pool, such as custom design software to help the customer order custom products and financial management tool to help the client doing business with the provider will follow. For organizations, providing software library and protocols to facilitate constituent businesses joining an extended enterprise will become common practice. We also expect particular systems and infrastructures be developed for the purpose of inducting new members into the cyber community, either as e-commerce providers or users. Some of them would be free.

The above possibilities do not exclude business-to-business e-commerce, although we discuss them mainly from the perspective of business-to-customer. In fact, an enterprise should not automatically separate these two models. Both business-to-customer and business-to-business practices belong in a holistic e-commerce model for the enterprise. This point will become more evident later as we discuss more aspects of the planning model.

2.2 Revenue: Turning Information Services into Products (Principle 1.2).

How to generate revenues on the Internet? Retailing sites generate revenue by selling products and marketplace sites by selling intermediary services. Thus, the Web sites to these companies could be mere expenses of marketing. However, portal sites (general or domain) must rely on the Web practice to make money. Even for the other sites, basic categories of information products can be created from information services: value-added proprietary information, customer base, online transactions, and in-house tools for information services.

Value-added information services are a natural step following free provisions. Many business Web sites set aside certain items that the viewers must pay to get. These items could be investment research reports, regular (not trial) software, or proprietary personal services. In this case, the free information they provide becomes the bait for the not free information. Investment portal sites, newspaper sites, and software vendor sites are frequent users of this sales technique. Another form of value-added services is usage fees and membership fees. Clearly, the power a site has to charge its viewers is entirely depending on the unique value it provides. However, uniqueness is an endangered species on the Internet. The competition in the Cyber community is near perfect and, hence, few proprietary information services have the staying power to remain for sale. Exceptions tend to be software products and information products that are protected by copyrights or patents, or by the sheer requirement for know-how. An example is the online trading industry. Competition is forcing online trading sites to include an impressing array of previously for sale, in-depth analyses in their free information services. Competition is also forcing personal relationship sites to waive their membership fees. Therefore, we expect the promising and lasting value-added information to come mainly from personalized services. Personalization of information services can lead to some easily justifiable information products for the viewers to buy, such as the custom services and the tools for personalization. Here again, personal means proprietary; these two "P's" are two sides of the same coin in both the dictionary and the e-commerce strategy.

Free information services help create the customer base. However, they do not identify the customers. Membership and cookies help identify the customer base. Therefore, many portal sites, marketplace sites and retailing sites have to require registration of the users in order to verify and authenticate the services or transactions. This is only the beginning, though. The moral of the story is that all e-commerce sites should consider this practice as a marketing weapon whenever possible. Membership registration represents a transaction cost to the user and, hence, is not welcome. The trick is the value added to the user. A commonly worked technique is to offer the user the ability to get personal services, such as free e-mail and free home page, and to conduct personal transactions, such as ticketing. Not every site can use the same technique. However, personalized information and services are really the common theme. Virtually all sites should be able to use this guideline. A ubiquitous way to obtain viewer information is to use cookies. Cookies could be unreliable and do not provide as much information about the viewer as membership. However, they are the easiest and cheapest way to comprehensively capture viewers for a Web site. The customer base has a three-fold use. An e-commerce site uses, naturally, its customer information to analyze for its business. This is an old practice. Another old practice is to sell their customer information to other businesses. This use of customer base is getting commonplace in e-commerce, but it involves complicate legal and moral issues. However, there is another use, which could be innovative and profitable. In the Internet age, every company could become an advertisement agent; i.e., it could accept, at a fee of course, other companies' advertisement in its e-commerce sites and, thereby, create an advertisement operation for itself. The company's customer (or viewer) base becomes a profit niche for it, just like for any portal sites. The Internet shows its equalizing nature here, too. It breaks down the traditional barriers between advertisement media and advertisers. In essence, every Web site could become a niche portal site in the way of advertisement and linkage to other (related) sites. Both the advertisement and the linkage could be treated as free information services, but they also have the promises to become proprietary and generate revenue.

Conducting actual business transactions is the basic way to make a profit for businesses on the Internet since it sells products - either information products or traditional commodities - that command significant prices. The producers rake in the revenue of the sales - this is well known and has always been the sole purpose of many company-owned Internet retailing sites and business-to-business procurement sites. However, just like the case with Internet advertisement, the Internet age also allows non-producing sites to include transactions in their money-producing operations. In fact, every e-commerce site can become a marketplace site and broker certain products, at least in its niche domain. This point is closely related to the discussion in the above section, about linking sites for the viewers (e.g., single-window for customer services). The planning concept here is the same point we used through this chapter: personal integration. Every Web site could strive to develop business ideas around the theme of providing related information and transactions for people who are interested in their particular products. "Alliance" with related but not competing sites is a natural way to become a broker for the customers and generate commission revenue. This is a win-win situation for the customer (convenience), the producer (sales), and the site (value-added). The customer information discussed above would be a pivotal element for this operation. Personalization (or customization, in the case of business-to-business e-commerce) would also be the differential among competitors since it drives the value added operation. Linkage without personalization probably can not add much transactional value to the user and most likely would not generate revenue. The enterprise might as well regard this level of linkage as free information services since customers could easily bypass the site once the linkage becomes known. Higher levels such as membership would have the power to keep the customers in the "brokerage." Membership, in turn, requires powerful information services to become a profitable information product. At the root, the situation is not different from the one facing any brokerage, traditional or e-commerce. For that matter, the situation is also the same with intermediary e-commerce sites. The differential is custom and value-added services. Just imagine, for example, that newspaper sites create linkages to publishers and publishers linking to other publishers. They can rival directly the bookstore sites. The latter would have to survive on the unique value they provide to their customers - personalized services, since they do not enjoy any inherent advantages of distribution channel on the Internet. Competing based on discounted price cannot last long unless the operation itself has the caliber of cost saving.

The final category of information product we discuss in this section is the tools, systems, and technologies that a company developed for its own internal operation (e.g., enterprise integration) as well as for creating personalized or customized services. The above discussion mentioned a number of possible information products, especially value-added personal or custom products. These products most likely would involve innovative business ideas and designs. To many companies, they could also involve home grown technical results. The former might be patentable in today's new patent laws, or at least would become their proprietary know-how. The latter would be good candidates for being turned into a profit center. In a similar way, the effort to integrate an enterprise and create effective extended enterprises will lead to new results that others can use. The concept of profit center for information products is more appropriate to certain types of companies than others. The point worthwhile to mention here is that the Internet also makes this possibility closer to reality for more companies than ever before. It is now possible for every person to auction - either buy or sell - his/her services on the Internet, so it is possible for every company to do the same, too. Therefore, it is worthwhile for an e-commerce site to employ a structured approach to developing its information products and carefully document the whole process. Another dimension of profit center is spin-off ventures. Significant advancement of the previously free services or internal solutions could become new information products transacted at their own e-commerce sites. A significant spin-off of personal information product is MyCFO. In the past, the most famous spin-off is perhaps the Sabre system by American Airlines. Innovative personalization and customization, discussed above, could evolve naturally into their own e-commerce sites for the niche market.

2.3 Intelligence: Tapping into Internet Resources (Principle 1.3).

How to study the market? Data mining and database marketing are well-known powerhouses for new product development and promotion. The Internet adds a tremendous dimension to the powerhouse. The big picture here is, again, the global connection of organizations and users and the low transaction cost that the new technology brings to the cyber community. Data mining and database marketing can now become real time and online practice and no longer have to be confined to historical data. The customer base discussed above is naturally important to the practice and is at the core of any e-commerce marketing, but is not the only core. The new information technology affords additional means for an e-commerce company to develop market intelligence and tap into this intelligence. A basic point to keep in mind is that organizations are connected with organizations.

Foremost of the new means is the Internet itself. Search engine sites scan the whole Web community periodically to create and maintain their information directories, on which the whole search operation is based. The same technology can be used to create and maintain marketing information directories. This practice is not big companies' exclusive privilege. Small-scale operations could use free search engines available on the Internet to build manually a good intelligence base. The marketing information could range from competitors and products all the way to users and target environments. Much of the information is available readily in the company home pages and requires only some customized search to locate and assemble. Other intelligence might involve proprietary data that the company has to pay to get. The significance is using free data alone might be sufficient for many types of marketing study and free data are plentiful on the Internet. Perceptive professionals of e-commerce would be able to integrate standard data and go a long way towards uncovering powerful marketing intelligence. With creative ideas and innovative design, the cost could be very affordable to virtually any sized e-commerce. This is a sharp contrast to traditional means to accomplish the same.

A second unique property of e-commerce that companies can use to gain marketing intelligence is the fact that users' every move in all transactions (either viewing information or conducting some business) could be recorded real time and analyzed online. The previous notion of linking with other related sites can lead to another joining of force among them: comparing notes on marketing intelligence. The trick is, of course, they must complement each other as opposed to competing against. The Internet makes it possible for different sites to use the same format, model, and techniques to acquire and process their marketing information and, hence, allows them to join their efforts on an online basis and at an affordable cost. New data mining techniques would have to catch up with this distributed and even real time practice. The progress, however, will come.

Finally, the whole enterprise could incorporate the Internet intelligence into its regular processes, too. The real time and comprehensive recording of a user's transactions with an enterprise provides a potent basis for the enterprise to integrate itself. That is, the data could become a driver to enhance and shorten the product development cycle, from marketing to design, manufacturing, and after sale service. From this perspective, the e-commerce venture can deliberately design a site with features that capture the marketing intelligence it envisions. It could also develop a number of sites to collaborate in the way of acquiring marketing intelligence, as well as perhaps conducting business. Some large portal sites have started to redefine themselves as a portfolio of sites. Many sites hold other sites, too. However, e-commerce enterprises are not accustomed to creating many different or even unrelated sites like their traditional counterparts routinely do. This could change. The investment on the additional sites would then become a strategic investment on marketing and enterprise integration. The same concept is applicable to extended enterprises, except that the scope of concern (the enterprise) in this case would be the scope of all extended constituencies.

3. The Enterprise Integration Principle (Principle 2).

Revenue and cost determine profit. The proceeding principle is concerned with revenue; thus, we consider cost with the second principle here. The general theme of the principle is that an enterprise must use the new information technology and must integrate its e-commerce processes with those of the traditional business. An enterprise is an enterprise. The same enterprise can not have two separate, parallel systems and still achieve the maximum performance at the minimum cost. There are two perspectives to the discussion. One is that an enterprise connects its existing e-commerce practice with its regular processes. The other is to put its regular processes on the Internet. The substance is the same.

3.1 Administration: Adopting E-Commerce for Business Functions (Principle 2.1).

The most natural way to start an e-commerce seems to be putting a company's administrative functions on the Internet. That means public relations, marketing, sales, procurement, customer services, human resources, delivery, and general administration. To some extent, accounting and finance can also use e-commerce, especially the part of them concerned with external operations such as billing and payment. However, cost accounting, inventory control, and similar activity-based functions would likely have to wait until the company's core production system has also used e-commerce practice. The reason for this choice is administrative functions tend to have a major connection with external constituencies and, hence, can benefit easily from the Internet connection with persons and organizations. The basic opportunities recognized in Section 1 apply readily to these functions, to reduce transaction cost. Furthermore, the definition and scope of the administrative connection are often fluid, entailing frequent or even random configurations either with intermediaries or with end users (e.g., mailing lists). Therefore, the Internet is poised to improve them. It provides universal and low cost connection to every one the Internet reaches without reconfiguration. The flexibility is a given, the process is simple, and the intermediaries become unnecessary. All these benefits spell savings in cost and time. Unsurprisingly, as indicated before, many companies have at least

31

put company brochures, job opportunities, and e-mail contacts on the Web. Many serious e-commerce sites put more of the administration functions on the Web. In fact, the entire practice of Internet retailing and procurement are a perfect part of the administration functions. Therefore, traditional companies would create their e-commerce in the image of the traditional administration systems. New e-commerce companies would also focus their attention on this realm. Although we consider this focus as only the first wave of e-commerce, we do not minimize its enormous impact in its own right. We must re-iterate the theme of Chapter 1, i.e., the equalizing power of the Internet has the promise to change the landscape of retailing. It could grow a company or help one to live up to new competition. Thus, it is absolutely sensible for any company to look into the possibility of applying e-commerce to its administration functions. The previous section, the principle of information services and products, provides certain analysis concerning the opportunities existing in this category. To go beyond, the notion of Intranet is a ready next step. Unlike the previous focus of external connection, this model looks inward for the internal connection of administration. As many companies have demonstrated, Intranet is a good tool to enhance productivity since it works on reducing transaction cost for internal connection in the same way the Internet does on external. An enterprise could simply use a Web server to support its employees communicating work through it. In this case, the company home pages become the company's common user interface to different software systems and employees use them to transfer files and conduct simple workflow functions. The Intranet is scalable, meaning that it can expand smoothly to other functions such as connecting with core production functions as well. As such, it would play the role of an integration agent (see below).

However, a more subtle and yet significant improvement over the above first wave practice of e-commerce is to integrate e-commerce processes with traditional processes. The administration e-commerce systems can be some add-on, stand alone operations to the regular administration; they do not have to replace or even alter the traditional administration systems that they duplicate. In fact, many companies are doing just that keeping a dual system of both. A classical example of a dual system using information technology is the automatic teller machine. Initially, banks treated ATMs as only some front end for human tellers. Even today when banks are starting to use ATMs as some online terminals to the banking system at large, many ATM transactions still require human tellers to verify and re-do. In this sense, they have always been a mere marketing tool and never been a productivity tool. E-commerce sites could be treated the same way, too. Companies that maintain a dual system would perceive their e-commerce sites as only collection points or a front end that is not part of the "real" systems. These sites would need primarily the first class of technology, document connectivity, only. This approach has all the benefits that precaution has to offer and precaution is not a bad concept for this fast moving field we call e-commerce. It also has the added advantage of security control against hackers. On the other hand, although dual system e-commerce might still be a potent weapon of marketing, it will never be able to reap the full benefit bona fide integration can. Only integrated e-commerce systems can affect positively the companies' overall productivity. There are two indicators of integration: the authority of decision making and the connection of application software. Parallel processes between the e-commerce site and the internal operation should have a streamlined decision structure. That implies that decision points are distributed and non-duplicate, and a single decision authority spans both sides for the same functions. The software connection is more tangible. The working definition of integration is to have administration systems connecting their application software with the e-commerce systems. Thus, the integration will make use of at least the second class of e-commerce technology, application connection. More often than not, it requires database connectivity as well, the third class of technology.

3.2 Production: Applying E-Commerce to Core Processes (Principle 2.2).

Every enterprise has its core production processes. For a hospital, production means medical treatment. For a bookstore - or for that matter a retailer, it is the acquisition, inventory, and logistics of books or the retailing goods it carries. For a university, it is education and research. For a financial institution, it is the execution of financial products. For an informational portal site, it is the information service/product - i.e., the acquisition, production, and utilization of its information resources for customers. For a search engine, it is the search; namely, the development, maintenance, and query of the information directories. For a transactional portal site, it is the transactional processing and management for clients. For a manufacturer, it is obviously the design, production, and inventory functions of its product development cycle. These core processes typically account for the lion's share of an enterprise's total cost, often in the neighborhood of 50%. More significantly, an enterprise cannot build core competence without building a competitive core production system. It certainly cannot build quality without building quality products. Thus, saving cost is not a job that can rely only on improving the administration functions; it must also tackle head-on the hard core of cost in the core functions. The fact that it might be difficult to do illustrates exactly why it has to be done in order to get ahead.

Manufacturing enterprises are among the most complicated of all to integrate. Results and lessons obtained in this field have always been momentous to compass other industries. Computer-integrated manufacturing, concurrent engineering, and agile manufacturing are some of the prime results developed in the past few decades. Their big visions and ultimate objectives are actually the same - to speed up product development and production at a lower cost, but each has its own unique contribution. Computer-integrated manufacturing brings to the field factory level manufacturing execution systems connected to shop floor level computer-aided manufacturing systems. Concurrent engineering excels on supporting distributed design processes across organizations in an extended enterprise manner. Agile manufacturing seeks to capitalize on these results and develop rapid response capability, such as custom manufacturing for custom design with mass production efficiency. The efforts are continuing as the technology gets more powerful and people get more encouraged to boldly go where no enterprises have gone before. The immediate possible benefit of seeking e-commerce practice for the core production functions is, again, to take advantage of the power of a universal user interface that is readily available at low cost. The technical issue of integration is, to put it simply, how to inter-operate all kinds of functional databases and applications using different models, formats, and software and hardware platforms. Web technologies do not solve the integration problem by themselves. However, they alleviate the problem by removing some of the obstacles of incompatible user interfaces. As such, integration solutions become easier to obtain, to operate, and to develop. Web-based concurrent engineering systems, Web-based workflow management systems, and Web-based enterprise resources planning systems have already come out in the market. Database connectivity further allows many legacy systems to inter-operate with each other and with new Web-based systems. Coupling all these developments with the increasingly pervasive use of PC on the shop floor, the problem has become less intimidating. At least, a manufacturer can adopt an evolutionary approach; whereby, it gradually incorporates major systems into a Web-based integration environment. At the beginning, the environment needs only to feature Web-based common user interface for standard application systems. Eventually, it could bring in EDI, shop floor data acquisition and control systems, and emerging integration tools (such as STEP) for computer-aided manufacturing. In the end, it could tie together all major application systems at, at least, the level of workflow to effect a full-scale integration. This approach is, in essence, to provide an Intranet for core production processes. The Intranet could include Web-based workflow management, Web-based concurrent engineering, and Web-based computer-integrated manufacturing. A central design concept is to link the otherwise sequential functions (from marketing and design to production and delivery) in a forward chaining manner - such as design for manufacturing or for dissembling and environment. The chaining must also seek to feed crucial information from each step back to every other step preceding it that estimated the information. In other words, the decision assumptions and parameters at each step should be updated using the actual conditions taking place in the subsequent steps, ideally on a real time and online basis. The manufacturing Intranet should be able to promote all the benefits of integrated manufacturing and more. Since the basic technical issues are similar for all types of enterprises, the idea of a manufacturing Intranet would be relevant to healthcare enterprise integration, financial enterprise integration, and all others.

The saving of cost does not stop here. The concept of internal e-commerce could lead to a paradigm shift, making an enterprise rethinking the way it conducts business among major core functions (divisions). Radical changes on its processes could result. Consider an Internet bookstore. Suppose the enterprise is an industry leader and enjoys the highest volume of sales. It excels on providing customers free information services, discounted price, and quick delivery. To be able to do the former, it maintains a state-of-the-art e-commerce site with a powerful information repository. To do the latter (price and delivery), it builds a huge inventory coupled with a network of logistic centers. The enterprise's administration is based on e-commerce; therefore, there is no such problem as maintaining a dual system. The core production system, however, is largely traditional. The enterprise has to sink in huge cost for the system just like any traditional bookstores trying to do the same must do. Its only major saving comes from the savings on the distribution channel; i.e., it does not need to maintain a network of physical bookstores. Competition has made this advantage insufficient to offset its discounted sales. Consequently, it loses money. The more successful its Internet retailing operation becomes, the more money it might lose. How come? The root cause is, of course, the fact that it must maintain a costly inventory and logistic system. Why does it have to maintain inventory and why can it not simply order the books for its customers and ask the publishers to send directly to them? The reason is simple. The publishers do not care to deal with retailing or with delivering books to individual customers. The fact that they do not handle direct sales is the very reason why there are bookstores in the first place. Creating and maintaining the necessary distribution channels is costly and complicated enough to deserve a whole new industry all to itself. Traditionally, publishers do not care for this business. However, is it not true that e-commerce has changed the distribution formula? Is it not true that publishers can now easily handle retailing through e-commerce? Is it not true that there are more and more publishers who are doing just that, Internet retailing? The bookstore in question has a perfect chance to convert its core production processes into a business-to-business e-commerce practice. It could position itself as a domain portal site for books and other publications, or even more, as opposed to using the traditional business model of bookstores. As publishers are now doing their own business-to-customer e-commerce, the Internet bookstore no longer needs to maintain its own inventory. The publishers' inventories are its inventory. It does not have to conduct its own physical logistics. Its logistics is its informational transactions with the publishers who do the rest. The new fundamental question that arises at this point is who needs the bookstore if publishers could sell directly to customers? Bookstores can never out-discount the publishers anyway. The honest answer has to be no one. Every publisher could become an Internet bookstore of a portal site for books. The key must be the unique value that the bookstore - or any Internet store - offers to its customers. The bookstore must earn the patronage of persons not with the books it sells, but with the information services and products it provides. Publishers would have their unique value added through their unique physical production systems, including the writers. Bookstores, on the other hand, could have their own unique value added through information products developed with extended enterprises. Personalization would be key here.

3.3 Enterprise: Connecting Administration Systems with Production Systems (Principle 2.3).

It is only natural to connect the administration Intranet with the production Intranet once both are in place. Hence, the notion of an enterprise Intranet with all the desirable functions could be a minimum working definition for enterprise integration. The desirable functions would include the connection of administration systems and production systems discussed above. More fundamentally, however, the enterprise Intranet must be fully consistent with the e-commerce practice. Although the physical enterprise systems probably have to be isolated from externally oriented e-commerce systems for security reasons, they must support directly the latter. In fact, a more comprehensive working definition for enterprise integration for e-commerce is the enterprise's ability to support and provide the advanced information services and products discussed in Section 2 of the chapter. In particular, the purpose of connecting the administration systems with the production systems is to make an e-commerce enterprise capable of tapping into integrated customer services, selling personalized (information) products, and capitalizing on customer information to enhance quality and productivity. The first principle is fully realizable only when the second is realized.

For manufacturing enterprises, the vision of agile manufacturing paves the way well to the notion of personalized products. Here, we push the traditional concept of small batch manufacturing at mass production efficiency up another notch. We emphasize that the meaning of custom design and custom manufacturing must extend to the personal level. Consider a scenario. The e-commerce site helps a customer (buying a shirt, a car, or some cosmetic products) to identify his/her personal needs and then create, through embedded decision and design tools, a personal specification for the product. The e-commerce site, in turn, obtains all crucial business and production data about the personalized design and manufacturing (or packaging) and quotes the customer a price and delivery date. All these transactions are performed online, real time, within a timeframe of a usual airline ticketing transaction. Both the price and the delivery date are, of course, nearly as good as they would be with buying the mass-produced products available in stock. This kind of efficient customization is impossible without powerful enterprise integration. The Internet retailing site and the enterprise itself must be one and the same in terms of processes. The marketing, production, and delivery systems must work fully together to be able to determine the resources availability, the total cost, and the competitive price on the fly.

To draw an illustration from present practice, integration of administration and production for an enterprise means connecting enterprise resources planning systems with concurrent engineering systems and computer-integrated manufacturing systems, plus marketing and sales. Clearly, Intranet using Web technologies, facilitates the integration. We might mention at this point that enterprise is a scalable concept. It does not have to follow organizational boundaries. The new information technology, noticeably the Internet, extends an enterprise beyond or even transcending organizational boundaries. We discuss this concept next.

4. The Extended Enterprise Principle (Principle 3).

Information technology makes the world a global village. The Internet recognizes only collaboration. The e-commerce inter-operates persons and organizations. Therefore, the notion of extended enterprise is perfectly natural to the Internet and e-commerce. Only the opposite needs justification. The Internet itself is an extended enterprise. It has a common structure (albeit open), and everyone involved has a common sense of purpose and belonging, yet constituent networks join or leave the venture at their own will. The Web community is also an extended enterprise. Every business-to-business e-commerce enterprise that conducts business transactions is an extended enterprise. Every portal site is an extended enterprise. In fact, all e-commerce enterprises garner momentum from the openness and extensibility of the Internet. Therefore, every e-commerce enterprise faces the competition of creating the most innovative and profitable way to extend its enterprising over the Internet. The prize is competitive information services and products. Personalization requires extended enterprising. The Person-Centered Commerce (see Chapter 1) depends on a web of extended enterprises.

4.1 Extension: Applying E-Commerce to the Extended Enterprise for Integration (Principle 3.1).

An enterprise has certain external constituencies, including customer, supplier, distributor, financier, and the like. An extended enterprise is an enterprise that includes them as additional internal constituencies. Traditional business models offer many good examples of extended enterprise. A defense contract, for instance, entails close collaboration of many contractors and subcontractor, even the government agencies. Often times, they have to link their own internal processes and systems or create new processes and systems to encompass every partner for the contract. The result is an extended enterprise centered on the contract. There were many organizations each doing some part of the design for, say, a new military aircraft.

Thus, there rose the need to integrate all the design activities across organizations. It is a small wonder that concurrent engineering stems from this type of extended enterprises. Supply chain integration is another example. The prime company links its procurement systems with its suppliers' production systems. In this extended enterprise, the overall planning processes for the chain encompass both the prime and the suppliers and become the defining processes for the virtual enterprise. When the extended enterprise tightens up control of the overarching processes a notch, then a just-in-time production and inventory control system will result for the prime. A healthcare enterprise is typically an extended enterprise, too. A community hospital, for example, does not have its own resident physicians and all the necessary laboratories. Thus, it collaborates with these constituencies to form an extended hospital for the patients. Many strategic alliances are another form of extended enterprises. The previous business model of virtual enterprises is yet another example. In the cyber community, linkage is the norm; hence, extended enterprises are the norm.

The concept of extended enterprises is particularly important for e-commerce because it is both easy and profitable to develop. Extension on the Internet is much more broad and flexible than the traditional connection of constituencies. Technically speaking, every cyber person and organization could be a constituency of any other persons and organizations in some enterprising. There are three levels of enterprising for an extended e-commerce enterprise.

• The first is concerned with information services and information products. An e-commerce site, especially for the business-to-customer market, could create linkage with other e-commerce sites that are relevant to the customer (not necessarily relevant to itself) to enhance its marketing. Virtually all e-commerce sites could do this, and many have done just that. Some formal collaboration among sites would be necessary to implement the more innovative and potentially revenue-generating ideas.

• The next level is transactional. The connection of sites is designed at a level that supports actual business transactions. This level requires the joining of real processes and, hence, the participating companies must have a formal process for the extended enterprise. All business-to-business e-commerce operate at this level of extended enterprising.

• The highest level is to apply integration to the extended enterprise as a whole, as if it were one organization. Everything we discuss in the previous section about the enterprise integration principle would apply to the extended enterprise as well. For instance, an Intranet could be developed for all constituencies of the extended enterprise. In fact, extranet is precisely an example of this concept. The extended enterprise could seek to connect its administration processes and systems across constituent organizations. Procurement and supply chain class of functionality will become available. It could also explore, to connect in a similar way, the production processes and systems. Just-in-time class of functionality will result. Finally, it could overarch and integrate all processes and systems for the entire e-commerce enterprise, in the light of creating innovative and personalized services and products. Enterprise connectivity class of technology is a must for this practice.

The driving force underlying these efforts would be the combination of the above two principles; that is, generating new revenue and reducing cost. Although traditional extended enterprises tend to focus on the cost side, e-commerce practice could focus more on creating better business opportunities than each alone could. The first principle of information services and products has indicated many such situations where a joint venture would be win-win for every partner. Again, extended enterprise is a natural business practice. The Internet has also made it an easy practice. We would submit that an e-commerce enterprise, without seeking extension or joint ventures in the sense of Internet connection, has not really discovered the Internet.

4.2 Growth: Recursively Cascading the Extension Throughout (Principle 3.2).

Extended enterprise is a recursive concept. That is, an enterprise has immediate external constituencies, which in turn have their own respective external constituencies and so on. This concept meshes seamlessly with the cyber community. Every user of the Web is accustomed to the notion of endless linkages to sub-pages and to other home pages at other sites. The cascading Web sites mimics perfectly the social and business nets where everyone is familiar with the notion that a friend has friends whose friends are helpful and a client has clients whose clients are relevant. The difference is the enmeshing in the cyber community is astronomically more powerful. As being the case throughout, the virtually unlimited direct connection of persons and organizations is the key. The Web allows and supports an exponential extension of the extended enterprise at an almost instantaneous speed with almost non-existent cost. Well, this is almost an exaggeration. Simple extension of extended enterprises (at, e.g., the information level) can be attainable easily. Advanced practice would be more difficult. However, the universal user interface always helps; it, for example, makes transactional extension feasible, too.

Technically, to grow an extended enterprise is no different from creating one. Conceptually, they are also the same. The only difference is the vision and perhaps the management philosophy. That is, the traditional model of extended enterprises still embraces the notion of a prime vs. its contractors while the cascading mentality does not. The traditional vision is inherently finite. It is too conservative and restrictive for e-commerce. This practice is comparable to insisting on using proprietary solutions when open systems are commonly used and easy to get for the same job. The Internet is open and practically infinite. The business-to-business e-commerce, for instance, allows an enterprise to select vendors from any number of choices and change them at any time - and so do the vendors choosing their buyers. An extended enterprise could perfectly be some chance endeavor, fluid venture, or task force that evolves quickly. In a particular enterprising, the prime is not always the largest of all participants, only the most significant for the project. It all depends on the role and the job. This practice is helpful for the new vision, too. Extended enterprises in e-commerce should open the traditional vision up to new models that are more democratic, agile, and distributed. In certain cases such as supply chain integration, there might still be the need to maintain some stability of the supplier pool. However, the basic point stands. In the age of e-commerce, two reasons would liberate the traditional confines of extended enterprises. The confines are counter-productive to the original purpose of saving cost, and the confines prevent the development of more and better information services and products, especially in the area of personalization.

We might point out that the vision of Person-Centered Commerce assumes pervasive practice of scalable extended enterprises. Many portal sites have already excelled on this premise. The first principle of information services and products emphasizes extended enterprises without predicating on the traditional model. Thus, we expect the open version of extended enterprises to become the norm of the extension for e-commerce.

4.3 Roadmap: Converting Societal Transaction Cost Reduction to Business Opportunities (Principle 3.3).

Asking what the customer wants is always the golden rule for new product development. Companies are good at identifying business opportunities that either improve current products based on customer response or reduce cost on prevailing practices. Both tend to focus on the status quo, seek incremental changes, and analyze for immediate needs. The new information technology, however, is good at bringing about sea change as discussed in Chapter 1. How to identify new opportunities for developing unprecedented products that no one knows yet? In particular, how to seize the moment to invent profitable extended enterprises and, thereby, creating innovative information services and products for which no one has asked yet? This kind of paradigm-shifting opportunity is the determinant of winners and losers in the new information age. We return to the roots of the new age to search for clues: reduction of societal transaction cost. We return to the basic business rule of analyzing the value chain; this time, we keep in mind that the direct and universal connection of persons and organizations in all possible combinations has altered the societal value chain.

Great business opportunities could come from the most unlikely places. One such place is person-to-person business. What opportunities are there other than baby-sitting and yard sales, people of the conventional thinking might ask. A surprising but resounding answer is offered by eBay. However, eBay covers only a tiny bit of dealings people do among themselves through agents or some intermediaries. The above discussion about Internet bookstores illustrates that the traditional value chain is no longer a given fact. There is the potential of transforming all retailing stores and all middle persons. Just like the case where information technology has helped corporations flattening their management hierarchy, the new Internet retailing is flattening the traditional hierarchy of distribution channels - so far, for businesses only. Could it happen for persons, too? In a sense, all stores stand not only in between businesses and customers but also in between persons and persons. As eBay proves vividly, with e-commerce people no longer have to rely entirely on auction companies or antique stores. Does the same hold true for all other stores and agents that connect persons to other persons? To push the analysis even further, is not it true that a company, or for that matter any organization, is some kind of middle layer between persons who produce and persons who consume? We emphasized the person-to-person connection in Chapter 1. This connection promises to change fundamentally the way our society organizes to do business. The previous value chain represents the best ways to reduce transaction cost for the society in the past. The new information technology is rewriting the book. Therefore, there is little doubt where the new opportunities reside. They must reside in the new value chains that represent the renewed reduction of societal transaction cost. Organizations are nothing more than facilitators for the societal transaction cost. When some organizations become an inhibitor themselves, they would not survive. When they facilitate better, they thrive. Either way, the societal selection represents tremendous business opportunities for others, if not for the original organizations. The open extended enterprises promise to be the instrument for developing innovative opportunities. A powerful question to ask is could we extend the current enterprise to reduce some aspects of societal transaction cost, especially for the persons? More specifically, the search could follow two strategies. The first is a push approach; that is, consider systematically three paths from the perspective of the (extended) enterprise: extended constituencies, extended value chains, and extended processes. The second is pull, reviewing completely from the person's perspective, following likely the life cycle of a person's needs and activities. The Person-Centered Commerce model illustrates the pull concept. There promises to be tremendous business opportunities for providers and vendors that enable and support the persons to acquire information and conduct transactions of the persons, by the persons, and for the persons.

5. The Planning Model.

Now, we can conclude with a summary of the planning model using the above three principles. The objective is to help develop innovative ideas of using new information technology to better e-commerce for an enterprise. We consider two basic types of e-commerce ventures, those created by traditional companies and those new; both face similar challenges. The basic strategy discussed in Section 1 of the chapter provides a ready starting point. More advanced planning follows.

- *Identification of the product.* A traditional company should always consider both Internet retailing and Internet procurement, regardless of its previous business model. It would have no problem to develop an appreciation for the transactional type of e-commerce. However, it should not ignore possible new information products or even new physical products made possible by the advanced practice of e-commerce. For this type of enterprises, principles 1.1 and 2.1 could guide the planning for their e-commerce objective in terms of initial goals and possibly personalized information services. The planning process should move on through every principle until reaching Principle 3.3. Then, it should use Principle 1.2 to develop new information products. For new e-commerce ventures without a traditional commodity base, the natural starting point is the information side of the e-commerce house. Principle 1.2 should lead the way of planning for innovative information products. What needs to reiterate is the importance of actual business transactions. Towards this end, Principle 3 might help a venture (especially the information type) identify possibilities for offering transactional services through joint ventures - or, extended enterprising. For any e-commerce site that does transactions, Principle 2 is important. It is, however, particularly useful as a checklist for Internet retailing sites that maintain a significant back end operation using traditional business models. These enterprises should look beyond administration functions. In short, when pushing the envelope for the enterprise, every e-commerce company should plan for both business-to-customer and business-to-business e-commerce, making money on both information and transaction products.

- *Innovation for Marketing.* We cannot over emphasize the significance of Principle 1.1. All Web sites are information providers, by definition. However, most of them take a push attitude; that is, here I am. They push out their information assuming that the cyber community will automatically appreciate it. The cyber community does appreciate, except that it needs some help from the provider. Principle 1.1 stresses a pull attitude; i.e., the customers pull. A site must consider for its prospective patronage from the perspective of the patrons. Successful sites have done that. The successful sites make their patronage feel that the sites are of them, by them, and for them. However, there is only a distinct minority of e-commerce sites striving towards the objective. Thus, there is only a distinct minority of e-commerce sites winning the new game. When all is said and done, the distinction between a company direct sale site and a portal site, especially a niche market (domain) portal, would become blurred. Ultimately, present distinction among different types (retailing, procurement, information portal, transactional portal, and so on) of e-commerce sites would fade away as all sites acquiring some elements of all types. Finally, Principle 1.3 should become a weapon of marketing, too. It is relevant to all types of e-commerce and all sizes of enterprises. The ultimate competitive weapon would come when the enterprise has fully explored Principle 1 and combined it with Principles 2 and 3. This is the theme of the planning model: integration. For e-commerce, integration empowers an enterprise to develop at ease innovative strategies and compete freely in any shape and form.

The rest of the book explores the planning model. We first review previous results about information technology planning and then evaluate the model in the next two chapters. The review and evaluation follow the normal paradigm of research, calibrating the model to the practices reported in the literature. The formal study would help provide confidence and accountability to the model.

41

3

STRATEGIC PLANNING IN GENERAL

Planning for e-commerce is planning for business. Therefore, it has the general properties of business strategic planning. The field has acquired tremendous knowledge about strategic planning for enterprises; hence, we would want to make use of the asset. However, generic planning models tend to lack sufficient punch for the particular industries that particularized models aim to provide. Thus, we would expect the new effort of e-commerce planning to incorporate the new features of e-commerce into the planning. We would also want to make sure that the new e-commerce planning is consistent with the proven general results that apply. This is the purpose of the next three chapters. First, we examine the proven results in this chapter. Then in the following chapter we evaluate the new planning model presented in Chapter 2 against previous methods and calibrate it on industrial cases. Finally, in chapter 5, we incorporate some proven results into a planning framework (methodology) using the new model.

1. The Investigation: an Overview.

We study the general literature of strategic planning from the perspective of information technology. Since e-commerce is a new field, companies have relied on generic strategic planning methods such as Value Chain Analysis and industrial benchmarks to develop their initial plans. Two representative examples are the two cases studied in this book, a major bank (Chapter 7) and a heavy machinery and ship builder (Chapter 8). Bench marking provides a reference model of sort. However, it could be tenuous and be easily hindered by trade secrecy. The bank case reflects this point. The Value Chain Analysis method and other generic information systems planning techniques tend to be too general to explore the technical insights of e-commerce. Yet, they also seem to be too specific about following the status quo to encourage new enterprises. Thus, by themselves, they might not be sufficient to generate visionary plans for e-commerce. E-commerce, after all, requires innovative employment and deployment of new information technology for new business opportunities. The heavy machinery case shows this point. Clearly, the field has a gap in the supply of strategic planning frameworks that are prescriptive at the level of visions (e-commerce goal setting) and are descriptive of the technical requirements on enterprise (information) integration that the visions require.

The root cause of the problem resides in the fact that the Internet is fundamentally an inter-organizational technology and requires particular visions to realize its promises while traditional strategies focus predominantly on an organization per se. This mismatch reflects a larger problem concerning planning for information technology in general. Information technology has played a number of quite different roles for organizations in the past decades. It initially was nothing but some number crunching machine. Then, it became some managerial report generator or managers' productivity tool. Since the early 1980's, it has assumed the role of a competitive weapon. Now, enterprises not only recognize information technology's promises for producing competitive advantage, they realized that it, in some cases, even changes the very basis of competition in an industry. However, the planning methodologies have not kept pace. Survey after survey, how to align information strategy with corporate strategy has remained the number one concern of information system managers and chief information officers. However, in seminar after seminar, how to explore new information technology to create new business opportunities has also become a serious question corporate leaders and chief executive officers ask. Many studies have attempted to respond to the former, using a traditional perspective that business strategy pushes information strategy; but very few addressed the latter since it requires a radically different perspective. The new perspective recognizes new information technology as a driver pulling business opportunities and visions and, hence, the strategy. We might add that this "pull" view permits and, perhaps, calls for a prescriptive reference model for strategic planning that is based on the promises of the new capabilities.

One of the few such reference models is due to C. Hsu [1996]. It is amenable to gradual refinement, increasing the granularity of the goals through a planning framework. The framework could start with using the reference model to set high level goals and then map these goals to specific business processes. It could employ generic planning methods to review or even re-engineer these processes and, thereby, determine the appropriate scope and domain of the application of the new technology for the enterprise. Finally, the framework could review the particular classes of information technology required for particular processes involved in the particular goals. At this point, the framework would have generated necessary details about processes and functional requirements to enable systems analysis and design implementing these goals. This is actually our approach in this book. We take the original reference model which is generic for all information technology, add the special properties of e-commerce to it, and make it a particular planning model expressly for e-commerce (see Chapter 2). We then proceed to develop a methodology including the procedures for using some of the proven methods from the literature to refine the results (see Chapter 5).

This approach requires a proven way to analyze enterprise processes. Value Chain Analysis [Porter, 1984] is the most relevant method for this type of business process analysis. It helps guide the mapping of goals on processes and the prioritization of possibilities. Some processes will be modified, some deleted, and some new processes will need to be created. Moreover, many processes, original or new, will also be linked or integrated and, thereby, give rise to a process re-engineering effort. These changes, in turn, become a working definition for the technical requirements of the new information technology, since the latter must deliver the changes. In order to verify the model, we apply it to significant empirical cases to ascertain that (1) the framework works and (2) it provides unique results unavailable from previous methods. A number of empirical cases reported in the literature are retro-fitted to the model, and some new ones are developed using the model. Therefore, scholarly speaking, the basic research method employed to establish the planning model is interpretive case study. The research method used has ramifications for the accountability of the model. We, hence, discuss the method below, too.

We now examine some details of previous results. Since the literature on e-commerce planning is young and the proposals tend to lack an established user base, nor the support of a sound long-term study, we cannot study them objectively. Therefore, we focus our review on the established literature of strategic planning for, especially, information systems. The literature has a proven user base for the development of information strategies, including even e-commerce systems development. We have included some of the typical papers and books about e-commerce and Internet enterprises planning in the References of the book. We expect the field to grow rapidly. Thus, some of the proposed planning methods and strategies will have the chance to be tested and verified in the practice of e-commerce in the near future. Albeit worthy, the evaluation work has to wait for another day.

2. Previous Results: Strategic Information Planning.

Information Systems (IS) is an interdisciplinary field encompassing technical and managerial subjects. Its literature is rich in both areas. The earlier results concentrated virtually exclusively on how to analyze, design, construct, and manage the system to deliver the required functionality. The scope was very much confined to the perspective of a data processing center or that of a management information system department. Since late 1970's, organizations have discovered the power of information as a strategic weapon (e.g., the famous invention of the Automatic Teller Machine). Information systems started to cater to the strategic demands of organizations, i.e., serving the business goals and creating competitive advantage as well as meeting their data processing and information management needs. Therefore, organizations have to plan for information systems as tools not only for cutting costs but also for value addition. The Strategic Information Systems Planning (SISP) literature is a response to the broadening of the old scope. Thus, the authors tend to deal with three broad issues concerning the strategic roles of IS in enterprises: conceptual models, SISP methodologies, and theory building. The literature dealing with SISP concepts promotes the need to plan for information systems as a strategic resource, as opposed to using these systems for mere data processing or management support. The authors stressed a few basic concepts that have now become professional common sense. They include the focus on creating strategic and competitive advantage, integrating IS and business strategies, and aligning top management with IS management and users. They also identified a few patterns of IS efforts, such as entrepreneurial (user innovation), bottom-up development, and top down analysis. The authors have also identified the major impact of information technology on enterprises as in re-defining, re-engineering businesses rather than in data processing roles. There are many representative results; some of them include authors such as [Pavri and Ang, 1995; Beath and Orlikowski, 1994; Martin, 1993; Porter and Miller, 1985; and Ward, 1990].

Our planning model has inherited many of the SISP concepts since, after all, e-commerce is also a testimony to the strategic promises of information technology. The more direct concern from the perspective of the planning model is the previous methods for developing strategic information systems. The literature describes around ten major strategic information systems planning methodologies, of which we have reviewed six in detail for the purpose of this book. We summarize them below.

[Vitale et al, 1986] classifies SISP methodologies into two categories: impact and alignment. Impact methodologies help create and justify new uses of IT while the methodologies in the "alignment" category align IS objectives with organizational goals. The SISP literature identifies Value Chain Analysis as a leading impact methodology and the Business Systems Planning (BSP), Information Engineering (IE), Strategic Systems Planning (PROplanner) and Method/1 as leading alignment methodologies. Critical Success Factors is recognized as both an impact and an alignment methodology. All six methods are industry level results that have been widely adopted and applied in actuality. They are also applicable to developing e-commerce information systems.

These six major SISP methodologies are summarized in Table 3.1 below (pp. 46-48). We compare their foci, main features, strengths, and weaknesses. The comparison is largely our interpretation of the known results in the literature, which has provided many critiques of previous SISP methodologies, including these six.

Methodology	Focus	Salient Feature	Strengths	Weaknesses
Value Chain Analysis	Impact	- A form of business activity analysis - Helps in devising information systems which increase profit - Concentrates on value-adding business activities	- Concentrates on direct value adding processes. - Is independent of organizational structure	- Doesn't address issues of systems development and implementation. - Doesn't define a data structure. -Difficult to apply to non-manufacturing firms.
Critical Success Factors	Impact as well as alignment	- Used for identifying key information needs of an organization and its managers.	- Focus on key information requirements	-Not comprehensive - Internally focused and analytical, not creative. - Ignores value adding aspects of Information Systems.

Business Systems Planning (BSP)(From IBM)	Alignment	- Combines top down planning with bottom up implementation. - Focuses on business processes. - Data needs and data classes are derived from business processes.	- An integrated method which combines top down analysis with bottom-up implementation. - IBM being the vendor, it is better known to the top management.	- Detailed, time consuming, and costly. - Does not incorporate a software design methodology. - Requires a high degree of IT experience within the planning team.
Strategic Systems Planing(PRO planner)	Alignment	- A business functional model is defined by analyzing major functional areas of a business. - Data architecture is derived from the business function model. - The above architecture is used to identify new systems and their implementation schedules.	- An integrated method which combines top down analysis with bottom-up implementation.	- Detailed, time consuming, and costly. - Requires a high degree of IT experience within the planning team.
Information Engineering (From James Martin)	Alignment	- Provides techniques for building enterprise, data, and process models. - These models are combined to form a comprehensive knowledge base, which is used to create and maintain information systems.	- A comprehensive methodology - Provides automated tools to link output to subsequent systems development efforts.	- Extensive user involvement - Lengthy - Difficulty in finding a team leader - Difficulty in securing top management support.

Method/1 (from Andersen Consulting)	Alignment	- A layered approach: - Top layer is methodology, middle layer is techniques supporting methodology, and the bottom layer has tools supporting techniques. - Techniques supported: DFD, Matrix Analysis, Functional Decomposition, Focus Groups and Delphi studies. - Supported by CASE tool Foundation.	-Comprehensive - Provides automated support	- Expensive - Too detailed - Time consuming

Table 3.1: Comparative Features of SISP Methodologies (pp.46-48).

The key question to ask now is whether or not these methods by themselves are sufficient or even optimal for the task of planning for e-commerce, especially setting the goals of e-commerce systems. The literature has recorded some surveys about their performance as goal setting tools for strategic use of information systems. For instance, [Lederer and Sethi, 1988] has classified the problems found in implementing SISP methodologies as resource, planning process, and output related problems. Interestingly, the survey results seem to suggest that the practitioners are not particularly satisfied with their methodologies when it comes to aligning IS objectives with business goals. The basic reason is the fact that many industrial planning systems require detailed, lengthy, and complex procedures and efforts that are not always deemed relevant to the purpose of goal setting. They could err on being tedious and focusing on the trees rather than the forest. Moreover, when the objective is to use new information technology to pull new business strategy, these methodologies might not generate useful ideas at all. [Barlow, 1990] even suggests that the large number of methodologies that have been developed can often "add confusion rather than clarity to the (IS) planning process."

3. Value Chain Analysis.

Value Chain Analysis of [Porter, 1985] is a popular generic methodology for strategic planning, not limited to IS only. According to Porter, "every firm is a collection of activities that are performed to design, produce, market, deliver, and support its product. All these activities can be represented using a value chain." A typical value chain is shown in Figure 3.1.

48

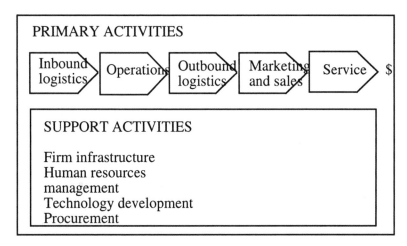

Figure 3.1: Porter's Value Chain.

Once the value chain is modeled, executives can rank order the steps in importance to determine which departments are central to the strategic objectives of the organization. Executives can then consider the interfaces between primary functions along the chain of production and between support activities and all of the primary functions. This helps in identifying critical points of inter-departmental collaboration.

Value Chain Analysis is a powerful tool used by strategists to diagnose and enhance competitive advantage. It allows the managers to distinguish how the underlying activities firm performs in designing, producing, marketing and distributing its product or service. These activities ultimately give rise to the firm's competitive advantage. By showing how all the activities of firms can be examined in this integrated way, [Porter, 1985] provided an original, practical perspective of competitive advantage.

Value Chain Analysis is an appropriate planning framework for many enterprises, including the use of Internet technology in businesses. Its strengths stem from its focus on the value added (and not merely cost saving) aspect of a system and, hence, is amenable to the analysis for changes, such as assessing the impact of information technology on the business. Information systems technology is particularly pervasive in the value chain since every value activity creates and uses information and, therefore, can substantially affect competitive advantage of firms. A firm that can discover a better technology or a better way of using a technology for performing an activity than its competitors gains competitive advantage.

Information technology is capable of changing the value chain. E-commerce has provided numerous pieces of evidence to this effect, as discussed in Chapter 1. In particular, one could easily identify how the Internet promises to positively affect all parts of the value chain of a firm. Some examples are given below in respect of Primary Activities, namely, Inbound Logistics, Operations, Outbound Logistics, Marketing and Sales, and Service:

- Inbound logistics -- low transaction cost connection to suppliers (business-to-business e-commerce).
- Operations -- Web-based user interface for enterprise connectivity (Intranets and extranets for enterprise integration).
- Outbound logistics -- low transaction cost connection to distributors (business-to-business e-commerce) or to consumers (business-to-customer e-commerce).
- Marketing and sales -- direct marketing and sales on the Internet to bypass the traditional channels (business-to-customer e-commerce).
- Service -- direct service for products and customers with much heightened quality and functionality (business-to-customer e-commerce).

The Internet also affects the support activities such as corporate structure, human resources, technological development, and purchasing positively. Some examples of e-commerce practice that change these aspects include:

- Corporate structure -- flatter organizations and extended enterprises (enterprise integration).
- Human resources -- employee recruiting and training on the Internet and Intranet for corporation-to-employees communication and dissemination of information (company Web sites).
- Technological development -- marketing intelligence and extended enterprises (enterprise integration).
- Purchasing -- low transaction cost connection to vendors (business-to-business e-commerce).

Besides the above visible effects of the Internet on the value-adding activities of a firm, the Internet offers many other significant benefits that are subtle to value chain analysis. As a case in point, an Internet retailing site could capture information not only about what consumers buy but also about what they might buy and will not buy. Such information can be very specific about target product promotion for target consumer groups and, hence, would help determine the company's market niche coverage. In other words, the subtle Internet benefits could change the company's marketing and sales value chain (e.g., abandon the traditional channels altogether). These benefits are not explicitly revealed by Value Chain Analysis [Kling, 1994], but are uniquely important to e-commerce planning. Having classified a firm's value adding activities in nine generic activities, Porter asserts that competitive advantage grows out of a firm's ability to perform these activities less expensively than its competitors, or to perform them in a uniquely productive way. Porter also emphasizes linkages between the activities that the firm performs, as no activities in a firm are independent; although, each department is managed separately. The emphasis here is on cost linkages that are involved so that the firm achieves an overall optimization of the production rather than departmental optimizations.

Porter classifies competitive advantage as cost advantage, differentiation advantage, and focus advantage. Cost advantage follows from the ability of a firm to deliver products of acceptable quality at the lowest possible cost. To sustain cost advantage, Porter gives a number of cost drivers that need to be understood in detail because the sustainability of cost advantage in an activity that depends on the cost drivers of that activity. These cost drivers include, for example, the scale of production, the learning curve of a firm, capacity utilization, linkages within value chain, timing about being a first or a late mover, policies that enhance the low-cost position or differentiation, location of individual activities, and institutional factors.

Differentiation advantage emerges from exploiting one or more characteristics of a product or a service that are widely valued by the customers. The purpose is to achieve and sustain performance that is superior to any competitor in satisfying those buyer needs. Successful differentiation leads to premium prices and, thereby, to above-average profitability if there is approximate cost parity. There can be numerous representative sources of differentiation in a firm. Differentiation is usually costly, depending on the cost drivers of the activities involved and a firm needs to find forms of differentiation where it has a cost advantage in differentiating. Focus strategies for advantage emerge from Porter's astute observation that a company that attempts to satisfy every possible buyer need does not have a strategy. Focusing, therefore, means selecting; the firm needs to select targets and optimizes its strategies for the targets, whether the strategies are based on cost or differentiation.

Porter's generic method is widely adopted for information planning. Authors either use it directly or adapt it to serve the particular needs of SISP. A good work in the second category is reported in [Wiseman, 1985], which extends Porter's thinking in many practical ways in the information systems area. He based his results on his experience with the previous SISP methodologies in work at GTE and other companies. Wiseman concurs that the significance of strategic information systems does not lie in the format of the reports they produce but rather in the role that these information systems play in the firm's gaining and maintaining competitive advantage. He made some interesting observations at the time. First, he points out that although the use of information systems may not always lead to competitive advantage, it can serve as an important tool in a firm's strategic plan. He further emphasizes that strategic systems must not be discovered haphazardly, *but those who would be competitive leaders must develop a systematic approach for identifying strategic information systems opportunities* (emphasis added). Both business management and information management must be involved. This is one of the first articulations on the "pull" philosophy in the field. A "systematic way" is precisely what a reference model of planning is meant to be - i.e., a tool for systematic discovery of competitive advantage through new information technology. The planning model of Chapter 2 is such a reference model for e-commerce planning. It is also pertinent to point out here Wiseman's criticism of popular SISP methodologies, such as IBM's Business Systems Planning (BSP) and the Critical Success Factors (CSF). He considered both methods as non-strategic since both are just ways to develop information architectures and to identify conventional information systems for merely planning and control purposes. This observation is similar to our analysis and is part of the rationale for developing the proposed planning model.

There are other parallels between Wiseman's work and Hsu's. Wiseman recommends developing a framework for identifying strategic opportunities. Since competition is bound to respond to any new development and deployment, Wiseman recommends the use of strategic thrusts based on information technology. These moves are just as important as other strategic thrusts as acquisition, major alliances with other firms, and other strategic thrusts. In this view of strategic opportunities, there are five strategic information thrusts and three strategic targets as shown in the Table 3.2. This opens up the range and perspective of management vision. Wiseman uses the term strategic thrusts for the moves that companies make to gain or maintain some kind of competitive edge or to reduce the competitive edge of one of the strategic targets. Information technology can be used to support or to shape one or more of these thrusts. Examining the possibilities of these thrusts takes imagination, and it is helped by what other firms have done in similar situations, which explains why so many examples of strategic IS implementation are presented in literature. We will continue this discussion in the next chapter when we analyze our reference model and compare it to the above methods we discussed.

Strategic Thrusts	Supplier	Customer	Competitor
Differentiation			
Cost			
Innovation			
Growth			
Alliance			

Table 3.2: Strategic IS Opportunities.

4. Enterprise Integration and Customer Information Service.

The original reference model of [Hsu, 1996] is built upon lessons and results obtained from the field of enterprise integration, concerning especially manufacturing enterprises. It embraces the "pull" philosophy, advocates the "strategy thrusts," and consists of a structure of planning directions for developing strategic information systems plans. The structure is useful as a roadmap for determining information systems goals in different categories. The goals so determined are based on a proactive review of information technology in light of yet developing competitive opportunities and are prescriptive in nature. This reference model is reprinted in the Appendix of the book. We evaluated the model in detail in Chapter 4. Since it is concerned with enterprise integration, we briefly discuss the literature that drove its development, especially such models as concurrent engineering, computer-integrated manufacturing, virtual corporation, and information enterprises.

Promoted by the U.S. Department of Defense, the original concept of concurrent engineering is a technical framework for various defense contractors to inter-operate their voluminous design information. The challenge was the simple fact that different companies and organizations used different software and hardware systems that are not compatible. Therefore, new methods and technologies become necessary in order to share and integrate engineering drawings and product design files among all contractors, sub-contractors, and design engineers working on the same weapon systems. Information technology has proven to be the single most powerful solution for this enterprise. It is a tool for integration, but its power has also changed the vision and the enterprises involved. It, for instance, promoted inadvertently the concept of extended enterprise out of concurrent engineering. The many lessons and evidence went into the pull view, the strategy thrusts, and the principles of the reference model.

Also prompted by Defense, the U.S. Air Force wanted a more cohesive manufacturing enterprise for its contracts. Its Integrated Computer-Aided Manufacturing (ICAM) Program initiated the worldwide race to integrate manufacturing with computers in the late 1970s and early 1980s. In essence, the ICAM vision extended the previous efforts of CAD/CAM (Computer-Aided Design/Manufacturing), a physical integration approach, into an approach that focused on the logical synergism among CAD, CAM, and eventually all other major functions of integrated manufacturing. It sought to integrate the islands of automation commonly found in manufacturing enterprises. Information technology has again proven to be the critical solution to this problem. Thus, CIM established the principle, since becoming operative, that information integration is the best means to achieve overall synergistic control of physical resources and operations in large-scale systems. This view of integration has also prompted new thinking towards new configuration of the previous manufacturing processes and cycles through new information technology. The core lessons of enterprise integration embodied in the planning model stems from the CIM practice.

The new information technology in concurrent engineering and computer-integrated manufacturing also created the model of virtual teams. This concept was later generalized into virtual corporation, networked corporation, horizontal corporation, and agile manufacturing. Its essence is to use information technology as the means to connect physically dispersed organizations and to encompass all aspects of an enterprise. Employees of a virtual corporation perform their assigned activities from anywhere, either within an independent consultant arrangement or under the virtual auspices of organizations that participate in the virtual corporation. As such, employees have a project-oriented association that precludes committing themselves to a fixed, traditional organization characterized by physical configurations. Clearly, the new information technology is not just a tool to enable the new model. Instead, the new model is inspired completely by the new technology. The new business model followed the new technology and aligned itself accordingly. Therefore, the same theme of information technology presented itself for the third time: extended enterprise, enterprise integration, and pull and strategy thrusts. Many details of this model went into the planning model, too, as described in Chapter 2.

We now turn to a harbinger to many of the concepts we include in the free information services principle of the planning model; that is, customer information service. A milestone result of this concept is the customer resource life cycle (CRLC) perspective of [Ives and Learmonth, 1984]. This model is, in essence, a quite comprehensive reference model for identifying possible information services for customers. Although it was not designed expressly for e-commerce, the e-commerce planning model can use it as a supplement to further refine some guidelines. In fact, the planning model has made used the CRLC concept in its principles. Therefore, it is worthwhile to describe the CRLC model in detail here. We should also mention that the CRLC model itself is a synthesis of many previous results on the topic.

According to the CRLC model, there are four main and thirteen sub-categories of a customer's resource life cycle, and each sub-category offers an opportunity to design information systems to facilitate the customer. The first category, requirements, deals with determining how much of a resource will be required by a customer and what will be the attributes of the resource that will best serve customer needs. Owens-Corning using data on energy efficiencies to evaluate insulation requirements for new building designs is an example. The second category, acquisition, focuses on customers' selecting source of the material, ordering it, paying for it, getting possession of the material, and testing it. American Hospital Supply's order entry system is an example of IS deployed to meet customers' needs in this category. Category stewardship deals with deploying IS to support customers during the operating life of the product. Examples include GE Supply Company's inventory management tool and Discover card's web site allowing customers to monitor their accounts. Retirement phase refers to transfer or disposal of a product by the customer, such as Avis car rental company's ATM-style car return system and Kelly's Blue Book web site, which facilitates customers disposal of used vehicles. The categories and sub-categories of the resource life cycle with the possible deployment of information technology to help customers through the cycle is summarized in Table 3.3 below (pp. 54-55).

Basic Model	Extended Model	Description	IT Functionality and Examples
Requirements	Establish requirements	To determine how much of a resource is required	IT is used to understand the customer's requirements. Examples are Owens-Corning using data on energy efficiencies to evaluate insulation requirements for new building designs and Wells Fargo Bank advising a business on the type of bank account best suited for their needs.
	Specify	To determine a resource's attributes	
Acquisition	Select source	To determine where customers will buy a resource	This is a major IT endeavor in its external orientation. IT is used to perform purchasing functions for the customer. Classical example in this category is American Hospital Supply's order-entry system. Auto-by-tel and Wells Fargo Bank's web sites are examples of such Internet based applications.
	Order	To order a quantity of the resource from the supplier	
	Authorize and pay for	To transfer funds or extend credit	
	Acquire	To take possession of a resource	
	Test and accept	To ensure that a resource meets specifications	

Stewardship	Integrate	To add to an existing inventory	IT functionality called for is to monitor a resource during its use by the customer. General Electric Supply Company's inventory management tool for its customers is an example. Charles Schwab's web site e.schwab for on-line stock trading by its customers and the Discover card's web site for account holder's monitoring of their accounts are two web based examples of IT deployment in this category.
	Monitor	To control access and use of a resource	
	Update	To upgrade a resource if conditions change	
	Maintain	To repair a resource, if necessary	
Retirement	Transfer or dispose	To move, return, or dispose of inventory as necessary	IT functionality required is to close a resource for the customer. Classical example is Avis' use of ATM-like machine to shorten the car return process. Kelly's Blue Book web site to help customers dispose of their automobiles is a web-base example in this category. Other web-based examples are cash management account reconcilement facilities offered to businesses by the Wells Fargo Bank from their web site.
	Account for	To monitor where and how much is spent for on a resource	

Table 3.3: Customer Resource Life Cycle (pp. 54-55).

The above paradigms are the building blocks of the reference model of Hsu. However, there are many planning methodologies in the field. How do we know that adding one more is worthwhile? We cannot answer the question directly since only the users of planning models can provide a definitive response. Still, we do the second best thing. That is, we evaluate the proposed model from a theoretical perspective. We will evaluate it in the context of the above SISP methodologies established in the IS field.

55

The evaluation uses the interpretive case study research method. It is one of the most common qualitative approaches used in the research of information technology. Although there is some confusion within the research community, the word 'qualitative' is not a synonym for 'interpretive' - qualitative research may or may not be interpretive, depending upon the underlying philosophical assumptions of the researcher. Positivists generally assume that reality is objectively given and can be described by measurable properties that are independent of the observer (researcher) and of his or her instruments. Interpretive researchers, on the other hand, start out with the assumption that access to reality (given or socially constructed) is achieved only through social constructions such as language, consciousness, and shared meanings. Positivist studies generally attempt to test theory in an attempt to increase the predictive understanding of phenomena. In distinction to this, interpretive studies generally attempt to understand phenomena through the meanings that people assign to them and do not predefine dependent and independent variables [Kaplan and Maxwell, 1994]. We elected to use the interpretive method simply because it fits the situation better.

4

EVALUATION OF THE REFERENCE MODEL

"If you like the new model, use it; if you don't, don't use it" (John von Neumann). What is the value of the planning model proposed in the book? There is an increasing number of planning methods proposed for e-commerce in the field. However, few have ever offered any formal justification for their prospective users to adopt them. We intend to break the rank. We endeavor to evaluate the planning model in the context of the literature, which is the best we can do for a new model. As discussed in Chapter 3, the literature only has established planning methods in the field of general information strategic planning. The field applies to e-commerce, albeit, too generic for e-commerce to be sufficient. Thus, we must evaluate the proposed model in the context of strategic planning for information systems, with respect to the established methods. For this purpose, we go back to the basis of the planning model, that is, the generic reference model for setting strategic goals for information technology. The Appendix reprints the model from [Hsu, 1996]. The only difference between the model in Chapter 2 and the model below is the orientation. The planning model is oriented expressly for e-commerce and presented in terms of e-commerce properties and opportunities while the latter is more generic concerning information technology in general. The substance is the same. The generic model compares directly to the generic methods established in the field. We use both the e-commerce cases and traditional cases to evaluate the model.

1. The Reference Model: a generic (re-)interpretation.

As stated in Chapter 3, the reference model is a proactive attempt to capture the promises of new information technology for new e-commerce opportunities or, for that matter, new opportunities for all enterprises. It takes the pull view and advocates strategy thrusts. The reference model emphasizes the need for effecting new regimes and paradigms through information-integrated and information-enabled enterprises to lift the organizational performance beyond the status quo. More than anything else, it is a holistic way of looking at an enterprise and optimizing the performance of the enterprise in its entirety, including its likely external constituencies. When applied to e-commerce, it highlights the notion of societal transaction cost, recursively extended enterprises, and personalization or customization. All these concepts are forward-looking and are consistent with many other authors' believes in the field of e-commerce and Internet enterprises. In particular, the reference model prescribes three distinct dimensions of a firm's business and then suggests three main attributes for each dimension. In total, these nine attributes serve as nine categories in which e-commerce opportunities and opportunities prompted by new information technology lie. To develop specific goals, the planner would systematically examine each category to look for relevance with the particular enterprise in question. The reference attributes would then be interpreted for the particular business attributes. We describe these dimensions below. They correspond respectively to the three principles of e-commerce planning in Chapter 2.

Management of External Environments.

This dimension corresponds to the Information Service and Product Principle for e-commerce. It focuses on the direct, external application of the Internet and other new information technology on the Internet to gain competitive advantages. The underlying theory is to manage uncertainty in the enterprise's environment.

- *Providing Information Services to Customers.* This is the e-commerce planning Principle 1.1. The generic idea is to lure and lock customers into the enterprise by investing in information technology that provides unique and crucial services to them. The added value is in external orientation. For example, an organization develops IT primarily for facilitating its customers' business rather than for its own internal use. Classic cases include the American Airline's Sabre system for travel agencies and Citibank's Automatic Teller Machine (ATM) for individual customers. There are numerous obvious opportunities for an organization to develop new generations of information services for customers and reap the same in strategic benefits, especially given extended enterprise and information integration. Generalizing the ATM to an on-line, free-of-charge banking and other services network for customers would be a natural potential. Interestingly, this is what Wells Fargo Bank has done. Healthcare Management Organizations have begun to explore the unlimited possibilities following along this line of thinking. Allowing customers to track their packages through an innovative use of their home page by FedEx [http://www.FedEx.com/] and facilities for on-line banking through the web pages of the Wells Fargo Bank [http://www.wellsfargo.com/] are two such web-based applications.

- *Turning Information Services into Products.* This is e-commerce planning Principle 1.2. The generic idea here is simple. The above notion of customer service can lead to innovative information products or information service profit centers. The Sabre system has become a major source of revenues for American Airlines since travel agencies pay significant fees for its extended services. In a similar way, proprietary information technology and services that an enterprise develops can be turned into dedicated information service providers or spin-offs in the market. Electronic commerce and global information enterprises seem to be especially ripe for this type of opportunity. Yahoo! [http://www.yahoo.com/] and similar web search services like Lycos, OpenText, etc. are examples of information services that have been turned into products on the Internet. The recent development of broadcasting content on the Internet in TV style adds a new dimension to the potential for providing information services to customers and turning those services into products. Some of the questions to consider in this category include the following: Is the firm in a position to develop the information product that it proposes to offer? Will the firm need to set up a different enterprise to support the information product (like SABRE Travel Information Network)? Will a firm need to set up some consulting operation to support its information product? Possible consulting services around such information products can be systems integration consulting, software consulting, and Internet consulting.

- *Monitoring the Market and Customer Behaviors.* This corresponds to e-commerce planning Principle 1.3. The generic idea is database marketing. Marketing databases have proven to be a potent weapon for gathering marketing intelligence and assisting in new product development. Their key is to exploit ubiquitous interfaces with customers (coupons, purchases, repairs, surveys, and the like) and turn them into intelligent information for strategic uses. A broader implementation of managing external environments would include not only the customer but also the suppliers and other constituencies of the extended enterprise, including external users of the Internet. Analyzing the information needs of these external users within the context of their respective enterprises and employing the Internet to satisfy their needs will work to the organization's benefit. Basic strategic gains result when an organization is able to do more in the way of extended contact and use the feedback gained to improve internal and external business processes. The web allows collection of marketing information that was not otherwise available. Analysis of the log files for the web server access show which pages are being browsed by visitors. The information to monitor include customer profile (their incomes, their spending patterns, their usage patterns of the Internet, etc.), market/competitors profile, and environment profile (economy, government regulations, international situation, etc.).

Maximization of the Internal Networking of Processes and Resource.
This generic dimension corresponds to the Enterprise Integration Principle of e-commerce. Its basic orientation is improving the production function of an enterprise, thereby, enhancing its productivity (measured through cost and quality). Linkages will be created across an enterprise to connect all stages of cycles, including differing levels of granularity (product, production, and part); flows (information vs. materials); and businesses (administration vs. production). The underlying theory is that, by connecting all stages of the business cycle, maximum channels of communications can be created to minimize the internal uncertainties facing an enterprise, and resources can be pooled and utilized throughout the extended enterprise.

- *Applying Information Technology to the Internal Processes.* This corresponds to the e-commerce planning Principle 2.1. The generic idea is that an enterprise that delivers higher quality at a lower cost than competitors enjoys the most fundamental strategic advantage of all. Information technology has proven to be an agent of progress in many applications. The point is there is never an end to the progress. Thus, applying information technology to the enterprise functions and processes that are not traditionally considered as ready target for application would find new strategic opportunities. Examples include the medical functions of a hospital (e.g., diagnosis, surgery, treatment, and pharmacy) and the educating function of a university (e.g., lectures, assignments, and laboratories). Although these functions have been using information technology - such as CATSCAN/MRI in medicine and studio style classrooms in education, the majority still follows a traditional paradigm where information technology is sequestered to number crunching jobs. Deepening and broadening the role of information technology to convert traditional enterprises into e-enterprise is the name of the game. Intranet and extranet are two recent examples.

- *Creating Forward and Feedback Linkages for All Production Cycles.* This generic category corresponds to e-commerce planning Principle 2.2. The common basis is the fact that an enterprise has three basic cycles: part, production, and product. The product cycle includes everything from marketing and product planning to recycling used materials; the production cycle satisfies the customer's orders and demands, and the part cycle processes the individual elements involved in producing a product. Previous visions of integration tend to focus only on a single cycle apart and aside of the other two. They primarily integrate the forward stages into a connected sequence in the cycle without closing the cycle through feedback. Forward linkage allows some jobs in the later stages to be performed simultaneously with earlier jobs; or, at least, the requirements of the later stages can be explicitly considered early in the product cycle. Both forward and feedback linkages are needed to complete a cycle. Furthermore, all three cycles are interwoven in a truly agile enterprise. Therefore, new strategic opportunities for information technology will arise from creating feedback to complete a cycle and from connecting all cycles through forward and feedback linkages. These cycles are actually inter-related processes. Thus, an enterprise will do well by mapping its processes and sub-processes to these cycles and reviewing for linkages. The concept of backward/forward chaining prompts organizations to look at the complete life cycle of a process as opposed to taking a linear view. Therefore, it has promises for guiding new strategic use of information technology towards process re-engineering. Since the Internet is an inter-organizational technology, organizations should pay extra attention to processes that extend beyond traditional organizational boundaries and see if the process life cycle concept extends beyond a physical organization. It is possible that some forward/backward chaining in the life cycle of a process will occur outside the confines of a physical organization. Such applications of the Internet technology are further discussed in the third dimension, extended enterprises.

- *Connecting Administration Systems with Production Systems.* This generic category corresponds to e-commerce planning Principle 2.3. It recognizes the historical dichotomy of administration vs. production when it comes to information technology applications. Information integration allows and asks that the walls come down, just as e-commerce abridges information flow with material flow. An interesting example showing the significance of this connection is activity-based costing and management in which the classical administrative function of accounting is conducted on the basis of monitoring the alignments of resources around activities. This monitoring certainly can be and should be made on-line and in real time. Total Quality Management is also based on performance information cutting across administration and production. Calibrating and aligning administration with production on an on-line, real time basis produces the ultimate decision-making information within an agile, lean, and productive enterprise. In essence, this is the basic logic underlying some principles of e-commerce planning, that e-commerce enterprises need to offer and connect both information and transaction services and that e-commerce systems must integrated with regular systems.

Transformation into Three-Dimensional Enterprise.
This dimension is the Extended Enterprise Principle of e-commerce planning. It is concerned with the generic need of enterprise scalability. The three categories below provide some logic guiding high-level information technology planning towards continuous enterprise integration and modeling. It also strives to incorporate the first two dimensions into the integration. They expand the scope of enterprise from the traditional organizational view to one that features collaboration with other organizations, through information enterprising. This dimension is especially crucial for planning for e-commerce and other types of Internet enterprises because the Internet, as mentioned earlier, is an inter-organizational technology.

- *Thinking Extended Enterprise.* This is e-commerce planning Principle 3.1. The general fact is simple; all organizations have business processes that encompass those of others. All the discussions pertaining to the internal production systems and administration of an enterprise are applicable to the virtual systems of an extended enterprise. Strategic opportunities for streamlining operations across organizations by way of Electronic Data Interchange (EDI), Just In Time (JIT), and Concurrent Engineering (CE) are practically unlimited. The healthcare industry, for example, is a fertile ground for this concept. Many opportunities are implicit in connecting insurers, hospitals, physicians, patients, government agencies, and research institutes through information integration. Other industries have similar opportunities. The Internet technology is a practical and inexpensive enabler of such integration.

- *Expanding to Information Enterprises.* This generic category corresponds to the e-commerce planning Principle 3.2. The fact that enterprises are linked through information and this linkage can go on recursively without a limit is easy to appreciate for e-commerce. It is not so obvious for others. Traditional business thinking focuses only on the material enterprises of products, resources, and the marketplace. Running parallel to the material enterprise is an equally large world of information enterprises in cyberspace that can utilize the same enterprise thinking. For example, a virtual medical center could be constructed by using personal medical instruments located in patients' homes and linking them with doctors and researchers through multimedia telecommunication systems. A third-party information server/clearing house could provide pooled inventories and other resources to its client organizations through information integration in an extended enterprise manner. An Army/Defense logistics system could be integrated in cyberspace with visualization, simulation, and global information management capabilities. A studio-style virtual classroom could result from combining virtual laboratories, multimedia courseware, and the Web technology to enable distance learning that is delivered to individual households. This kind of electronic commerce and global information enterprise opportunities can often be uncovered by applying familiar paradigms to the information side of the world. Recursive extension of enterprising possibilities would become natural and so does transformation of the perspective of the enterprises. Essentially, this category is a scaling up of the preceding concept.

- *Evaluating Information Technology on Micro-Economic Bases.* This generic notion is the e-commerce planning Principle 3.3. The common observation about information technology application is its often limitation to cost/expenditure savings. Even when information technology has established an eminent role in Corporate America, there is a lack of proper ways to evaluate its development at the strategic level and, hence, guide its innovative application. To move ahead, the prevailing valuation criteria must change. An enterprise can evaluate information technology and its application on three micro-economic criteria: transaction cost reduction, utility improvement (value/benefit added), and organizational design. In theory, the best accounting for the contribution of information technology is its impact on the basic production function of the enterprise. This accounting is hard to come by in practice since the complete production function is usually unavailable for individual enterprises. Transaction cost would be the best choice. Although it is not quantitative in most cases, it is sufficiently appreciable in qualitative terms. The value of the Internet is an overwhelmingly telling example. Transaction cost reduction, therefore, is the overarching guideline for e-commerce planning.

All three dimensions are inter-related. Together, they constitute a three-dimensional enterprise. For example, an organization can apply the concept of customer information services either to the customers of the original (physical) enterprise or to the customers of the extended (information) enterprise - customers' customers and suppliers' suppliers and so on, or both. The same principles for analyzing customer requirements will apply to either case but will prescribe different applications in the extended category. Similarly, the concept of providing information services can also be applied to a virtual (information enabled) enterprise. Finally, this very concept of providing information services can be justified either on traditional economic basis (cost reduction, utility enhancement) or on transaction cost reduction. Thus, the last dimension has a multiplication effect with the first two. In other words, the first two sets of categories (six in total) can couple respectively with extended enterprises, virtual enterprises, and transaction cost reduction. Therefore, there are potentially four perspectives (these three in the third dimension plus the tradition perspective) for the six categories, resulting in a total of twenty-four (24) possible categories of information technology goals.

In this chapter, and indeed chapters throughout, we would not consider the multiplication potential and would treat the third dimension as only three additional categories to the first two sets. These nine categories are tabulated below in Table 4.1 (pp. 63-64).

Category Of IT Goal	Description	Sub-categories Of IT Goal	Examples
Management of External Environments	The focus of IS applications under this category is on direct external applications of IT as a strategic weapon to gain competitive advantage.	1. Providing Information Services To Customers (E-Com Principle 1.1) 2. Turning Information Services into Products (E-Com Principle 1.2) 3. Monitoring the Market and Customer Behaviors (E-Com Principle 1.3)	Citibank's ATM, Federal Express's web-based package tracking system, Wells Fargo Bank's Internet-based on-line banking, American Airlines Sabre system, Yahoo!.
Maximization of the Internal Networking of Processes and Resources	IS under this category is oriented towards improving the production function of an enterprise, thereby enhancing its productivity (measured through cost and quality). IT is focused upon creating linkages across an enterprise to connect product, production, and part cycles, to connect information and material flows as well as administrative and production functions.	1. Applying Information Technology to Internal Processes (E-Com Principle 2.1) 2. Creating Forward and Feedback Linkages for All Cycles (E-Com Principle 2.2) 3. Connecting Administration Systems with Production Systems (E-Com Principle 2.3)	CIM, CAD, CAM, CATSCAN/MRI, web-based virtual classrooms, Intranets, Total Quality Management (TQM).

Transformati on into Three- Dimensional Enterprise	IS in this category is used for enterprise integration and modeling. IT is employed to expand the scope of enterprise from the traditional view into both extended enterprises and information enterprises.	1. Thinking Extended Enterprise (E-Com Principle 3.1) 2. Expanding to Information Enterprises (E-Com Principle 3.2) 3. Evaluating IT on Micro-Economic Bases (E-Com Principle 3.3)	EDI, JIT, Extranet, Virtual Corporation such as Auto-by-Tel.

Table 4.1: Reference Model Categories (pp.63-64).

2. Appropriateness of the Model for Information Goal Setting

The reference model described above has some properties that are consistent with the nature of information technology goal setting, in general, and e-commerce planning in particular. We submit a few below.

- The model explicitly targets strategic uses of information technology in the light of yet developing IT-based competitive opportunities. Since it is forward looking, the model is consistent with planning for the use of technology that is evolving rapidly. This suits the needs of the pull view of the technology driven strategy thrusts.

- The reference model is rooted in the paradigm of enterprise integration through information. Beneath the hype of the Internet and the Web is essentially a technology of enterprise integration. The technology connects a firm with its vendors, customers, suppliers, and various other constituencies, but it also connects the firm itself in the same manner. Thus, the model is consistent with nature of e-commerce and other new information enterprises.

- The reference model highlights some subtle but important areas for organizations to focus upon during a planning effort. Distinction between merely providing information services to customers and turning those services into information products is one such example. In a way, it is consistent with the use of a roadmap or checklist for strategies.

- The reference model prescribes competitive advantage through re-configuration and re-engineering of business processes. Some of nine categories focus explicitly on reviewing and redesigning enterprise processes and organizations. Therefore, it is also consistent with the prevailing practice and findings of the information technology field, which recognize the need for business process re-engineering and organization redesign when pondering innovative strategy thrusts using information technology.

- The reference model explicitly recognizes the cyberspace as a viable medium of conducting business and processes (information-enabled enterprises) and suggests formal integration of this space with the traditional business model. This orientation is consistent not only with the results in the field of enterprise information technology leading to the model but also with all major findings since then in the field of e-commerce and other practices of information technology. In other words, the model has shown its lasting value in the turbulent world of planning for information technology applications.

We now review a number of industrial cases available in the open literature to see if the reference model is consistent with the practice. We will note whether the model covers all major applications and strategies. We will also examine whether the model is able to shed further light on the established practices. We review both the traditional cases and the e-commerce cases. For consistency, we refer to the generic model (for general goal setting using information technology) for traditional cases. When it comes to the e-commerce cases, in the next section, we indicate their match with the e-commerce planning principles discussed in the extended planning model of Chapter 2.

Sabherwal and King reported 34 cases of strategic applications of information technology by businesses in their 1991 paper entitled, "Towards a theory of strategic use of information resources." They used these cases to discover useful propositions of a theory for customer information services (discussed in Section 4, Chapter 3). We now re-examine these very cases to illustrate how they match up with the strategic goals of the reference model. We briefly describe these 34 cases below (all taken from the above paper) before we show the match in the matrix of Figure 4.1.

The Cases.

The 34 cases (in brief) are:
(1). American Airlines developed the Sabre reservation system which lists flight schedules of major airlines in the world, and American gets paid for any reservation made via Sabre on other carriers. The system, initially, also gave American preferential treatment, which was changed due to legal/government pressures.

(2). American Hospital Supply Corporation (which is now a part of Baxter Travenol), a leading manufacturer and distributor of health-care products, set up computer links with hospitals. This system simplified ordering processes for both AHSC and the customer and led to increase in customer loyalty and AHSC market share.

(3). American Express Co. uses information resources to provide preferential services for its customers. The services include arranging itineraries while at the same time cutting travel costs. Computers search for the lowest airplane fares, track travel expenses for card-holders, and issue monthly statements. This preferential service provides American Express with a significant differentiation advantage.

(4). Starting with data-processing and card issuance services for Merrill Lynch, Banc One has made agreements with other brokerage houses and its Financial Card Services Division processes credit-card transactions for several companies. It has grown at a tremendous pace, from $150 million in assets in 1959 to $15 billion in assets in 1986, and a major factor in its growth has been the way it has used its information resources.

(5). Car/Puter, an automobile dealer, maintains information on "pricing packages," including for each make and model of car a dealer carries, the manufacturer's list price and dealer cost, option costs, dealer freight and profit. It locates buyers and sells them a computer printout listing the pricing package. Computer printouts help convince buyers they are getting the best deal in town.

(6). Citicorp utilized ATMs for customer servicing and marketing by creating much "friendlier" machines than the earlier ones, which had already proved unsuccessful. It reduced considerably the cost of processing low-profit consumer transactions at branch offices. The ATMs have helped Citicorp move closer to its goal of becoming a nationwide consumer bank despite federal laws prohibiting interstate banking, as Citicorp has access to over 6500 ATMs in the US alone.

(7). Citicorp is also taking a lead in global banking telecommunications through its Global Transmission Network, which provides up-to-the-minute investment information in 190 cities around the world.

(8). Delta Airlines uses data obtained from the Air Traffic Publishing Company to monitor the daily fare changes by their competitors. Its system monitors reservation data, comparing current sales against historical patterns, and advises agents to shrink or expand the number of discount seats available on particular flights. Using the reservation system, Delta can respond to competitors' actions within two hours.

(9). Digital Equipment Corporation uses two expert systems that help configure equipment orders. This helps reduce the time needed to fill orders and increases accuracy, thus differentiating DEC as a quality provider.

(10). Dow Jones & Co., publisher of the Wall Street Journal, has used its page transmission technology to reduce the costs of producing a national - and international - newspaper to the point where it is economically feasible to do so. The company has, consequently, been able to expand into the global market while maintaining control over its operations.

(11). Dun & Bradstreet recycles and repackages the accumulated information from its various divisions into new products to increase revenue. To obtain information on Company A, Company B not only pays Dun & Bradstreet but must also submit its own financial information and, as a result, new information is always coming in.

(12). Equitable Life Assurance, the nation's third largest insurer, has developed an on-line system that ties the firm's field offices with its regional offices, warehouses, and the corporate headquarters. The on-line information from the inventory control and purchasing system gives the company leverage during vendor negotiations. The system has resulted in large annual savings for the firm and has also enhanced the reliability and quality of its deals with its suppliers.

(13). Federal Express Corporation has a database management system, Cosmos, which tracks all letters and parcels sent by the company. As a result, the company can tell its customers where their packages are in 30 minutes or less. The company maintains a very high delivery rate and high market share.

(14). The newspaper chain Gannett Co. has successfully used satellite transmission technology for its national daily, USA Today. The system transmits the four-color paper from its area editorial offices in Washington, DC to 30 U.S. printing plants and to Singapore and Zurich.

(15). General Electric has built, and continues to augment, a database from the information obtained through a toll-free hotline for customer complaints and questions. The accumulated experience and knowledge is used to provide improved customer support, to improve existing products, and to develop new ones. Some 94 percent of the customers who use the system express their satisfaction with the results.

(16). McGraw Hill Inc. has set-up several systems to enable its magazines, books, newsletters, economic forecasting units, and financial data operations to pool information and, in some cases, be cross-marketed. Instead of gathering data for a single publication, reporters store their file in giant computer databases which some call the McGraw Hill turbine. The turbine churns out several new products from specialty print publications to on-line services for customers with personal computers.

(17). McKesson Corporation, the nation's largest drug distributor, provides its drugstore customers with terminals. It allows customers to enter orders directly in return for which they are guaranteed delivery within a certain specified period. This has led to broadened product lines and increased customer loyalty.

(18). Mead Corporation's subsidiary Mead Data Central Inc. has used electronic delivery of information to provide users with quick access to vast amount of information. It spent $30 million on a communications network and special software and, in 1973, launched its Leis service, which helps lawyers do extensive case research on short notice. By 1986, most law firms used Leis, which accounted for Mead Data's $154 million in annual revenue and generated pretax profits of about $20 million.

(19). Merrill Lynch & Co. combined information on a customer's checking, savings, credit card, and securities accounts into one computerized monthly statement with the idle funds being automatically "swept" into interest-bearing money market funds. The product, Cash Management Account, has shattered the traditional boundaries between the banking and securities industries. Introduced in 1978, the product had about 1 million customers by 1983, bringing Merrill Lynch $20 billion in assets.

(20). Metpath, a large clinical laboratory, keeps records of patient data on file and offers financial processing services through billing and accounts payable applications, thus achieving differentiation in an otherwise commodity service. This differentiation increases the loyalty of physicians who normally have a tendency to switch from lab to lab in search of lower costs.

(21). Navisar International, earlier International Harvester, offers a system Focus to truck fleet operators. The system which runs on a portable computer, helps customers to estimate the number of maintenance personnel, the investment in spare parts inventory, and the size of the maintenance facility needed to maintain a particular truck or bus fleet. The company has used the system to develop an ongoing relationship with large fleet owners who can now benefit from a more tightly run maintenance operation. Since the system is based on data Navistar has collected over a long period of time, it is difficult for competitors to compete.

(22). Owens-Corning Fiberglass Corporation uses data on energy efficiency to help builders evaluate insulation requirements for new building designs. It provides the package "free" to builders as a service for their customers, the home buyers. In return, the company demands the builders to carry its insulation materials exclusively, resulting in considerable increase in company sales.

(23). Pacific Intermountain Express, a California based trucking firm, uses an information system that allows shippers to call the computer to track the status of a shipment. This is important for misplaced or delayed shipments, emergencies, etc. Strategically, it created a way for the company to differentiate its services from its competitors and to attract shippers, thus increasing its profit opportunities.

(24). Procter & Gamble Co. uses phones and terminals to log and disperse customer complaints. It acts as an early-warning system and enables Procter & Gamble to continually refine its products, correcting deficiencies and making improvements.

(25). Red Lion Inns chain uses a computerized inventory-control kind of system to monitor the status of rooms in its 52 hotels, to set discount rates, and to enable guests to make reservations from its hotel lobbies. The system enables the chain to have a 70% room-occupancy rate, 2-3% above the national average, and a repeat business rate of 85%.

(26). Red Lobster's nationwide communication network provides management personnel with next day access to sales data at both corporate headquarters and divisional offices across the country. This enables the management to monitor and evaluate results and, if necessary, modify prices or re-target promotions. This pricing strategy ensures some consistency in pricing nationwide while still permitting menus to be carefully tailored to regional audiences.

(27). Red River Construction, serving the heavy utilities industry in Texas, uses computerized bids for construction contracts. This permits the company to make numerous last minute changes in a reliable fashion, and, as a result, the bids are more accurate. Such use of information resources helps the company to wait till the last possible moment to finalize its cost and that increases the number of times it was the lowest bidder.

(28). Using its computerized data and retrieval system for banks and stocks and commodities, Reuters has become a gatherer and disseminator of financial data for world capital markets. As a result, Reuter's profits rose tenfold to $58 million in the five-year period 1977-82. Sales of data dwarfed sales to news organizations by 9 to 1.

(29). Toys "R" Us, the nation's leading toy chain, relies on a sophisticated information system and point-of-sales terminals in its outlets to keep track of what's selling so that it can take quick mark downs to rid itself of slow movers. While the toy-retailing industry grew 37% from 1980-1985, Toys "R" Us sales increased 185%. Clever use of information resources is commonly considered to be a major factor responsible for the company's success.

(30). United Airlines, working with IBM, developed its own Apollo reservation system five months after American developed Sabre. Sabre lists flight schedules of major airlines in the world, and United gets paid for any reservation made via Apollo on other carriers. The system also gave United preferential treatment, which has been now reduced due to legal/government pressures.

(31). A series of systems that automate policy and claims processing have enabled USAA to do sales and service over the telephone, eliminating agents that boost premium. The company ranks near the top in customer satisfaction with automobile and homeowner claims handling.

(32). Wetterau, a large wholesaler, diversified into the retailer arena based on its expertise with electronic check out scanners and computerized inventory systems. Wetterau's scanner-equipped stores are on-line with its host computer, which updates prices, tracks reordering information, generates shelf labels, and performs other functions.

(33). Xerox Corporation has developed a customer support system that provides the customer service representative with information about the problems he/she will encounter and parts most likely to be needed. It also provides useful information to field support representatives for scheduling the customer service representative to the next site. The system has improved customer satisfaction through faster, high quality response time, and improved productivity of the large technical representative force by increasing the number of calls each can make.

(34). Xerox Corporation has a system that supplies master manufacturing schedules on-line to major suppliers so they can ship parts precisely at the time Xerox needs them, thus enabling the company to keep its inventory low.

The Mapping Matrix.

The above 34 cases are tabulated in the first column of the matrix of Table 4.2. The first row of the matrix is an abbreviated list of the nine sub-goals of the reference model. There are three sub-goals under the goal category: Management of External Environment, namely, Providing Information Services to Customers (PISC), Turning Information Services into Products (TISP) and Monitoring the Market and Customer Behavior (MCB). The second category of goals, Maximization of Internal Networking of Processes and Resources, is abbreviated in the matrix as 'Internal Networking.' The three sub-goals under this category are Applying Information Technology to Internal Processes (AIT), Creating Forward and Feedback Linkages for All Cycles (FFL), and Connecting Administration Systems with Production Systems (CAP). The third category of goals, Transformation into Three-Dimensional Enterprise, has been abbreviated in the matrix as '3-D'. Three sub-goals under this category are Thinking Extended Enterprise (TEE), Expanding to Information Enterprises (EIE), and Evaluating Information Technology on Micro-

Economic Bases (EIT). Wherever a strategic goal in a reported case corresponds with one or more of the nine sub-goals in the reference model, an X is placed in the appropriate column. For example Case #1 (The American Airlines Sabre reservation system) meets the two sub-goals in the reference model, Providing Information Services to Customers (PISC) and Turning Information Services into Products (TISP). This match explains the two X's in the second and the third columns of the second row. Table 4.2 is printed in pages 70-71.

Strategic Goal -> Case	PISC	TISP	MCB	AIT	FFL	CAP	TEE	EIE	EIT
American Airlines	X	X					X		
American Hospital Supply	X	X					X		
American Express Co.	X								
Bank One		X							
Car/Puter	X								
Citicorp (I)	X								
Citicorp (II)	X								
Delta Airlines	X								
Digital Equipment Corp.	X			X	X		X		
Dow Jones & Co.				X					
Dun & Bradstreet				X					
Equitable Life Assurance							X		
Federal Express		X							
Gannett Co.							X		
General Electric	X	X							
McGraw Hill Inc.				X					
McKesson Corporation			X						
Mead Corporation	X	X							
Merrill Lynch	X	X							
Metpath	X	X							
Navisar International	X						X		
Owens-Corning	X	X							
Pacific Intermountain Exp.	X								
Procter & Gamble Co.	X	X							
Red Lion Inns	X		X						

Red Lobster			X						
Red River Construction				X					
Reuters		X							
Toys "R" Us			X						
United Airlines	X	X							
USAA					X	X			
Wetterau			X						
Xerox Corporation (I)	X								
Xerox Corporation (II)					X		X		

Table 4.2: The First Validation Matrix For the Reference Model (pp. 70-71).

Analysis.

A total of 51 strategic goals are identified in the 34 cases. That gives an average of 1.44 strategic goals per case. Of these 50 strategic goals, 36 (72%) fall under the first category, Management of External Environment. Within this category, 19 (38%) fall under the category Providing Information Services to Customers (PISC), 12 (24%) under the category Turning Information Services into Products (TISP) and 5 (10%) under Monitoring the Market and Customer Behavior (MCB) category. There are 8 of the cases (16%) that fall under the second category of goals, i.e., Maximization of Internal Networking of Processes and Resources. The break-up under three sub-goals under this category are Applying Information Technology to Internal Processes (AIT) - 6 (12%), Creating Forward and Feedback Linkages for All Cycles (FFL) - 2 (4%), and Connecting Administration Systems with Production Systems (CAP) - 0. Finally, there are 7 (12%) of the goals that fall under the third category of goals, Transformation into Three-Dimensional Enterprise. All these goals fall in one category: Thinking Extended Enterprise (TEE).

A few salient points emerge from the above analysis:
- The strategic goals delineated in the reference model are consistent with all the goals reported in these cases. That is, we have not found any goal that the reference model does not cover, nor any that it could not explain or foretell.

- In 24% of the cases, the strategic goal sought is accomplished by turning information service provided to customers into a product. The reference model is unique in the literature in its prescribing this goal and its integrating this goal with the goal of providing better information service to customers.

- A whopping 72% of the strategic goals subscribe to the dimension of Management of External Environment. This concentration is understandable as these cases are from the 80's and early 90's, before the advent of e-commerce. The strategic value of information resources was still perceived to be mainly in external orientation and providing unique services to customers. The three most popular cases of strategic use of information technology from that period, the American Airlines Sabre reservation system, Citibank's ATM, and the American

Hospital Supply Corporations automating order processing system are a testimony to such external orientation. They all used costly proprietary systems to provide the connection and processing and, hence, took a long time to diffuse to a finite domain (in today's standard). Comparing these harbingers with today's e-commerce, one could better appreciate the value of the Internet as an inexpensive and readily scalable means of connection and processing. Furthermore, two of these cases (American Airlines and AHSC) also exploited a hidden promise of information technology: the concept of an extended enterprise. Their practice went way beyond simply "providing service to customers" and helped achieve competitive advantage by jointly optimizing productivity with their dealers, suppliers, vendors, etc. The Wal-Mart-Warner-Lambert joint collaboration case (CFAR case) focuses on extended enterprise. The reference model recognizes explicitly this dimension, which is missing in many other results. The value of this concept becomes evident to others only when the Internet becomes a basis for business. This fact shows that the reference model is suited for serving as a roadmap for planning for e-commerce and other enterprises using information technology.

- None of the cases analyzed that fall under the category 'Thinking Extended Enterprise" has also shown characteristics of the other two categories in the 3-D dimension. The difference is subtle but illustrative. The other two categories represent the continuing growth of enterprises and extended enterprises by information technology. "Expanding to Information Enterprises" is the virtual corporation type of applications. As opposed to traditional material enterprises of products, resources, and the marketplace, virtual enterprises require heightened commitment and sophistication in information technology to develop. Transaction cost reduction is another step up in business thinking. We expect more enterprises will come down this direction as the application of new information technology deepens and broadens. An example is the virtual team reported in the Ford Company's designing of its Contour car. The Internet technology has made these two categories more relevant than when the reference model was first proposed. E-commerce has started to explore opportunities in these areas (e.g., marketplace sites). This observation supports our claim about the prescriptive nature of the reference model and its suitability for planning for the use of Internet technology.

- Three of the nine strategic goals, namely, Connecting Administrative and Production Systems, Evaluating Information Technology on Micro-Economic Bases, and Expanding to Information Enterprises, are not explicitly discovered in any of the cases analyzed. This situation could be due to factors such as that they are embedded in other goals. However, as discussed in Chapter 2, there could be definitive indicators for whether or not these principles of planning apply. Therefore, a second possibility is simply the lack of sufficient information about the cases reviewed. A third, and perhaps more significant, possibility is that they belong to a more matured stage of new information technology. Their application requires the use of information technology in some other areas and at some other levels first. Thus, we would expect the continuing progress of e-commerce to see more uses and opportunities in these categories. The Person-Centered Commerce is a possible example.

- Interestingly, from a different perspective, there are six distinct categories of strategic information technology goals, three each in the two broad categories of "Management of External Environment" and "Maximization of the Internal Networking Of Processes and Resources." Each of these six goals can apply to one or more of three arenas: the traditional single enterprise applications, extended enterprise applications, and in the cyber-space. Each of the six goals can also be evaluated differently by changing the perspective of micro-economic evaluation. For example, each goal can be evaluated in traditional cost-benefit analysis perspective or, newer, value-added and reduction in transaction cost perspective. A static Web site, for example, may not be justified in terms of cost-benefit, but from the perspective of reduction in transaction cost, it might be amply justified. Production functions of a firm in traditional, single enterprise settings will be different from those in an extended enterprise or in the cyber-space. Hence, we can examine totally 24 strategic categories from the above combinations. This extension of the reference model is not reflected in the above analysis, but its possible role for e-commerce planning is positive.

3. The Planning Model: a reality check.

We now turn expressly to the extended, e-commerce version of the reference model, the planning model of Chapter 2. In this section, we discuss some prominent and representative cases of the strategic use of the Internet technology for e-commerce. The objective is again to examine the appropriateness of the reference model for e-commerce planning. The format here is the same as the analysis above for traditional cases.

(1). Amazon.com. In some sense, we have discussed this famous and leading e-commerce practice in both Chapters 1 and 2. We focus on some of the more mundane aspects here. Amazon.com is an Internet bookstore doing business out of its Web site, www.amazon.com. Dubbed as the "largest bookstore on earth," the web site provides customers with a capability to buy almost any book in print and any music in recording in the English language, any time and at a discount price. Its yearly revenue has exceeded $1 billion in 1999, compared to $17 million in 1996. Only the Internet that universally connects persons with organizations can fare this sort of fairytale growth. Amazon.com has been among the top three e-commerce sites from the beginning. For the record, the other two top sites in 1995-96 were Virtual Vineyards and Software.com (www.virtualvin.com and www.software.com). All are business-to-customer retailing e-commerce. The landscape has changed dramatically since, of course. At the heart of the successful web site is a database system that allows visitors to Amazon.com to search for books by author, subject, or title and place an order with a credit card. The system simultaneously places an order with the publisher to get the book to the company's Washington State warehouse overnight, and Amazon.com then ships it out to the shopper the next day. Incidentally, the company is expanding its warehouse into a network of traditional style, regional logistic centers to cope with the vastly expanded business. The Internet has allowed Amazon.com to do things that traditional bookstores cannot. These unique customer information services include library-style notes on book titles, the opportunity to "chat" with other readers with similar interests on electronic bulletin boards, e-mail messages to the authors, and notifications of new books published in a given area. Another big advantage Amazon.com enjoys from being a

virtual bookstore is the unlimited display space the information world affords it. It assembled, from early on, five times as many books as the largest bookstore in the physical world carries. It changes the value chain on distribution and saves great deal on real estate by removing the need for an extensive network of retailing bookstores. All these savings enabled the company to discount its prices, especially on the top selling 300,000 books distributed by traditional wholesalers. More recently, the company is diversifying its business into, for example, eBay style market and selling information on its huge customer base. Despite its stellar success and being an earliest mover on the market, it still loses money. We might point out that Amazon.com has been conservative on creating information products and applying e-commerce to its core production functions. Principle 2 (especially 2.2 and 2.3) and Principle 3 (3.1-3.3) should be helpful for the e-commerce enterprise to develop innovative products. Nonetheless, Amazon.com is an exemplified Internet retailing enterprise that creates revenue on transactions. More precisely, the company makes money on reducing transaction cost for readers and book buyers. However, it does not really change the societal value chain. It, itself, is still a middle agent no different from any other bookstores. It just competes better with other, traditional bookstores. In this sense, we do not grant Amazon.com the vision of creating its business opportunity based on societal transaction cost reduction.

(2).Yahoo! Inc. Contrast to Amazon.com, Yahoo! Inc. generates its revenue from information products, including advertisement, e-commerce shopping mall for small retailers, and marketing intelligence. Both its cost and sales are relatively low because of this concentration on information. Being the leading portal site based in Sunnyvale, Calif., Yahoo! Inc. provides an easy way to search the enormous amount of information on the Web by using its highly organized and edited directory of all kind of content providers and e-commerce sites. Founded by two Stanford University graduate students, the company grew entirely out of enthusiasts' free information services search engine. According to one study in 1997, 24 percent of Internet users use a search service daily while 44 percent use one weekly. Yahoo!'s website at www.yahoo.com is a testimony to the reach of the Internet. It has recorded over 10 million visitors a day. Besides a powerful search engine, additional facilities offered include Yellow Pages, People Search, Maps, Classifieds, News, Stock Quotes, Sports Scores, My Yahoo!, Yahooligans! for Kids, Beatrice's Web Guide, Yahoo! Internet Life, Weekly Picks, Today's Web Events, Chat, Weather Forecasts, Random Yahoo! Link, Yahoo! Shop, among an array of ever renewing services, all free. Yahoo! has also extended its operations overseas by way of national Yahoo!s in a number of countries such as Canada, France, Germany , Japan, United Kingdom, Ireland, and Taiwan. Within the U.S., Yahoo! has specific web sites covering Atlanta, Austin, Boston, Chicago, Dallas/Fort Worth, Los Angeles Minneapolis/St. Paul, New York, S.F. Bay, Seattle, and Washington D.C., just to name a few. We might single out one particularly commendable feature of this enterprise, its attention to personalized information services and products. Its personal home pages, disk space, and financial portfolio, for instance, have been powerful marketing tools giving the company competitive advantage over other portal sites. We might also mention, however, that this e-commerce enterprise has been slow in moving into the much larger market (in terms of sales) of transactional services. It excelled on the realm of extended enterprises, which should make the company poised to develop innovative transactional products for its huge customer base. Starting with information and turning into transaction is precisely the path that eBay took, which became the talk of the Wall Street in 1998. Although eBay also started with free information service, it

has never amassed the kind of customer base Yahoo! has. We would grant Yahoo! the most comprehensive and innovative e-commerce enterprise on the information side, but it is lacking on the transaction side. Thus, we grant it all principles of e-commerce planning but the last one, Principle 3.3, creating opportunities based on reducing societal transaction cost. We would also discount its performance on other principles that call for both information and transactional products.

(3). Auto-By-Tel and similar sites. Besides providing consumers with information, Internet automotive services such as Auto-By-Tel, Autosite, and DealerNet help dealerships reach more customers and increase sales. While experts agree that such Internet services are not likely to eliminate visits to a dealership, they are increasing competition. These companies pick dealerships against one another in search of the lowest vehicle price, eliminating the stressful negotiating process for consumers. In short, they offer transactional service to reduce the customers' transaction cost involve in the car purchasing experience. For dealerships, Auto-By-Tel and other similar e-commerce companies charge them membership fees (typically in hundreds to thousands dollars a month) depending on the features they request. For buyers, however, the service is free. Once a car buyer submits a new-vehicle price request, Auto-by-Tel relays the request to the dealer that is closest to the buyer. That dealer contacts the prospective buyer within 48 hours, delivering its best possible price. Half of the purchase requests typically result in sales. Manufacturers are even stepping up efforts to get their dealerships on-line. General Motors, Ford, and Chrysler have all decided to offer free Web sites to their dealerships. Internet car-buying programs continue to add features, such as parts availability and national search for used car prices. More significantly, these sites are joined with related businesses to offer single-window transactional services to customers, based on the formation of some extended enterprises. Customers, for example, can submit a General Motors Acceptance Corporation credit application through the DealerNet service, and Auto-By-Tel entered into an agreement with American International Group Inc. to let customers buy low-cost auto insurance. It is also interesting to note that the car manufacturers offered free information products to their customers - namely, dealerships - in a manner similar to the car buying service sites offering free information services to their the buyers. Their customer bases, the buyers, earned them the other types of customers, the membership fee paying dealerships. Thus, all the manufacturers and car buying sites have demonstrated the information service and product principle (1.1-1.2) and the extended enterprise principle (3.1-3.2). Other principles, however, would be areas they could further explore for e-commerce opportunities.

(4). Dell Computer Corporation. Dell Computer excelled on being the low cost manufacturer of personal computers and workstations. It is also the largest direct sale (branches, not dealers) PC manufacturer in the world, even before the advent of serious e-commerce in 1997. Thus, it is a small wonder that Dell is also one of the first and one of the most successful Internet retailing e-commerce enterprise. Its Web site handles over $20 million of direct sales every day at the turn of the millennium. If the site were an independent business, it would be a top two business-to-customer e-commerce enterprise along with IBM. The Internet fits perfectly into its business model since it stresses the principle of customization and direct delivery to thrive in the swiftly changing and expanding global business community. Dell emphasizes extended enterprise and enterprise integration. Through cooperative R&D, the company benefits from the expertise of its technology partners. Dell partners benefit

from feedback received by the sales and tech support groups as well as from the users directly. Through integrating operations distributed around the world, the company benefits from reaping the best that each place has to offer. A build-to-order (customization) manufacturing system combines customer demand with the latest technology offerings. Therefore, the company is perfectly poised to take full advantage of the Internet and other new information technology since its two overarching principles - direct sale and customization - mesh perfectly with the principles of e-commerce. Carrying out customer-related administration processes on the Internet and connecting them with the manufacturing processes have been a natural match for the company. Besides reducing the transaction cost involved in PC purchasing and services, the company also uses the Web site to establish good relationship with their customers. Dell offers to create customized Intranet sites for their corporate customers to simplify their procurement and support processes. The company also creates personalized web pages for individual buyers. Customers can also track their orders from the company's web site. We would grant Dell an excellent transactional e-commerce enterprise. It certainly has achieved Principle 1.1, Principle 2 (2.1-2.3), and Principle 3.1. We could grant the enterprise Principle 3.3, too, since the direct sale approach does alter the societal value chain in a sense. However, we would also expect the enterprise to achieve much more by way of information, both in creation of innovative information products and in the recursive extension of their integrated enterprise to reduce societal transactional cost further. The company's proven capacity of creating customization and direct connection should ready them for personalization. We might add that Dell Computer's e-commerce practice has started to diversify in 1999 in a way similar to Amazon.com.

(5). E*TRADE. E*TRADE Group, Inc., based in Palo Alto, California, is a provider of online trading services. The company started offering online stock and options trading to independent investors in 1992 and, hence, was perfectly poised to explore the promises of the Internet when it came about. The situation was not unlike Charles Schwab and a few other traditional brokerage houses. However, it was among the first to recognize the potential of the Internet and adopted the right strategy to put itself on the Web and, thereby, put itself in the spotlight. E*TRADE gives its customers a range of portfolio management tools and access to company research, market analysis, news, and other information services. It earns customers' business by means of offering unusually low commissions, due again to the unusually low transaction cost the Internet has to offer. Although it is not the largest brokerage house on the Internet, E*TRADE is arguably the fastest growing brokerage house ever because of the Internet. It created a sensation among predominantly young and male cyber citizens in 1996-1997 when it claimed roughly 1.5 % of a typical day's trading volume for the entire New York Stock Exchange. Fundamentally, E*Trade is similar to Amazon.com in terms of its strategy and application of the Internet technology. It, of course, is far from being able to achieve the same industrial leadership as the latter. They face quite different competitive challenges, to be sure. In the bookseller business, saving physical cost on the distribution channel is a fundamental thing. For brokerage, however, money games, such as margins, could be more important concerning both profit and cost. Still, in a way, the enterprise failed to capitalize on many promising opportunities it is poised to exploit. We single out the principles about extended enterprise and innovative information service and product. It has the benefit of doing business entirely in the cyber space (meaning no material flows involved other than paper work); thus, it is better integrated than Amazon.com.

(6). InfoTEST. We include this case to point to the real meaning of using the Internet as a marketing weapon. This Web site serves one purpose for the company: it provides company brochures to the public. InfoTEST International is a non-profit company that tests how world-class corporations and institutions can gain a competitive advantage using Internet technologies. Through collaborative business trials and private consulting services, InfoTEST evaluates how the Internet and other information technologies can improve internal operations and strengthen enterprise marketing, sales, customer service, and other essential business priorities. InfoTEST is supported by over 30 U.S.-based organizations including corporations, government departments, laboratories, and universities. Together, they form a business-focused research and testing consortium – the InfoTEST alliance. The Web site becomes the propaganda site for the enterprise. It does not show off, nor demonstrate, what they can do or what they have actually done to attract the prospect clients (user companies). The site does not serve any portal functions for the viewers either. It could have easily provided some standard information services, such as connection to the relevant functions of the member organizations or to relevant sites that provide further information on the topics. This is a very telling case since it represents the vast majority of Web sites. Even companies that sell e-commerce, such as e-commerce services, technologies, or marketplace, do not typically apply what they preach to their Web sites. Propaganda sites might be fine for most Internet enterprises that have nothing to do with e-commerce, but it cannot be the positive showcase for any e-commerce sites. Providing electronic brochures is still a form of information service and is still better than doing nothing. Thus, we grant the site Principle 1.1, minor.

(7). Federal Express. Federal Express and Dell Computer share many common characters in their business philosophy and business practice. They both stress direct linkage to customers, running a tight ship, and base their competitive advantage on the innovative power of information technology. Both were poised for e-commerce, and both embrace it. Thus, both practiced e-commerce in quite similar way. They are important differences, too, of course. FedEx sells logistics while Dell makes physical goods. Thus, FedEx must handle the material flow both from the customer and to the customer. Different from Dell, it cannot just do the ordering business with the customers in the cyber space and, hence, cannot do away with the traditional branch offices, yet. Its e-commerce site, therefore, has to focus on providing the customer a different kind of transaction service, that of tracking the parcels or packages. Its transactional service on tracking the logistics is a well-known industry leader. This tracking serves the dual role of being pertaining to both information and transaction. It is certainly a major tool for marketing. As an additional service, the company distributes free software to enable personalized transaction at home or office. For instance, customers could fill in an on-screen form to request a courier and to print a bar coded, plain-paper shipping document and receipt. FedEx might like to realize that their vast customer base is a huge asset for them to develop innovative information products. The enterprise is very conservative about the information side of e-commerce. It might want to recognize that the information side is neither far away from their core business nor conflicts with it. Its powerful information infrastructure would also allow the company to develop extended enterprises with, perhaps, independent teamsters and other carriers. Many possibilities that are unthinkable or unattractive before e-commerce might just reverse themselves with e-commerce. We grant Federal Express similar principles as we did to Dell Computer

for Enterprise Integration (2.1-2.3) and Information Service and Product (1.1), except Extended Enterprises. FedEx is way more conservative than Dell in this category.

(8). Sandia National Laboratories. The Web site at Sandia is a good, pioneering example of Intranet for some administrative functions. The Intranet succeeded to become the single, virtual source for all enterprise information its employees seek. In addition to posting things, such as policy manuals, memoranda, and vacation balances, employees could reserve conference rooms for their meeting from a list of several dozen specifications (overhead projector, whiteboard, handicap access, coffee machine, etc.). There is also a project-management tool with which the users can enter a project case number and find out immediately how much is being spent on procurement, labor, and other factors about their projects. Other internal tracking tools remind employees what inventory they are responsible for, where it resides, and what is the status of anything they may have ordered. Like any venerable organization, Sandia possesses a wealth of information and experience that resides principally in the heads of its employees. In order not to lose this resource as people retire, the organization was videotaping departing staff members as they hold forth on their subjects of expertise, then putting transcripts of those sessions on the Web. The Intranet provides other support as well, including travel reservation and publication, which are important to the laboratory researchers' core activities. The recently heightened concerns of security at national laboratories might hinder the openness of this Intranet, but it has proven to be a productive booster for the enterprise. This case clearly covers Principle 1.1 and Principle 2.1. We would think that others could apply if the enterprise define e-commerce broadly. It, for instance, certainly has procurement and other common business processes for e-commerce to contribute.

(9). Ford Intranet. Ford Motor Company is one of the corporations that developed an Intranet to help improve its internal processes early on. The corporate Web site provides information to employees about different aspects of their product development. The effort was prompted by Ford's in-house surveys in 1994 and 1995, which showed that nearly half of the company's professional workers did not have access to the information they need to do their jobs. So, Ford developed Ford Hub to disseminate this information. It works like an internal portal site. The menu for the competition category, for example, tells users what are the places to go for information on benchmarking, auto shows, global market information, competitor news, product-cycle plans, and patent information. If the vision is extended to include real time information about marketing, design, production, and other aspects of the core processes, then the system would be quite close to Mr. Bill Gates's digital nervous system. If it also supported the professional workers to conduct their jobs through the system, such as updating product designs or production schedules, then the enterprise is indeed integrated. Finally, if it could also connect with suppliers, dealers, and so on to do the same, then we would have an extended enterprise that is integrated. The difference between Ford Hub and such a complete e-commerce enterprise is eight principles beyond Principle 2.1, which is Ford Hub.

(10). The Boeing Technical Libraries. The Boeing Technical Libraries were an extension to its previously developed electronic information delivery systems. The new system uses the Web technology as an integrating tool for both internally generated and externally published information across the Boeing Company. The physical library has four separate geographic locations in the Seattle area with

smaller independent libraries in Philadelphia, Wichita and Huntsville which share the on-line catalog system for their documents. The notion of library makes this practice an isolated case. However, when combined with the ideas of Ford Hub, the possibilities of technical information suddenly become unlimited. The technical libraries could very well be a repository of job-related information or even be a switchboard for the assembly and dissemination of such information. Its possible connection to e-commerce should become not only evident but also relevant. The point here is, again, that e-commerce sees and recognizes no boundaries between functions, processes, and organizations, insofar as their complementary possibilities are concerned. The successful e-commerce enterprises will see relations in places where traditional companies only see isolation.

Analysis.

We use the same matrix as in the previous section to summarize our analysis of the e-commerce cases. However, instead of using the generic model as in Section 2, we use directly the e-commerce version of the model. Therefore, the nine categories correspond from left to right to Principles 1.1 - 3.3, respectively. They pertain to the e-commerce planning model of Chapter 2.

Strategic Goal -> Case	P 1.1	P 1.2	P1.3	P 2.1	P 2.2	P 2.3	P 3.1	P 3.2	P 3.3
Amazon.com	X	X	X	X			X		
Yahoo!	X	X	X	X	X	X	X	X	
Auto-By-Tel	X	X					X	X	
Dell Computer Corporation	X			X	X	X	X		X
E*TRADE	X			X	X	X			
InfoTest	X								
FedEX	X			X	X	X			
Sandia National Laboratories				X					
Ford Intranet				X					
Boeing Technical Libraries				X					

Table 4.3: The Second Validation Matrix For the Reference Model.

The above table is illustrative in many ways. The applications of the Internet technology mentioned in this section are representative of such use of the technology by businesses. Most of these applications include some match with Principle 2.1 because e-commerce is almost by definition a practice of administration over the Internet. Any Web site that does not match this principle is hardly a real e-commerce site. InfoTEST does not, and so it happens that it is not an e-commerce practice. Just a handful of years ago, when the business uses of the web were relatively new, most applications belonged to the first category, providing information service. In fact, most companies only put up home pages that were the electronic equivalent of flyers and billboards. One of the first (then) popular interactive Web site that enabled the viewers to do something real was the Pizza Hut web site. It, in certain locations in California, allowed customers to order a pizza through the site. We could justifiably consider it a pioneer of e-commerce. However, the Web site became popular because of its novelty, not because of its functionality since it is not much more convenient to order a pizza through the Web than over the telephone. As the novelty wore off, so did the popularity. However, the Pizza Hut Web site demonstrated that using the Internet to do business is not just a far-fetched possibility. It is a reality. The rest is history. Many of the above applications have gone way beyond the initial vision of business use of the Internet. All of them, at the same time, still have a great deal more to explore, to develop new opportunities for their e-commerce enterprises.

We discussed some further possibilities for the above applications in our analysis of these cases. We summarize a few comments below.

- Both information and transaction are important. Every e-commerce enterprise could and should endeavor to develop novel services and products on both the information side and the transaction sides of the e-commerce world. The two sides complement each other much more than they appear. We expect, in particular, Yahoo! to develop its transactional services as new information products and Dell and Amazon.com to develop information services.

- Extended enterprises hold the key to further expansion. Yahoo! must ally with transaction providers to create meaningful transactional products. For the same reason, Dell and Amazon.com must leverage the expertise that portal sites have accumulated on information services if they want to profit on significant information products. For e-commerce, the alliance is much easier to pull off than with the case of traditional business, albeit still challenging.

- Enterprise integration is the basis for competitiveness in e-commerce as well in traditional business. Dell and Federal Express both show that they were bound to be successful in e-commerce even before they really started because both emphasized direct connection with the customers and customized products or services. Both are what e-commerce requires of the new business model and both require the integration of the enterprise.

- Intranet is a powerful tool for integration. Its beauty is its scalability. An enterprise could start with some easy to do yet very helpful functions, such as the three Intranet cases illustrated above. It can be expanded later to include more functions or be connected with other existing systems. A comprehensive environment can eventually result. As long as there is a proper plan for the enterprise, the gradual approach will work well.

4. The Reference Model and Previous Planning Methodologies

The above two sections mapped some representative experiences in the actuality to the reference model. They seem to suggest the consistence between the model and the findings of the field. Most significantly, the mappings seem to suggest that the planning model is comprehensive in its categories, indicative of additional possibilities, and reflective of the continuing progress of information technology. We now compare directly the reference model to Value Chain Analysis and Wiseman's framework for strategic information systems planning. Both works are discussed in detail in Chapter 3 along with a review of other pertinent results in the literature.

The reference model logically sits on top of the Porter model in the sense that it seeks to provide goals that could feed into the application of Porter's value chain analysis. Cost, differentiation, or focus strategies of Porter are general, intuitive building blocks of a business strategy, but they are too general for strategic information technology planning. A basic reason this is so is because the information technology has undergone tremendous change since Porter's writings. For example, in their article, "Exploiting the Virtual Value Chain" [Rayport and Sviokla, 1995], the authors bring out a new, second dimension of competitive advantage to update the old analysis. They write, "every business today competes in two worlds: a physical world of resources that managers can see and touch and a virtual world of information. The latter has given rise to the world of electronic commerce, a new locus of value creation." The reference model explores, expressly, this information world to find out what are the precise impact and possibilities that information technology bring out for enterprises. It attempts to analyze and catalog what the value chain model leaves out. The three dimensions of possible competitive advantage identified and prescribed in the reference model are useful starting points for an analysis of real or virtual value chain. Conversely, goals and the information world by themselves do not change the physical processes. A firm will still need to perform physical activities to produce products with physical material flows. The reference model recognizes the proven value of the Porter model for this purpose. Coupling of the Porter model with the reference model seems to be a logical thing to do. It would superimpose information technology-enabled goals on the enterprise value chain to guide the re-engineering of business processes that would deliver competitive advantage. This is a framework that we propose (see Chapter 5) for e-commerce planning.

Finally, we conclude our evaluation with a comment on the differences between the Wiseman's framework and the reference model. Wiseman's framework extends Porter's three generic categories (low cost producer, differentiation, and focus) to five categories: differentiation, cost, innovation, growth, and alliance. Still, the framework is informal about information strategies, similar to the generality of the Porter model. It explicitly accounts for the fact that sustainable competitive advantage can mean different things to different firms. Competitive advantage may be with respect to a supplier, a customer, or a rival. It may exist because of a lower price, because of desirable features, or because of the various resources that a firm possesses. The reference model, on the other hand, stresses commonality. It provides a formal way to systematically enunciate strategic goals (in nine categories), which is what Wiseman recognizes but does not provide.

To conclude the comparison with other works, we would like to think that the role of information and information technology has evolved significantly since the time of the previous results. The basic difference between the reference model and the other works reviewed here might be attributable to the worldview that the continuous evolution has created. Information and information technology, to the reference model, is nothing short of a leading player of new enterprises, nor anything that is too specific or too technical to be a strategy driver. Information plays a much more pivotal role in various enterprises in today's world than ever before. For e-commerce, in particular, information often is *the* product that businesses make and sell, and hence live or die by it. With this in mind, we now turn to an attempt of testing the reference model in actuality. Both versions of the model, the generic and the e-commerce, are employed and tested. The next chapter prepares the test. It proposes a methodology for applying the reference model to the planning for e-commerce practices.

5

PUTTING THE REFERENCE MODEL TO WORK

The previous two chapters compare the planning model to other methods established in the literature and show how it helps analyzing some of the representative practices of e-commerce. In the process, it becomes clear that the planning model could couple with value chain analysis to set up detailed action plans for e-commerce enterprises. We elaborate on this template in this chapter. Its basic design is to implement the "pull" approach of information strategy formulation. The methodology described in this chapter consists of five stages, progressing from general to specific. It starts with a procedure to develop strategic e-commerce goals using the planning model. This procedure is illustrated in Chapter 6. It then suggests a way to identify business processes in the enterprise and to redesign the ones that are related to the goals with a prioritization design. Finally, it leads to technological requirement analysis and, ultimately, to structured systems analysis and design, based on redesigned processes. Chapters 7 and 8 illustrate the whole process through two exploratory studies with a bank and a heavy industry company.

1. Stage 1: E-Commerce Goal Setting.

Chapter 2 describes a comprehensive model for setting strategic e-commerce goals. It first outlines a quick and simple procedure, then nine planning principles (that is, the extended e-commerce version of the generic reference model), and finally a conclusion for more advanced planning. We summarize the essence of the planning approach and suggest below a basic procedure to use the planning model for particular enterprises.

- Form a planning team, including necessary players in the e-commerce enterprise. This team must involve both business and technology leaders so that meaningful deliberation of ideas and identification of opportunities are possible.

- Define the meaning of information and transaction for the enterprise. Industrial benchmarking could be a good technique to use for this purpose. There are a number of examples given in Chapters 1, 2, and 4, too.

- Define the meaning of administration, production, and extended enterprise for the particular business. Define all types of customers, including those that the enterprise pays to attract and those that pay to the enterprise.

- Define the competitors and external constituencies (in addition to customers). Identify their competitive nature in terms of the degree to which they are complementing and/or duplicating with the enterprise. In addition, categorize how each complements the enterprise's indigenous capabilities in areas other than their current relationship with the enterprise. Even a competitor could become a collaborator and a collaborator a competitor in e-commerce.

- Identify the possibilities of connection with persons and organizations. Note that a customer could be an organization and a supplier a person. Each possibility of connection should include alternatives and an understanding of feasibility.

- Conduct a first, quick pass through all nine principles in all three dimensions. The purpose for the first pass is to establish some reference point for further planning (and brainstorming). List possible goals in each category.

- Identify the information products, transactional products, and free information services, based on the result of the first pass. Assess the technological requirements, alternatives, and feasibility (including financial and organizational issues due to the technological implications).

- Examine the first set of goals from the perspective of enterprise integration, again. Emphasize customization. For example, review the previous definitions of information, transaction, constituencies, extended enterprises, and so on in a deliberate effort to revise the previous visions for information products and services. Some products could become services and services become products. Seek new classes of information and transactions. A new set of goals would result.

- Reexamine the revise set of goals from the perspective of extended enterprises. Emphasize personalization. Reexamine integration and every other enterprise concepts from the perspective of a particular extended enterprise. Revise the definitions. Revise the information products and services. Seeks new visions. Examine different possible extended enterprises along different paths (customer extension, supply chain extension, virtual value chain extension, and so on). A new set of goals would result.

- Use the best results to challenge the prevailing business model, especially the conventional value chain (from the perspective of both the enterprise and the economy or the society). Review the connections and try to alter the value chain by making new uses of the connections. The notion of Person-Centered Commerce should be useful here. For each promising use or possibility, redefine the constituencies, information, and transaction. Revise services and products. Finally, another set of goals would result.

- Prioritize and synthesize these goals. The purpose of this final step is to come up with a definitive set of e-commerce goals (specific things to produce or provide) for the next stages of planning. There is no need to vote down or up any particular goals at this stage. The only requirement is to understand their meaning.

- Articulate the goals in two ways: business strategy and information system. High level goals tend to take a business tone in their wording. This is fine at the top managerial level. However, in order to direct the analysis for implementation and technical implications, it helps to solidify the semantics from a technical perspective. Thus, a second version could simply call the goals e-commerce information technology goals or, even more specifically, just call them e-commerce information system (IS) goals to assist system development effort. The essence of both versions is the same, just the articulation would customize.

2. Stage 2: Business Process Analysis.

Value Chain Analysis of [Porter, 1985] is used at this stage for analyzing business processes. There are a number of case studies and methodologies developed in the literature to assist this analysis. This analysis process is quite commonplace and has rather standard procedures to follow. It centers on activity analysis and uses liberally published results to guide the work for particular enterprises. In this sense, the usual analysis for value chain starts with a reference model of common industrial processes. These processes could be customized for the enterprise in question. A typical value chain classifies processes into five generic primary activities: inbound material handling, operations, outbound logistics, marketing & sales, and service, and four generic secondary activities: procurement, technology development, human resource, and firm infrastructure. These nine generic categories are broken down into sub- and sub-sub- processes that comprise an enterprise. Besides the value chain of a firm, there are value chains of the suppliers and the channel value chains. Value Chain Analysis also considers linkages between processes within a value chain or across value chains (firm and supplier value chains, for example). We refer to the literature for the details. We might also add that, for the purpose of this analysis, other process modeling methods could also be used in the place of value chain analysis. We just need a good handle on the processes of the enterprise. One way or another does not matter too much as long as the business processes are identified properly.

3. Stage 3: Business Process Redesign Using the Goals.

The "pull" approach for e-commerce planning is, in part, a business process redesign approach. Thus, this stage is at the heart of the template after the goals are set. It is imperative that businesses redesign their processes in order to implement the goals correctly and derive maximum benefit from the new information technology. The previous chapters have shown that this point is anything but a cliche. A lesson to learn is the mistake made by businesses while adopting PCs in the 80s. At the time, businesses merely computerized their old processes without redesigning or integrating them. Consequently, the promised productivity gains of computerization remained elusive. It was only later, when businesses started to connect their computing power and redesign their processes to eliminate wasteful activities, that productivity gains started to become visible. The concept of business process redesign is not new, of course. There has been a rich literature about this concept and about how to conduct it. For e-commerce enterprises, especially those that launch e-commerce out of a traditional business, the lesson articulated by [Hammer and Champy, 1993] is particularly relevant. It says that simply automating a process as it exists prior to automation may, at best, be a missed opportunity and, at worst, lock the organization into outmoded ways of working. In order to make the best possible use of information technology, it is necessary to design optimal processes that take into account both the automated and non-automated parts of those processes. This is the Enterprise Integration Principle (2.1-2.3).

In our planning methodology, the e-commerce goals drive business process redesign. The business process redesign stage entails three activities. They are (a) evaluation of existing processes in terms of their adequacy for achieving the goals, (b) prioritization of business processes in view of the e-commerce goals for the enterprise, and (c) creation of new processes. All this analysis is achieved with the help of a few matrices described below.

3.1 Goals to Process Mapping (Impact).

The purpose of the first mapping is to determine the nature of changes the proposed e-commerce systems would require of the status-quo business processes. When an enterprise adopts some new e-commerce information technology to create new systems or apply the technology to its internal operation, its current business processes are bound to be affected. Technologies, such as the Web and the Internet, could alter the basic way the enterprise conducts its business. Thus, the first matrix is a tabulation for evaluating the impact of e-commerce system goals on the business processes of an enterprise. Fundamentally, these goals will impact processes in three ways: creating new processes, changing a process, or using the process as-is. Processes could change in two ways: deletion or modification.

A sample impact matrix is shown in Table 5.1. In the sample matrix, the specific e-commerce information system goals 1 and n need a new process, Process 1. In addition, for meeting the IS Goal 1, Process 2 needs to be modified while IS Goal 2 uses the process as-is. Is there a potential conflict here? The decision rule is simple. If the modification could be of such a nature that the modified Process 2 would continue to meet the requirement of IS Goal 2, then no new process is required. An M and a U would be entered into the appropriate cells as shown. On the other hand, if the modification would render it unfitting for IS goal 2, IS goal 1 actually entails a new process while IS goal 2 continue to use the current Process 2. The sample matrix would show an additional C for an additional process in the row of IS goal 1 instead of showing an M for Process 2. The same decision rule applies to Process 4 and Process n. A process can be deleted only if no other goal uses it either as-is or modified. In the example, Process n-1 can be deleted. The matrix can help summarize the impact and reveal potential contradictions. Any inconsistency or conflict exposed by the matrix should lead to a next round of review to resolve them, using decision rules such as the one discussed here. In any case, the analysis at this step is only preliminary in nature since the final decision of business process redesign must take into account the next matrices of analysis.

Processes \ IS Goals	Process 1	Process 2	Process 3	Process 4	•••	•••			Process n
IS Goal 1	C	M			U			D	U
IS Goal 2		U	C	U					M
IS Goal 3				M		C			
•••									
								D	
IS Goal n	C								

C = Create New		D = Delete
M = Modify		U = Use As-Is

Table 5.1: The Impact Matrix.

3.2 Goal to Process Mapping (Prioritization)

The purpose of this mapping is to prioritize the existing business processes in terms of their adequacy in meeting the e-commerce system goals, as well as creating new processes. The matrix is employed towards mapping the system goals to organizational processes. All goals are each assigned a separate weight according to some weighting scheme the enterprise chooses. A scale is used to show the correlation between a particular goal and a particular process; e.g., a scale of 0-4 where 0 *is no correlation* and 4 is *very high correlation*. Both values are pre-determined by the enterprise before constructing the matrix. Value that goes in the cell is the product of the corresponding weight of the goal and correlation coefficient. The resulting matrix will look like the one shown in Table 5.1 where $w(1)$ to $w(m)$ are the values of the corresponding goals, $cc(i,j)$ is the correlation coefficient between the i-th goal and the j-th process, and process value $pw(1)$ to $pw(n)$ are the aggregate values obtained from adding all cell values in a column for a process. Note that the processes considered could be new processes that the reengineered system calls to create, as well as revised, combined, or preserved previous processes. This matrix highlights the impact of e-commerce goals on processes. We might also mention that the goals here could take either version of articulation, but the IS version might prove to be more illustrative.

	Goal Weight w(i)	*Process 1*	*Process 2*	...	*Process n*
		w(i) × cc(i,1)	w(i) × cc(i,2)		w(i) × cc(i,n)
Goal 1	w(1)	w(1) × cc(1,1)	w(1) × cc(1,2)	...	w(1) × cc(1,n)
Goal 2	w(2)	w(2) × cc(2,1)	w(2) × cc(2,2)	...	w(2) × cc(2,n)
.	.	.	.	...	.
.	.	.	.		.
.	.	.	.		.
Goal m	w(m)	w(m) × cc(m,1)	w(m) × cc(m,2)	...	w(m) × cc(m,n)
		Process Value pw(1) = • w(i) × cc(i,1) for i = 1 to m	Process Value pw(2) = • w(i) × cc(i,2) for i = 1 to m	...	Process Value pw(m) = • w(i) × cc(i,n) for i = 1 to m
		Process P(1)	Process P(2)	...	Process P(n)

Table 5.2: The Prioritization Matrix.

The idea behind prioritizing processes in the above manner is to identify all processes that contribute to particular goals. The contribution of each process is weighted by the priorities of the goals to which it contributes. Thus, the aggregate value pw(j) indicates the contribution of a process to the overall e-commerce effort according to the priority scheme of the e-commerce goals. Having thus identified high priority processes, the enterprise can focus on developing e-commerce systems and applications using the new technology for those processes. It also facilitates optimization of limited resources, especially under a resource crunch. The enterprise would have a reference point for expending resources on the processes that best meet its e-commerce goals.

3.3 Process to Process Mapping.

Besides looking at the implications of the e-commerce goals on business processes, an enterprise also needs to look at the interaction among its business processes. In addition to obvious sequential linkage, where the output of one process is used by one or more other processes, business process redesign calls for two other types of relationships among processes. The first is logical overlap such as common information resources or decision space among seemingly disconnected processes, and the other is concurrent execution of processes. The universal, common user interface and scalable connection discussed before allow unusual collaboration among processes. For example, with the creation of an interactive web page, the advertising and order receiving processes can both be carried out from the same web page. The order that the customer enters can then flow over an Intranet and automatically provide input to marketing, manufacturing, and procurement processes. Electronic Data Interchange over the Internet links an organization's inventory process with the material ordering and vendor payment processes. Explicitly recognizing such linkages is crucial to redesigning those processes.

The idea of concurrent processes is also characteristic of new information technology and has to play a role in e-commerce enterprise. Instead of performing processes sequentially, the above technologies can enable processes to be carried out in parallel and, thereby, reduce the cycle time. For example, a company with a web-based recruitment system can drastically cut the application processing time by carrying out certain jobs in parallel. The company could post its job openings and invite and acknowledge applications through a dynamic web page, then avail his/her resume on a corporate Intranet for the appraisal of the concerned department(s). The same idea is readily applicable for business-to-business e-commerce systems such as procurement and supply chain, too. The status information could be made available to all parties concerned instantaneously and simultaneously. Certain decision-making jobs could also join when the workflow is concurrent. Obviously, concurrent execution of processes must be a hallmark of any serious planning for e-commerce systems. We deploy the matrix of Table 5.3 to indicate linkages among processes. An **L** in a cell indicates that the two corresponding processes have a potential or a promise to link in an e-commerce enterprise; although, no formal linkage may apparently exist in the status quo environment. The best way to tell usually is to check the information requirements of processes. If two or more processes share similar information resources, then they are likely candidates for concurrent execution.

Proc-esses / Proc-esses	Process 1	Process 2	Process 3	Process 4	•••	•••		Process m
Process 1		L						L
Process 2								
Process 3				L				
•••								
Process m								

Table 5.3: The Process Linkage Matrix.

The above matrices alone certainly do not result in any business process redesign, but they can help in the redesign. We would like to think that these analyses add to the conventional methodology of value chain analysis and business process redesign for, especially, e-commerce systems. Again, a system perspective would be a good idea for the analysis. It often helps clarify the meaning of processes and linkages when the planning effort forces the issue of concrete ideas on the planning team. The system perspective does not solve the problem of semantics, but it adds new dimensions to the semantics and allows for more meaning to help provide a working definition.

4. Stage 4: Technology Requirements Analysis.

This is an important stage in the whole process because e-commerce hinges on appropriate technology. We present the framework in a sequential manner, stage by stage, but the real essence of e-commerce planning is the interaction of strategy and technology. The first stage of planning embeds this theme. Here, we primarily take a system development angle to review the technical requirements when the big issues of technology (visions, alternatives, and so on) are settled above along with strategy. Chapter 2 has listed four basic classes of common Internet technology that e-commerce systems use. We add one more in this section, that is, the plain Internet technology for completeness. The plain technology, including e-mail, would be useful by itself for certain processes as a part of an e-commerce enterprise. Thus, although e-commerce can never rely on this class alone, it has its role in the technology requirement analysis for processes - see below.

The current Internet technology rests on the robust suit of communications protocol to allow information processing and interchange among various networks on a global scale. TCP/IP are two of the most significant in the suit. The first, TCP (transmission control protocol), connects individual computing devices with the Internet, and the second, IP (Internet Protocol), connects networks of the Internet. The suit also includes file transfer protocol (FTP) for point-to-point transfer of files and the e-mail (SMTP/MIME) protocols for direct point-to-point communication. During the evolution of the Internet, a series of applications have been created to meet the specific needs of users and systems. The Mosaic technology for Web (browser and server) and the HTML syntax as the language of the Web are two most famous examples. The new generation, Internet 2 expands the bandwidth and other features to include wireless connection and mobile computing. It will also support enhanced data, voice, and image applications such as video conferencing and virtual reality. Accordingly, the new generation of protocols, IP v.6, provides many new capabilities for flexible use and division of bandwidth, layered security control, and usage accounting functions. E-commerce has brought a boon to Internet software vendors. An extensive array of e-commerce technology is now available for Internet applications. Altogether, we divide them into five categories to assist our analysis at this stage.

(1) Communications Connectivity. Electronic mail was the 'killer application' of the Internet till the World Wide Web arrived on the scene. Based on Simple Mail Transfer Protocol (SMTP), e-mail allows plain ASCII text to be transferred from one computer user to another. Multipurpose Internet Mail Extensions (MIME) allows non-textual data such as graphics, audio and fax to be sent over the Internet as attachments to e-mail. File Transfer Protocol (FTP) is a client-server technology allowing a user to transfer or receive files over a TCP/IP network. A variation of FTP is the anonymous FTP which is an interactive service provided by many Internet hosts allowing any user to transfer documents, files, programs, and other archived data using file transfer protocol. The user logs in using the special user name "ftp" or "anonymous" and his/her e-mail address as password.

The user then has access to a special directory hierarchy containing the publicly accessible files, typically a separate area from files used by local users.

(2) Document Connectivity: create a Web site to process documents and similar files.

(3) Application Connectivity: run regular application software through the Web.

(4) Database Connectivity: run regular database systems (including applications).

(5) Enterprise Connectivity: inter-operate multiple database systems.

Please refer to Section 1 of Chapter 2 for a discussion of the last four categories of technology. We now use these classes to indicate the technology requirements of business processes pertaining to an e-commerce enterprise.

We propose a Technology Requirement Analysis matrix as a first cut analysis of the information technology implied in the e-commerce goals. The analysis seeks to map the business processes obtained from the preceding stage onto the five categories of the e-commerce technology. An indicator of 1-5 is used to map processes to the technology capabilities. In the scheme, an indicator of 1 shows that a particular process will only require communications connectivity capabilities for its execution, 2 means document connectivity, 3 application connectivity, 4 database connectivity, and 5 enterprise connectivity. These categories are progressive in capability, and a higher capability includes all lower capabilities. As discussed in stage 2 above and illustrated with the sample matrix of Table 5.3, some processes may be executed together beyond a naturally occurring sequential linkage. If two processes are thus linked, and one process makes use of a higher level capability of the technology, then the other process will also be enabled by the same level of capability. For example, if processes P1 and P2 are linked, where P1 is enabled by document connectivity (a static web page) but P2 requires database connectivity, then P1 will also be enabled by database connectivity. Unless the organization decides to forego the linkage between the two processes, the higher category always dominates. In the schema of information technology and enterprise integration, the domination implies economy of scale more than excessive capability. A sample of the analysis matrix is shown in Table 5.4.

Processes / IS Goals	Process 1	Process 2	Process 3	Process 4	●●●		●●●			Process m
IS Goal 1	3	3								
IS Goal 2	4		3							
IS Goal 3	5	4								
●●●										
IS Goal n	1									

Table 5.4: The Technology Requirement Analysis Matrix

5. Stage 5: Design of E-Commerce Information Systems.

As has been repeatedly emphasized in this book, an e-commerce Web site is much more than just some attractive looking web pages. The site is at least an Internet-based information system that not only disseminates information but also interacts proactively with external users and internal processes to achieve its business goals. This is also why we mentioned earlier that the e-commerce goals could be interpreted as e-commerce information system goals when it comes to developing the required environment. There are many tools and techniques available for system development. A classical example is the Data Flow Diagramming technique.

Data Flow Diagrams (DFD) are useful for modeling the processes of an information system and documenting its the logical design. It captures four basic elements of a system: the process (P), the online data flow among the processes, the external storage of data (DS), and the external sources or destinations (EE) of data flow. A representative DFD is shown in Figure 5.1 to illustrate how this technique can help in designing applications.

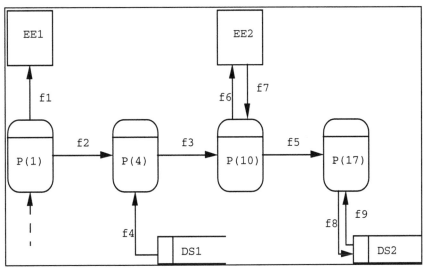

Figure 5.1: A Sample Data Floe Diagram.

In this example, P(1) has a flow to external entity EE1 while P(10) has a flow from and to the external entity EE2. This points to the need of the user interface with a capability of "writing" information to a user while process P(10) also accepts data from the user. An interactive Web page is implied, which might need application connectivity. The other implications of the diagram to the Web site design include that the site needs to support the information flow f1 and f6 and also needs the capability to interface with data stores DS1 and DS2. Depending on the nature of the application software implementing P(4) and P(17), DS1 and DS2 might be two separate systems or two images of the same database. The technical nature of the interface will depend on the details, which would be a task for the ensuing system design after DFD analysis. In fact, the rest of the system development effort can follow perfectly the standard methodology for structured systems analysis and software engineering. We stop here.

The above five-stage methodology puts the planning model to work. It develops e-commerce goals and gradually refines them to a level that is amenable to serving as input to feed into traditional system development effort. It, therefore, connects two sets of previously isolated results together for e-commerce enterprises: strategic goal setting and system development. We now put the reference model to work for a few industrial cases in the next three chapters. The first is a case of supply chain integration reported in the literature.

6

SOME IDEAS FOR A SUPPLY CHAIN ENTERPRISE

Procurement is an important aspect of supply chain, but it is not the ultimate concern of supply chain. The essence is integration; i.e., tying up the demand and supply processes across the extended enterprise of the demand or supply chain. Just in time production is a special case of supply chain integration. Procurement is the origin of business-to-business e-commerce and still represents the majority of the field. The main reason is the previous EDI practice, which has primed many enterprises for a sensible adoption of e-commerce in this area. We discussed this point in previous chapters. The new point here is that the rest of the supply chain - namely, integration - is a ready candidate for immediate expansion of the procurement e-commerce. Therefore, we examine a representative case of supply chain integration to discover how readily the e-commerce practice could apply to the non-commerce aspects of supple chain, which is a part of enterprise integration. The case is an extended enterprising project by Wal-Mart - the retailer - and Warner Lambert - the manufacturer. The system from the perspective of Wal-Mart is a supply chain, but it is a demand chain for Warner Lambert. We refer to it as, simply, the supply chain. The two companies applied Web technologies and used the Internet to integrate Wal-Mart's marketing information with Warner Lambert's manufacturing systems. We employ the planning model to compare notes with the project. We indicate additional, immediate possible goals for the project, over and above its reported applications using the planing model.

1. The CFAR Project.

The motive of the project between Wal-Mart Stores Inc. and Warner-Lambert Co., Listerine's maker, is reportedly to demonstrate a way for all retailers and suppliers to save billions of dollars by more accurately forecasting demand for individual products. While Wal-Mart is famous for how it analyzes daily cash-register data and works with suppliers to avoid building up inventory, it now hopes to go a step further. Like other retailers, it does its own forecasting but shares little of it with suppliers. This results in estimated errors of as much as 60 % in the suppliers' forecasting of their demand. The project, dubbed CFAR -- Collaborative Forecasting and Replenishment, offers a standardized way for manufacturers and merchants to work together on forecasts across the Internet. Using the CFAR model, retailers, carriers, and manufacturers can extend collaboration from operational planning through execution, enabled by the universal Internet technology. Publicized in 1996, with effort continuing afterwards, the project has a vision to become the basis for a new industry standard (e.g., its protocols) in forecasting and replenishment. The following description of the case is based on articles in trade magazines and information available from company Web sites (the list is given in Section 2).

Traditionally, for a single product, retailers and manufacturers may have twenty or more different types of forecasts between them, each developed for a special purpose and all trying to predict consumer behavior. Having multiple forecasts inherently causes problems because it means that the sum total of actions is uncoordinated. A retailer's promotional buyer may buy to one forecast, but the manufacturer's production line will build to another. Meanwhile, store operations may be allocating promotional shelf space according to yet another forecast. Each party goes its own way, and the other worries that "the other" is not going to hold up their end of the process. The manufacturer/retailer relationship becomes adversarial under these conditions. Manufacturers allocate orders against on-hand inventory rather than capacity (i.e., the manufacturers also build up "just-in-case" inventory to give themselves a safety margin against unpredictable retailer demand). At the same time, retailers frequently over-order from manufacturers because they have come to expect only partial deliveries. Both retailers and manufacturers often have access to very sophisticated decision support systems, but these systems are not fully integrated with the current forecasting and replenishment processes across the supply chain. In a similar way, the manufacturers' sophisticated factory planning and shop floor scheduling systems are not integrated with the retailers' forecasts of demand, which ultimately feed into the demand for the manufacturers.

The driving force behind manufacturer-retailer collaboration is in building sales, market share, and profitability. Therefore, the two companies decided to jointly develop sales forecasts that incorporate information about everything, ranging from planned changes in store layouts to precise meteorological data about pollen counts and when flu season will hit certain regions. This move helped them to eliminate 2 1/2 weeks of the lead time from the supply chain for a test product, Listerine. They have also halved order cycle times and eliminated incidents of stock-out. The forecasting data are directly fed into SAP/R3 by Warner-Lambert for their production planning.

The design of the forecast workbench employed in CFAR follows the inter-enterprise work flow design given in Figure 6.1.

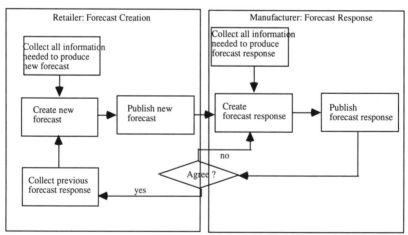

Figure 6.1: Work flow Design for Joint Forecast.

The figure illustrates the global process for the extended enterprise of supply chain, irrespective to the organizational boundaries. It, then, divides the job for each party. There is clearly a need for collaborative, global decision space cutting across the two companies. Thus, this flow model is also a working definition for the extended enterprise. It is worthwhile to note that the enterprise also slates bigger extension for the supply chain, including the integration of planning among stores, distribution centers, and suppliers to Warner Lambert. The ultimate goal is to achieve more accurate inventory systems; whereby, the retail industry could minimize uncertainty and eliminate inventory for the most part.

2. Strategic Goals Actually Employed By Wal-Mart & Warner-Lambert.

We now derive the strategic goals of the project based on the information obtained from the public literature. These goals will be calibrated to the reference model later. The perceived goals of the CFAR project for Wal-Mart and Warner-Lambert are summarized in the table 4.1:

Wal-Mart	Warner-Lambert
• Reduction of inventory	• Reduction of inventory
• Reduction of order cycle time	• Reduction of order cycle time
• Better shelf space management	• Streamlining production -- fewer changes in production schedule
• Better customer service (not being out of stock)	• Better customer service (timely supplies)

Table 6.1: CFAR Benefits.

All these goals are consistent with the promises of Internet-based enterprises but are beyond the prevailing practice of business-to-business e-commerce. These goals are not concerned with procurement per se but are envisioned for the companies' internal operating systems. Also implicit in the case are the activities pertaining to the extended enterprise of the value chain. We give below some quotes from reports in three magazines: Business Week, Information Week, and ComputerWorld, plus the Web site of Benchmarking, Inc., which is the software company that developed the CFAR protocol (http://www.benchmarking.com/cfar.html). These materials helped us in drawing out the implicit goals for the case.

Quotes:

- "The bottom line is, collaboration works in building sales, market share, and profitability," said Robert Bruce, vice president of supply chain management at Wal-Mart (ComputerWorld). *Inference*: Building extended enterprise is a strategic goal sought by the planners - corresponding to Principle 3.1.

- "The two companies have eliminated a full 2 1/2 weeks from the supply chain for a test product, Listerine. They have also halved order cycle times and eliminated incidents of a product being out of stock." (ComputerWorld). *Inference*: Better inventory management and better customer service are two strategic goals. They correspond to enterprise integration, i.e., Principles 2.1 - 2.3. We do not grant Principle 1.1 since the notion of customer service here is not information based and is embedded already in a tighter operation that enterprise integration effects.

- "Technologically, the Internet-based CFAR protocol poses no major implementation issues, according to its developers. Instead, the major challenge lies in creating links to in-house scheduling and manufacturing systems." (ComputerWorld). *Inference*: The Internet needs to connect to internal application systems of the core production functions. This is Principle 2.2.

- "As the 'see-far' acronym implies, a key benefit of the new system, Wal-Mart is proposing as an industry standard, is to provide more reliable, longer-term views into the future." "So far, supply-chain partners have cooperated only over the short term, via orders," says Michael Hammer, co-author of Re-engineering the Corporation. "What they need to do is get their overall forecasting and planning systems integrated for a long-term view." (Business Week). *Inference*: Major strategic gains lie in the industry-wide pervasive collaboration or recursive extension of enterprises, Principle 3.2.

- "If everybody can agree on a forecast and stick to it, you don't have to be changing your production schedules back and forth," says Ernest R. Lazor, chief information officer at Prestone Products Corp., in Danbury, Connecticut. "That's the way to get better margins." (Business Week). *Inference*: Integration of the enterprise - or, extended enterprise - results in strategic gains. We recognize Principle 2.3 and Principle 3.1 here.

- "CFAR (ultimately) could (help) eliminate uncertainty and eliminate inventory," says Andre Martin, a principal of Retail Pipeline Integration Inc., a consulting firm in Essex Junction, Vermont. "(current) CFAR," he says, "is just the tip of the iceberg." (Information Week). "The plan is to expand the CFAR pilot to include at least 200 other companies by the year's end." (ComputerWorld). *Inference*: The vision is, again, based recursive extension of the enterprise, Principle 3.2.

- "CFAR is different because it offers a standard set of processes and a protocol for all parties to share a much wider range of data over the Internet." (ComputerWorld). *Inference*: This is enterprise integration and integration of the extended enterprise, Principle 2.2 and Principle 3.1.

We now apply the reference model to the CFAR case and derive possible additional goals that might be applicable for its ensuing effort.

3. Strategic Goals Obtainable from the Planning Model

The CFAR project is about supply chain integration, not about e-commerce as originally perceived. However, it is a cliche to say that current e-commerce practice, especially the business-to-business procurement systems, could easily connect with the Internet-based CFAR environment. However, could the CFAR enterprise easily extend itself to include revenue-generating e-commerce? We examine the CFAR case from this perspective and apply the planning model to analyze for pertinent goals.

Chapter 5 suggests a simple procedure for applying the planning model to develop e-commerce goals - see Section 1. The first order of business according to the procedure is to define certain basic concepts of the reference model as applied to the particular enterprise. Thus, we first define the notion of enterprise here. There are three distinct enterprise views in the CFAR project: Wal-Mart's view, Warner-Lambert's view, and the extended enterprise view of the CFAR project that spawns both these views. In the Wal-Mart view, people who shop at their stores are the external customers. In the Warner-Lambert view, retailers like Wal-Mart are the external customers. In the extended enterprise view, not only both types are the customers, the other retailers and suppliers that the project wants to recruit are customers, too. Next, we consider information, transaction, and products.

- *Transaction.* There are two types of obvious transactions pertaining to the logic of CFAR. The first is the supply chain transactions, and the second is the transactions involved in the forecasting activity. Both types of transaction are the immediate candidates for which the enterprise could develop its e-commerce practice. The most obvious practice is procurement. The CFAR environment includes a set of standard processes and a protocol for data interchange. Therefore, both companies and, for that matter, all other user firms of CFAR could readily conduct their procurement transactions over the Internet through CFAR. In other words, CFAR is as much an information infrastructure for business-to-business e-commerce as it is an integration tool for product forecasts and inventory. Evidently, the practice can easily include additional administration functions as well. The forecasting transactions involve immediately all parties in the production of sales and marketing data, and in the production of the forecasts. This could lead to another practice, business-to-business e-commerce - collaborative, joint forecasting over the Internet. Perhaps even more significantly, it could lead to the end users of these two companies, their customers. After all, these customers generate the sales data. Sale transactions become a logical part of the CFAR enterprise.

- *Information Product.* The CFAR enterprise produces information products to its customers. The core product is the processes and the protocol the companies use to collaborate. A less direct product is the forecasts and sales and marketing information resources. Wal-Mart and Warner Lambert sponsored the CFAR enterprise to obtain these products, so will other retailers and manufacturers. Thus, the enterprise could make money out of these products. It could sell them or charge usage fees to, especially, users other than the two sponsoring companies. It could even sell the infrastructure of CFAR as a marketplace for business-to-business e-commerce. From the perspective of marketing, some of the products or transactional services could become free offerings to prospect customers (other retailers and suppliers) in order to allure them to the business.

- *Information Service.* By definition, information products are always a part of the information services. But in addition to the above information resources and software that CFAR produces, the enterprise could also consider for the customers who generate the sales data that become a part of its information resources. In this sense, information services to the companies' customers become relevant to the CFAR enterprise. Wal-Mart has always used its retailing data as a marketing tool. Thus, it is a wonder why the company has been conservative about Internet retailing. Perhaps, it is worried about cannibalizing possibly its own retailing stores. However, the company should at least be able to appreciate the marketing value of a direct business-to-customer site, as it could be a potent tool to collect additional data about customers and the market. Such an informational site, with limited transactional services for the retailing customers, should complement, not threaten, the regular business and would add good value to the CFAR environment. Wal-Mart Online is a cautious start.

We would confine our discussion to the immediate concern of the CFAR enterprise. Therefore, we would not attempt to analyze for Wal-Mart as a whole, nor for Warner Lambert. With this limited scope in mind, we then conduct a quick and simple pass of the nine principles of e-commerce planning to set some possible goals for the enterprise.

The Information Service and Product Principle

We consider in some details the CFAR enterprise's information services and products. The discussion makes direct use of the recognition of information and transaction defined above.

(1). Marketing: Providing Free Information Services to Customers.

The CFAR project has not reported any goal that falls under this category. An immediate concern to the enterprise is to recruit a significant number of other retailers and suppliers. They are the customers of the enterprise's information products, and they are the customers of the enterprise. Wal-Mart and Warner Lambert have good reason to sponsor the joint venture; however, others must also see value in it to participate. Thus, CFAR could offer to provide standard software libraries, process templates, or even consulting services to ease the effort (transaction cost) required so that even small retailers and suppliers could join. It should also customize, or help the other users to customize, its information resources and tailor the applications to their own strategic goals. The service must go beyond the mundane job of, e.g., converting data formats. It must address the customers' wants of the additional information resources not covered in the needs of the immediate work agreement. Information services to another type of customers, the company customers, would have different specificity but the same logic. Wal-Mart, for instance, could expand Wal-Mart Online to provide attractive information services to its customers and use the site to collect marketing information. Warner Lambert probably could do the same to collect data about its products. In particular, the CFAR enterprise solidifies large amount of external data, such as flu updates and allergy alerts. These data are valuable to their customers, too. Similarly, the enterprise can also turn much of the marketing intelligence, including information about Listerine-like products, whereabouts of stores, and consumption patterns into information services to customers. There would be little effort required of the information service since the enterprise collects these data anyway. It would cause little harm to the companies, too, since it determines what information to go public. Imagine a novel 'flu-map' on the Web to help people learn about the spread of flu in particular areas. This service would be an easy "double dipping" of the information power for the companies but would be a tough act for others to follow. To collect data about products and customer behaviors, a whole slew of services would be available. The site could add some ordering transactions to the usual sales announcements or even provide delivery service to certain types of products or customers. This practice would be good business-to-customer e-commerce as well as good marketing tool to obtain information about the effects of special sales, customer preferences, and trial balloons, just to name a few. We stress that the Web-based marketing process could be accessible to both Wal-Mart and Warner Lambert, or extend to other partners. The basic point we make here is straightforward. Since CFAR is about forecasting sales and sharing of the forecasts, the marketing power of Principle 1.1 for constituent companies is very pertinent to the enterprise itself. The information resources that Wal-Mart possesses could be a significant competitive advantage, especially when it decides to enter e-commerce in earnest. The company has the potential to become a major dispenser of information on consumer goods on the Internet and, thereby, leverage its information services to gain on competitors.

(2). Revenue: Turning Information Services into Products.

There has been no goals reported under this category. However, the CFAR enterprise produces marketing information and collaborative technology (including the networking protocol, reference model, Web designs, and the like). It attracts other retailers and suppliers based on these products. They are its livelihood. It has no reason not to become a bona fide product for the enterprise and generate revenue for it. It has full potential to become a spin-off and operate in its own right. As mentioned above, the CFAR is a small step away from the capability of serving as a business-to-business e-commerce marketplace. Companies that want to do procurement over the Internet could come to it, and companies that want to do more supply chain integration and more marketing could come to it, too. Its tremendous information base should serve it very well in competition in the domain marketplace. The idea here is similar to American Airlines Sabre reservation system, which is now spun-off to become an information service company of its own. In fact, if the CFAR technology should become the industry standard as envisioned by Benchmarking Consultants, the creators of the CFAR protocol, the domain marketplace goal would be more than pertinent.

(3) Intelligence: Tapping into Internet Resources.

The current CFAR enterprise has not reported any goals to build a marketing database over the Internet nor use the Internet data to do marketing. A quick example of tapping into Internet resources is to analyze the Web sites of their prospective company customers. The enterprise could better position its recruitment effort and better design its information services and products for the target market. Understanding their company clients' needs is pivotal to its vision of becoming the industry standard. This understanding does not have to rely on the physical contact with the companies any more with the Internet. Furthermore, the CFAR enterprise is an extended enterprise for its member companies. Therefore, it could join all members' marketing information and other information resources to form an extensive coverage of the market that no single members alone could achieve. Members could collaborate in database marketing as well as in forecasting and supply chain integration. As long as there are benefits for the collaborating companies, the goal of joint information resources would be a probability. CFAR itself is a product of the collaboration in the first place. E-commerce practice would make the collaboration even easier to pull off. The CFAR community Web sites could be the medium of the collaboration. In a straightforward manner, Wal-Mart would have the opportunity to use its presence on the Web to determine if some substitute product for Listerine is becoming popular with its customers. The company could also study consumers' responses to various factors of marketing as well as to location and operation of retailing stores. The study would no longer be limited to its own stores. Trade secrecy should not prohibit all possibilities for collaboration, as proven by the CFAR project.

The Enterprise Integration Principle

The CFAR enterprise is about integration. It has reported a number of goals under this category. In fact, it has covered all Principles 2.1-2.3. All these goals, however, are concerned primarily with the integration of its member companies' supply chain. Is the enterprise of CFAR itself integrated? We examine this question as well as the supply chain.

(4). Administration: Adopting E-Commerce for Business Function.

The CFAR enterprise has its own administration functions. It needs to recruit members, handle workflow for the community, and maintain the CFAR environment. It is unclear how the companies communicate among themselves other than transferring forecasts data files over the Internet. All CFAR administration functions, especially those that interact with member companies, could be put on the Internet, too, using a community Web site. In other words, the CFAR enterprise could develop an administration Intranet for member companies to use and reduce the transaction cost of interacting with each other. They could also use the CFAR Intranet to inter-operate their respective business processes that pertain to the extended enterprise of CFAR. From the perspective of Wal-Mart and Warner Lambert, this principle (2.1) would immediately suggest a business-to-business e-commerce practice for them, to handle all paper works and payments pertaining to the supply chain. For the CFAR enterprise, the community Intranet would be a basis for an e-commerce marketplace facilitating members to conduct business-to-business transactions.

(5). Production: Applying E-Commerce to Core Production.

The production system for the CFAR enterprise is the functions and processes involved in the making of its information products and in the execution of the CFAR environment for its company customers. A production Intranet for CFAR is certainly a possibility. It could use the Intranet to link all players in the production of the information products, perhaps in a concurrent engineering manner. It could also use the Intranet to integrate better the retailers' forecasting processes and the suppliers' scheduling processes. The linkage would go beyond file transfer per se. It would include the conduct of the activities that produce the files. Even from the company customers' perspective, this principle (2.2) promises to further integrate their supply chain and provide heightened benefits. In the CFAR project, Wal-Mart feeds forecasts to Warner-Lambert. This is a forward chaining of the production system overarching both companies. The feedback, or backward chaining, is not included. Opportunities exist for Wal-Mart to make use of the production data from Warner-Lambert, too. For example, the company could exact its prediction on delivery of certain products and use the accurate estimates to adjust its shelf space management, marketing, or even pricing policies. The premise is simply that it has the real time, actual data, on Warner Lambert's manufacturing. The retailers could improve its supply chain management first by helping the supplier to do a better job scheduling and then by helping itself better predicting. The production Intranet would make chaining in both directions easier.

(6). Enterprise: Connecting Administration Systems with Production Systems.

Principle 2.3 would suggest that the administration Intranet and the production Intranet be connected for the CFAR community. A comprehensive e-commerce practice for the CFAR enterprise itself would help sell its information products and would facilitate its member companies inter-operating among them to reap the best benefits of collaboration. More intriguingly, it would also help the community to leverage each other's marketing activities and information resources. The transaction records on the CFAR Intranet would reflect market activities concerning demand and supply. Thus, they automatically provide valuable data mine for companies to utilize and obtain all kinds of marketing intelligence. Simply put, it would make many innovative applications possible and support Principles 1.1 - 1.3.

The Extended Enterprise Principle

The CFAR project is an extended enterprise. It has also set good and sophisticated goals using the concept. Thus, we would only briefly review some comments as applicable to the CFAR enterprise.

(7). Extension: Applying E-Commerce to the Extended Enterprise for Integration.

The community Intranet mentioned above is an application of this principle, already. We consider some further ideas here. The CFAR enterprise itself has possible external constituencies, just as any other enterprise would have. Its immediate constituencies could include the partners of the CFAR technology developer, Benchmarking, Inc. It could also include the information technology community that develops CFAR-related solutions. A case in point would the industry standard setting organizations and the Internet 2 consortium. The extension could include the external constituencies of its company customers. The other suppliers of Wal-Mart and the other customers of Warner-Lambert are the other possible external constituencies of CFAR. This notion would become more relevant and clear when the CFAR enterprise embraces e-commerce. If it becomes a business-to-business marketplace and/or it discovers business-to-customer opportunities, too, then the extension of the CFAR enterprise follows naturally. We might add that a community Web site that includes Wal-Mart or other retailers would lend itself easily to business-to-customer e-commerce. Here, again, we see the CFAR case demonstrates the same fundamental theme; that is, the separation of business-to-business and business-to-customer e-commerce is meaningless in the long term when the whole field matures.

(8). Growth: Recursively Cascading the Extension Throughout.

The CFAR enterprise has always had a broad vision in terms of its user community. Thus, it is already consistent with Principle 3.2. We would only add that if the enterprise decides to embrace e-commerce, as opposed to a not-for-revenue Internet enterprise, it could consider more than the supply chain industry. There are many business-to-business marketplace sites, as well as domain portal sites. The nature of CFAR could be complementary to some of them. Thus, a growth path for the extended CFAR enterprise could be some alliance with these e-commerce businesses. Principles 2.1-3.2 above could actually be applied recursively to the alliance. We believe that the future e-commerce will not see the merging of business-to-business and business-to-customer e-commerce, but also feature collaboration of domain portal sites and marketplace sites. In fact, as many company e-commerce sites become a kind of domain portal sites, too, the distinction between these sites will also become less meaningful. For instance, Wal-Mart could become a marketplace site for many manufacturers who used to be its suppliers but then choose to have their own e-commerce practice. Our earlier discussion about Amazon.com vs. publishers applies here as well.

(9). Roadmap: Converting Societal Transaction Cost Reduction to Business Opportunities.

Does the CFAR enterprise bring about any fundamental change to the societal value chain and hence societal transaction cost? The answer is similar to the case of Amazon.com. The supply chain is still the supply chain, except that CFAR makes it perform better. If the enterprise applies e-commerce to itself, as we advocate in this section, it would affect the supply chain more significantly. It would not, however, change the supply chain itself. If it becomes a marketplace or even joins force with some domain portal sites, it would have the promise to really alter the value chain. Although Wal-Mart and other retailers would always have their suppliers, there would not be the (stable) supply chain that we know today. Therefore, if we examine the situation from a converse point of view, we could regard altering the current supply chain as a basic strategy for developing new business opportunities. The middle layer, retailers, could face a paradigm shift in the new age of e-commerce. Even suppliers who play a role of intermediary could be in for some prolonged surprises, too.

4. Remarks.

We applied the planning model to the CFAR case, following a methodology suggested in Section 1 of Chapter 5. The planning model indicated certain possible goals that an enterprise such as CFAR could have considered to use. The case, of course, is only an exercise in order to illustrate how to develop strategic goals for an e-commerce practice using the planning model. The CFAR project was a significant and famous industrial effort in the field of supply chain integration. The project, sponsored by Wal-Mart and Warner Lambert in collaboration with Benchmarking, Inc., has had an impact on the industry. Although its original vision as publicized in 1996 might be bolder than what it has actually accomplished in 1999, the case remains inspirational to similar efforts. Its original goals are still relevant and eloquent as ever. E-commerce was not a prevailing thought at the time of the CFAR effort. Then, its use of the Internet was quite a forward thinking in the field. What we attempted to do was a re-examination of the original goals in the new light of e-commerce and see what more could have been done, all with a conceptual review. We believe that this reexamination has served a purpose. It shows a few things:

- E-commerce is a powerful tool to use for supply chain integration. While the CFAR project has demonstrated how the Internet technology improved the previous practice of supply chain integration, we hope that our discussion has shown how e-commerce would further improve the supply chain applications.

- Since it is beneficial for supply chain integration, e-commerce must be a powerful tool for the integration of the internal operations of an enterprise, not just some application of the Internet for externally oriented commercial activities. We hope our discussion has helped illustrate this point.

- E-commerce immediately leads to broad opportunities beyond the traditional vision and practice of supply chain integration, even when it was initially applied only to supply chain integration. The reason is that e-commerce brings to the fore the business possibilities that the new information technology provides.

- The planning model helps to shed light on these possibilities. All nine principles of the model are useful and are consistent with the requirement of e-commerce strategic goal setting. All its basic concepts, such as information vs. transaction, enterprise vs. extended enterprise, and service vs. product, are shown to be relevant to e-commerce and useful to its analysis.

The next two chapters report a couple of exploratory studies applying the Internet to a bank and a heavy machinery corporation. These studies used the reference model to guide the development of strategic goals.

7

AN INTERNET BANKING PLAN FOR AN ASIAN BANK

A banker of an Asian bank explored the possibility of employing the Internet to enhance some customer processes for his bank. He did the work in collaboration with the authors while he was on leave to pursue his Master of Business Administration degree at Rensselaer Polytechnic Institute. The reference model served as the basis of the study. The banker later submitted the exploratory plan to the top management of the bank and presented to a managerial level internal meeting. We withhold the identity of both the bank and the banker upon his request. We describe the exploratory study below.

1. The Background

The bank was established in 1967 as a Development Finance Corporation, the country's first private financial development institution. In 1980, it became the country's first long-term credit bank when the bank launched an aggressive campaign to expand its operations beyond basic banking. Presently, businesses of the Bank range across a comprehensive list of financial services and products in international, corporate, and private banking, and capital market analysis. The Bank comprises 35 domestic branches and 7 overseas offices, representative offices, or subsidiaries. The Bank is also the flagship of its group consisting of eight affiliates covering every significant aspect of the financial industry. The Bank perceived its potential competitors to be foreign banks, as the government has started to open the country's financial industry under pressures from the U.S. and the World Trade Organization. The Bank was especially concerned about the one advantage that the U.S. banks always enjoy: information technology. The bank executives were confident for their position in the tightly knit society and their grass root connection with the local customers. These savvy bankers, however, did not under-estimate the newcomers. They knew, based on their professional contact or even personal education and work experiences in the U.S., what U.S. banks could do and have done with information technology. So, they watched attentively as the Internet emerged as the talk of the community. They were not impressed with what they saw in the informational Web sites that dominated the corporate use of the Internet at the time. Thus, they wanted to look into their enterprise itself.

The banker who worked with the authors realized that Internet holds many promises for a bank. The banker was fascinated with the notion of banking over the

Internet, or cyber-banking as many called it. He was aware that a comprehensive Internet plan for a bank could not merely confine itself to the present information processing needs of the bank. The introduction of the Internet technology would affect processes and functions throughout the bank. He appreciated a planning methodology that encompasses the whole range of activities from strategic goal setting to analysis and design of an Internet-based information system. Thus, the collaboration began. The generic reference model (see Section 4.1) served as a primary mechanism for setting goal for the new Internet-based systems supporting cyber-banking. The rest of the planning process followed the methodology described in Chapter 5. In the subsequent sections, we describe this planning process for one particular aspect of deploying the Internet in the Bank: on-line banking. The first stage has yielded seventeen information goals, which then serve as drivers for the ensuing process redesign effort.

2. The Goal Setting Stage.

One major objective for the planning process is to establish a basic set of goals for the practice of Internet based banking. Conceptually, the objective looks outward from a bank rather than inward. However, it still has to deal with internal processes that are, at least, directly connected to the external activities targeted. The Bank had an understandable desire to look outward when it started contemplating an application of the Internet. It is perfectly intuitive to relate the Internet to external processes; besides, changing internal processes would imply too much of a cultural change. The planning process obliged itself to the premise. Consequently, we limited the systematic search of possible goals to externally oriented activities that require seemingly the least change to the status quo.

The objective of providing on-line banking must consider four types of customers: individual customers, small businesses, large businesses, and international businesses. For individual customers, on-line banking services will mean owning checking and saving accounts, paying bills, approving and managing loans, and facilitating buying and selling of stocks. Services provided to small businesses will include transferring funds, opening and operating checking and savings accounts, processing transactions (credit card processing), and establishing a financial center that extends loans and lines of credit to businesses. For larger businesses, a bank also provides services that entail providing short term working capital for seasonal purchases, office supplies, travel, vehicles, equipment, entertainment, long term expansion, and debt refinancing. These services are traditionally offered through transactions at a local branch, either in person or via ATM, telephone, mail and so on. Banks also offer the facility of handling checks by storing checks for a business. Additionally, a bank can provide businesses with payment processing, e.g., collecting payments on behalf of the business. This service offers security to businesses and their customers as well as providing a source of short term finance for the businesses. All these services are amenable to the practice of e-commerce. Offering them over the Internet saves transaction cost for both parties. Furthermore, an Internet bank adds a dimension of security to e-commerce businesses and customers when they handle payments through it. The added security is a combination of a few factors: dedicated security control mechanism (scale of economy), escrow capabilities, and trust. The third factor might be more important than the first two; at least, it is uniquely associated with the institution we call bank. This means that cyber-banking actually increases business opportunities in the area of payment processing since this service becomes much more strategic, or even vital, to a bank's business customers in the cyber space than ever before.

In the area of commercial banking, a salient feature is that a large business usually deals with multiple banks. Therefore, an Internet bank fits easily into the role of being the business' "central bank". The on-line bank can provide comprehensive cash management service that establishes one account, one statement, one transaction for the business, and takes care of multiple dealings with other banks and financial institutions. This service is not unique to Internet banking, but Internet banking and e-commerce make it more significant and easier to operate than traditional banking, especially when it is combined with payment service or other transactional services. In this sense, a cyber-bank can justifiably boost its potential to become a one step financial and transactional services provider on the Internet for e-commerce businesses, including handling most of their business dealings with customers.

In the realm of international trade, a bank provides services on currency exchange, currency management, overseas letter of credits and import/export documents. These services can benefit from the added convenience that Internet based connection avails to banks. However, the unique, strategic opportunity lies in the notion of the virtual bank. A bank could collaborate with other banks in other countries where its business customers operate to form a virtual bank. The virtual bank could provide the financial and transactional services to its international business customers as a domestic bank does within its country. To be sure, many of the traditional banks, especially multinational banks, have always been providing similar service to their large business customers. The difference here with virtual banks is the scale and the threshold. The idea of one-stop transactional service center extends beyond bank-to-bank business. It includes business-to-business and business-to-customer transactions. Only the Internet could allow for large-scale application of this idea, which would be at the heart of a virtual bank. Because the transaction cost of providing the one-stop service is lower with cyber-banking, the bank could provide it to more and smaller business customers than traditional banking. Again, the low transaction cost of Internet based connection avails the elite services to the mass market. Try to imagine virtual banks joining force with marketplace e-commerce sites that have global appeals.

In sum, banks have a traditional business. The Internet brings some convenience to some of the traditional business because of its universal and low transaction cost connection. Examples include services to individual customers and small businesses. The Internet greatly enhances some traditional services and makes new business opportunities out of them. Payment processing and credit clearing are among the easily noticeable. These services can link directly to e-commerce. Finally, the Internet also opens entirely new business opportunities for cyber-banks. E-commerce services and virtual banks for cyber-banking are two major possibilities we mentioned above. The analysis for the Bank includes some of these opportunities. We summarize in Table 7.1 the particular goals developed by conducting a systematic search according to the generic reference model.

Type of Business	Reference Model Category	Internet Banking Goals
Individual Banking	1. Providing information services to customer 2. Turning information services into products	1. On-line opening of accounts - savings and checking 2. On-line transfer of funds between accounts 3. Facility to pay bills on-line 4. Facility to buy and sell stock on-line
Commercial Banking (Domestic)	1. Providing information services to customer 2. Turning information services into products 3. Thinking extended enterprise 4. Extending to information enterprise	1. Provide short-term working capital. 2. Provide long term loans. 3. Provide check-handling facility. 4. On-line opening of accounts - savings and checking. 5. On-line transfer of funds between accounts. 6. Credit card processing for businesses. 7. Provide secured transactions between customers of the on-line business and the business. 8. Provide secured business to business transactions on-line. 9. Authenticate transactions between on-line businesses and their customers as well as between on-line businesses. 10. Provide a virtual marketplace for businesses. 11. Dispense expertise about cyber-businesses.
Commercial Banking (International)	1. Providing information services to customer 2. Turning information services into products 3. Thinking extended enterprise 4. Extending to information enterprise	1. Provide currency exchange, currency management, opening overseas LCs, and handling import/export document services to businesses. 2. Create virtual banking corporations with other banks/financial institutions in order to provide banking/financial services overseas.

Table 7.1: Internet Banking Goals.

110

3. Web-Based Banking Processes.

The existing processes of the Bank that will be affected by the above goalsare the following: (1). savings account management process, (2). savings account transaction management process, (3). checking account management process, (4). checking account transaction management process, (5). other transactions management process, (6). loan management process, and (7). international finance process. These processes are comprised of sub-processes. This section details the specifications of some of the changes required of the processes in meeting the above Internet banking goals.

Savings Account Management Process.

Sub-processes:

(i) *Savings account opening process.* In regular (off line) banking, the customer goes to a branch to open the account and fills out an account opening form. For Internet banking, this process would need to be modified. Instead of the customer going to a branch of the bank to open the account, s/he should be able to open the account on-line. This will need to address two issues: (a) design and technical issues - designing the on-line form and program(s) to accept the user input and update databases and (b) security issues - establishing the identity of the customer and obtaining his/her signatures. Before digital signature technology gets robust enough to provide an alternative to physical signatures, the customer still needs to make an initial contact with the bank in person. A straightforward way the customer could open a savings account is the following: the customer logs on to the Bank's Web site and fills out an on-line account opening form. The bank opens the account for deposits alone. To activate the account for withdrawal and/or transfer of funds from the account, the customer will need to visit a branch of the bank. Upon establishing the customer's identity and obtaining the signature, the Bank will issue a personal identification number (PIN) and passwords so that the customer will use them in the future to carry out all transactions from anywhere on the Internet.

(ii) *Savings account transferring process.* This process enables customers to transfer funds between their savings and other accounts, either with the Bank or with other banks. Presently, customers use phone/ATM/tellers to effect such transfer of funds. The process of funds transfer between accounts owned by the Bank alone is straightforward. In the case of funds transfer involving another bank(s) or financial institution(s), a customer needs to log into his/her account on the Bank and, from there, connects to the other banks and financial institutions. There are three scenarios to this case, each implies different requirements on the protocols and processes. The first scenario assumes customers have access to the Bank via the Internet; the same holds true for customers of all other banks. However, the banks are connected among themselves using private networks. The situation is depicted in Figure 7.1 where the Bank is dubbed KLB. Under this scenario, a simple way to make the transfer work is to make use of the regular channel and mechanism for handling funds transfer among banks. In other words, the banking Web site will serve as a virtual, extended ATM to help the customers "register" their intended transfer but will not actually conduct the transaction on line. The transaction will take place at the backend by the clerks of the regular processes. The second scenario calls for banks using the Internet for their inter-bank transactions, too. Here, everyone uses the Internet. Figure 7.2 depicts the

111

situation. The Bank could entertain an advanced possibility where it sets up a banking portal site. Its Web site will not only provide links to other banking Web sites but will also include provisions that allow these different banking home pages to inter-operate. In particular, these sites will connect their respective withdrawal and deposit transactions under an overarching virtual process of fund transfer. Needless to say, the Bank alone cannot make it happen. It is a joint venture among banks, and all involved must agree to collaborate, of course. The technology required is reasonable; XML alone might be sufficient to develop a protocol for online fund transfer.

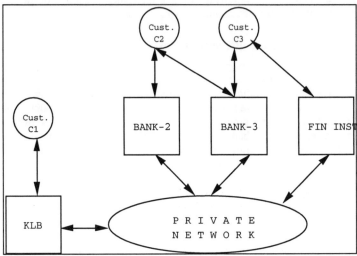

Figure 7.1: Savings Account Transferring Process (I).

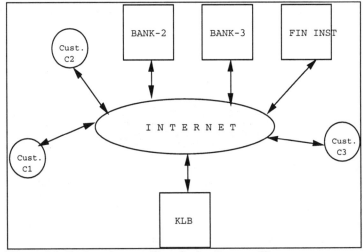

Figure 7.2: Savings Account Transferring Process (II).

There is a third possibility where some banks and financial institutions are on the Internet and others are not. In that case, customers of the Bank will log into their accounts at the Bank through the Internet and, in turn, will connect to other banks through the Bank. The Bank will build its banking portal site via the Internet and a private network, as shown below in Figure 7.3. This hybrid configuration could complicate the vision and the system design. A high road possibility is to expand the role of the cyber-banking system to become a sort of bank-to-bank e-commerce marketplace practice, somewhat similar to a traditional service bureau. A low road alternative is to keep everything simple and close to current practice. We describe next such a strategy, using Figure 7.3 as the example.

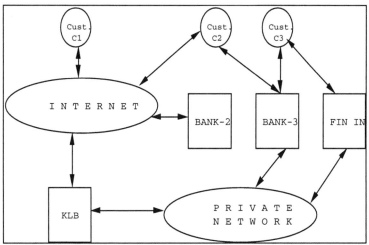

Figure 7.3: Savings Account Transferring Process (III).

The savings account transferring process will need to require that the customer logs into her savings account at the Bank using the Internet. This is a secured transaction, and the customer uses her PIN and password to log into her account. From this point on, she is presented a menu of choices - transfer funds between accounts on the Bank or Bank XYZ/Financial Institution ABC. For the customer, the fund transfer is transparent. However, the internal processes for the Bank conducting a funds transfer will change substantially. If the transfer is between two accounts of the Bank, the funds transfer process need not to invoke the process of establishing a connection with another bank/financial institution. For inter-bank funds transfer, the process will involve establishing a connection and the protocol for EDI. This process could be different for the case of Internet connection and that of a private network. At least, the authentication/security procedures will be quite different in the two cases. The Bank and the participating banks will need to work out and develop appropriate protocols for effecting such transfers.

(iii) *Savings account problem maintenance process*. This process deals with customer problems in using their savings accounts (for example, a customer may forget her password). For the Bank to go Internet, this process will expand slightly. If a customer cannot log onto her savings account online after three attempts, she will be presented with a standard trouble-shooting page to help her out. In the common case that the customer forgot her PIN or password, the page could walk her through a procedure by which she provides alternative information to authenticate her identity. Then, the system could send the correct PIN or password to her. Alternatively, the

113

page could simply guide the customer to call a number or to go to a branch of the bank and accomplish the same. This practice is commonplace now with e-commerce. The reason we describe it here is to remind us of a simple but significant point: the interactive home page allows the banking site to develop more authenticating algorithms in user-friendly ways than the traditional practice.

Savings Account Transaction Management Process.

Sub-processes:

(i) *Saving account transaction process.* This process is used to effect transactions such as balance inquiry, requesting statements, requesting checks, etc. in a customer's savings account. Changes required in respect of this process for Internet banking would be similar to those in the above savings account management process. Internet implementation of this process would require design of appropriate forms and database connectivity. These are some of the examples that would have a bearing on the technological requirement analysis for the Bank's Intranet project.

(ii) *Withdrawal management process.* This process effects withdrawal of cash from a customer's savings account. Cash withdrawal takes place traditionally at a branch or at an ATM. However, this process will be altered for Internet banking. The Internet does not deliver physical material flow, and cash is a physical material. Thus, the banking site must direct the customer who chooses to withdraw money to some convenient branches or ATMs. A simple way is to ask the customer to enter her zip code and use that zip code to display a list of all available ATMs along with a map and instructions on how to get to there. The similar technique could be used to add services or even information products for the customer who is going to get some cash. Using an example closer to home, if the customer chooses 12180-3590 as the zip code to query on the ATM location, the system will display a list of ATMs in the Rensselaer Polytechnic Institute area. If the customer chooses Troy Plaza among the list, she is presented with the location of the ATM in Troy Plaza along with the banner advertisement for the Friendly's restaurant and Price Chopper which flank the ATM in the plaza. (The Bank could have established a virtual bank with Troy Savings Bank, and the customer could be a visitor from the Asian country to the Home of Uncle Sam.) We included this simple example to show that even a banker is entitled to having some fun. Semi-seriously, cyber-banking allows for all kinds of breaking away with traditional thinking. It is a coup to the traditional paradigm and, hence, all banking processes deserve a new look and new thinking when being transplanted to the cyber space.

Checking Account Management Process.

This process is a mirror image of the savings account management process and has exactly the same type of sub-processes. They would need to be modified for Internet banking in the same manner as before, too.

Checking Account Transaction Management Process.

This process is also a mirror image of the savings account transaction management process. Their sub-processes are twins, too. This process would require similar changes to be put on the Internet.

Other transactions management processes.

Sub processes:

Transaction with affiliates and subsidiaries. Unlike most of the above processes, whose external activities and internal activities could have clear boundaries, this process pertains entirely to the internal operation of the Bank. When the external data enter the banking system in the form of EDI or by other e-commerce means, the core of the banking processes needs to adapt to this electronic transaction, as well. Therefore, Internet banking would probably spawn many Intranet applications. The process would need to be reengineered so as to obviate the need to renter the internal exchange of data between branches and the head office, for example. The e-commerce Principle 2.1 or even Principles 2.2 and 2.3 might apply. At this point, we could recognize a simple fact. That is, even when the Principle of Enterprise seems remote to an e-commerce practice, it is still relevant. Taking a clue from Chapter 2, we would suggest that Intranet is a way to go. The internal Web site with clever interface could help transferring data across affiliates and subsidiaries as if they were in one system.

Transaction for affiliates and subsidiaries. This process deals directly with the inter-operation of affiliates and subsidiaries without also involving the headquarters and branches. Its technical nature is the same as the above process. Hence, the above discussion applies to this process.

Loan Management Process.

Sub processes:

Loan planning. These processes are internal to the bank and do not directly affect banks dealing with its customers. The Bank could choose to include it in its Intranet, but that would be another issue outside the immediate concern of this exploratory study.

Loan approval management. This process comprises of loan application and loan approval processes. The loan application process not only needs to be online but should also be automated as much as possible. For example, the bank can create templates for various types of loan applications - homes (in the price range I), homes (in the price range II), automobiles, boats, etc. Guided by the pull down options, customers would be able to fill out an online application much more conveniently than filling it off-line. The application process can also include embedded algorithms in filling out the application and handling all processing. The loan approval process should be automated to provide faster customer service and eliminate time consuming and expensive human intervention. For certain classes of loans within certain limits, an automated loan approval system could approve some loans instantly and online. In the absence of digital signatures, the customer would still need to sign some physical documents before the loan is actually disbursed to her. Still, the

Internet would help speed up the process further, compared to implementing similar ideas without it.

International Finance Process.

The international finance process would make direct use of the above other transactions management process. At the basic level, the same enterprise Intranet could serve to facilitate the workflow among branches and subsidiaries in different countries. More comprehensively, it could be connected to some of the banking processes illustrated in Figures 1-3. For inter-bank workflow, the Intranet could be extended to form an extranet with other banks, especially those with which the Bank does extensive business.

4. Remarks.

What we described in this chapter is an initial attempt to explore some of the possible impact of the Internet on the Bank. Its scope is intentionally limited, focusing only on some of the mundane activities of a bank. The contribution of the Internet to these activities tends to be significant but, nonetheless, does not change the current paradigm. In this sense, the goals explored are incremental to the prevailing practice. The limitation has an advantage. It made the study down to the earth and put some blue-sky ideas to test. Throughout the information goal setting process for the Bank, technology capability was clearly the main player. In the end, the banker was comfortable with the notion of Internet banking. We were comfortable with using the reference model to assist the planning process. We should add that there were quite a few more goals identified during the processes, but they were not included in the formal analysis because they pushed the envelope too far. Some examples are virtual (extended) bank and the notion of extending elite services that banks used to reserve for large business clients to smaller businesses. All these examples are a step more sophisticated than the previous goals and promise since they make fuller use of the Internet capabilities to extend their previous products into much heightened and renewed business. The change would no long be incremental. We discussed these ideas in Section 2. A few other interesting ideas also emerged during the process. The bank, as these ideas go, could consider hosting Web sites for its customers and creating a virtual marketplace for banking and virtually any other domains that the Bank cares to explore. The Bank would then become a comprehensive e-commerce enterprise featuring the banking marketplace, financial portal site, and cyber banking. This would be a coup to the traditional paradigm. Section 2 discussed this idea, too. All the bigger ideas were results of a search using the other categories of reference model that the basic study ignored. We might also mention that banks do not want to get access to customers through other banks. However, all three levels of Internet banking would involve other banks in the access of customers for the Bank at various degrees. Is this issue a show-stopper? We do not think so. Airline companies always want to monopolize their customers' access to ticketing processes. They do not want their customers to go to other airlines to reserve tickets on their flights. However, the customer says otherwise; the travelers want just the opposite since they need to use more than one carrier to optimize their travel. Finally, the information technology settled the issue once and for all. Now, computerized reservation systems such as Sabre that serve as a ticketing marketplace for the whole airline industry are a fact of business life. Airlines must live with this fact and thrive on it. Would the same happen to the banking industry?

We take another step further on that note. Is there any common logic in the above three progressive levels of goals? We think so. The logic is the progressive diffusion of banking services. The traditional model for the banking industry is to provide the most powerful service to the largest business clients, which usually means thoroughly customized service. The one-step service, "my central bank," is the case in point. The basic level of Internet applications does not touch this model at all. The next level makes use the equalizing power of the Internet (low transaction cost - see Chapter 1) to expand its information products and offer this central bank to more businesses. In a way, the Internet pools the smaller businesses to a scale of economy and lowers the cost of the elite services for the bank so that more businesses could afford the services. The third level reaches out to individuals as well. What is the next step? "My central bank" for businesses will become "my central bank" for everyone, the individual customers. The same logic works here and makes this happen, sooner than many would predict. The new venture, MyCFO, is a personalized information product for the wealthy investors to enjoy one-step services. Its services cover investment, portfolio management, and many aspects of ordinary transactions found in daily life. The same idea would become affordable in its own way for most people since the underlying technology is not so intimidating. Most people, so it happens, need to use more than one bank or financial institution to optimize his/her financial life. This would be the Personal Finance Wizard idea we discussed in Chapter 1. Personalization would be the name of the game. Following the analysis of societal transaction cost, all the above levels of new banking help, but to vastly different extents. The third level started to alter the societal value chain in force. It is personalization, using the direct connection of persons and organizations from the person-centered perspective that would alter the societal value chain most. The alteration would spell the biggest business opportunity. To summarize, we have recognized four levels of new banking the new information technology enables:

- Web-based banking (see Section 3). The bank uses the Internet as the extended Automated Teller Machine for all types of customers.
- Commercial banking for small businesses. The bank becomes a virtual financial division for businesses to deal with their payment and other financial transactions.
- E-commerce banking and other related business. The bank becomes a provider of all types of promising finance-related services and products for e-commerce, globally.
- Personalized financial and banking business. The bank becomes a personal Chief Finance Officer for individuals as well as organizations.

The above discussion is clearly applicable to many banks in the world. The first level, Web-based banking, is largely a reality for an increasing number of major banks in the U.S. Many customers find the "Web ATM" especially convenient for dealing with credit card transactions, payments, and inquiries; which are unavailable with current ATM technology. The lesson here is clear. The customer appreciates new classes of services and these new classes would come from the capacity to conduct inter-bank transactions. Credit card payment, for instance, is inter-bank.

We might comment on the cost issue here. Internet banking could be a cost saver to banks. According to one study, one teller-effected transaction costs a bank $3.00 on average while a similar online transaction (e.g., through an ATM that is connected directly to the banking database engine) costs only $0.22. Therefore, the Bank might want to invest significantly to promote Internet banking. The traditional way to do this would be to offer some frequent user programs, giving customers, for example, bonus points for each on-line transaction and rewarding them with some gifts. We submit that this would prove to be a lousy way. It is an old trick that promises to have little effect on the new breed of e-commerce shoppers, shoppers who trade online and buy cars online. This group is primarily young and intelligent. If they would go for Internet banking, they do so for the core value of Internet banking. They would never be patronized by marginal cash rewards or junk prizes. The only way that could work on them is to develop innovative personal services and products that speak directly to the core reason why they bank online. The personal financial service idea, spanning both information and transaction, would work. Finally, we happen to uphold the position that security is not an intractable issue. Secure transaction is a crucial issue that must be addressed sufficiently; however, the current technology is already sufficient for many innovative ideas mentioned here. There is a will, there is a way. The real issue is the organizational inertia.

8

CUSTOMER SERVICE FOR SAMSUNG HEAVY INDUSTRIES

Dr. Hyun Taek Sim, a senior consultant at Samsung Heavy Industries Corporation, Ltd., collaborated with the authors to develop an exploratory plan utilizing the Internet for his company. The work was conducted in 1996-1997 when Dr. Sim was a resident visiting scholar at Rensselaer Polytechnic Institute. He was a leader in the company's business process reengineering effort until his visit to Rensselaer. Samsung Heavy Industries involves many complex processes and functions. Therefore, Dr. Sim concentrated the exploration on a customer service function. The choice was both reasonable and prudent. The company approved the exploration. The study considered primarily this question: What does it mean to put the customer service function on the Internet, and what processes would be affected and have to change? In essence, the study was an effort to set strategic goals for a sensible Web-based information system that would convert some of the previous customer service processes into an Internet-compatible operation. Customer service at the company includes ordering and after sale service, thus representing a typical e-commerce practice. However, Dr. Sim's charge was to enhance the existing functions as opposed to using e-commerce to expand into new practices or businesses. In a sense, the perceived use of the Internet in this study is comparable to that of the CFAR project (see Chapter 6); both are concerned with using the Internet as a tool to boost some traditional enterprise processes. Both, therefore, are a first major step towards full-fledged e-commerce. The study used the planning methodology of Chapter 5. The generic reference model was employed for the goal setting stage and value chain analysis for the second business process analysis stage. The third stage, business processes redesign used the analysis matrices as suggested for the methodology.

1. Company Background.

Headquartered in Korea, Samsung Heavy Industries Co., Ltd. (SHI) is a part of the Samsung Group that includes Samsung Electronics, Samsung Data Systems and close to ten other corporations. The SHI is a major international conglomerate in its field. The company operates the following divisions: shipbuilding and plant, industrial systems and machinery, and construction equipment. It has approximately 13,400 employees and annual sales of $3.8 billion; almost half of which comes from the company's business outside its home country, Korea. Samsung Heavy Industries Co., Ltd. has a network of ten branch offices and five subsidiaries in twelve countries. The Construction Equipment Division of SHI, the domain of the study, is

Korea's leading manufacturer of such equipment as excavators, loaders, bulldozers, hydraulic cranes, and forklifts. The total number of models available exceeds 100. Customer service and quality products are two business drivers for the division.

The company launched a business process reengineering project in 1995, which used Value Chain Analysis as a tool to identify the company's enterprise processes. The corporate value chain for SHI is shown in Figure 8.1. The value chain has three primary and six secondary activities. The primary activities include the Material Processes, Customer Processes, and Customer Service Processes. Material Processes correspond with Inbound Logistics, Operations and Outbound Logistics activities of a traditional Value Chain Analysis. Customer Processes describe Marketing and Sales activities of a typical value chain, and Customer Service Processes cover Service activities of a value chain. The six secondary activities are listed as Organization and Infrastructure, Human Resources, Administration, Evaluation Processes, Development Processes, and Planning Processes.

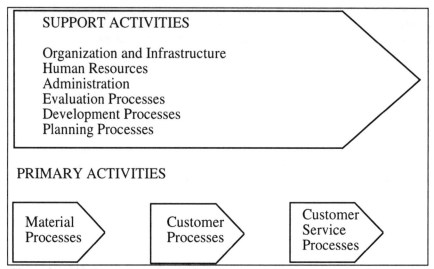

Figure 8.1: SHI Corporate Value Chain.

Some of the activities are more complex than the rest. The planning processes comprise six sub-processes and sixteen sub-sub-processes. Customer Processes comprise four sub- and twelve sub-sub-processes. Material Processes comprise manufacturing processes, including control material flow, control materials, shop floor control, and product control. Customer Service Processes are also a major component of the value chain. For our study, we focused on Customer and Customer Service Processes. The scope of customer service at SHI ranges from meeting customer orders for new machinery expeditiously to providing customers with service parts with a minimum of delay. Selling service parts for existing machinery is a lucrative business in heavy machinery industry. Besides which, providing service parts on time to customers is a core competence issue for the industry. A case in point is Caterpillar, a strong competitor of the company that delivers parts to

120

its customers anywhere in the world on a next day basis while SHI is behind that benchmark.

The company was aware of the possible application of the Internet in other areas besides customer service. The industry has reported, for instance, a case where a heavy machinery manufacturer used the Internet technology to reduce product cycle time for earth moving equipment to five days. The application was similar to the CFAR project in nature. The company, nonetheless, decided to explore some possible goals for the customer service activities using the Internet.

2. Choice of Internet Goals (Stage 1).

The study considered some basic possibilities of using the Internet to enhance the company's ordering processes, product service processes, and customer relationship processes. The reference model calls for applying the Internet to the internal processes. Thus, the first goals we identified were to put the customer-interfacing processes on the Internet. These processes are internal processes dealing with customers. They are most suitable for an immediate application of the Internet. The ordering processes always need to reach the customers and receive work flow (orders) from the customer, using whatever means the traditional system has to offer - mail, fax, telex, and so on. The Internet could easily replace these means. The after sale service is in a similar situation. Basically, any processes that involve workflow or other contact with customers can use the Internet to either substitute for the traditional ways or complement them.

Next, we searched for simple ideas to enhance the internal processes under the first dimension of the reference model, that is managing the external environment (corresponding to the information service and product principle of e-commerce planning). The notion of free information services (Principle 1.1) and information product (Principle 1.2) provided some structure for the search. The company was open to the concept of information product as long as the ideas are immediate to their basic products and business. It was not considering additional possibilities at all. The limited scope allowed a realistic analysis of the changes required of existing processes during the course of the study. It also made possible a reasonably comprehensive application of the analysis matrices as suggested (see the sections below).

After reviewing the existing processes of SHI and simplifying many possibilities, Dr. Sim identified the following specific Internet goals for the company to consider initially:

(1). Provide information to customers about orders
(2). Fill customer orders for service parts
(3). Provide information to customers about new products
(4). Provide information to customers about product modification
(5). Provide geological information to customers
(6). Provide project management tool to customers
(7). Create Intranet for customer's project
(8). Sell geological data to customers

121

(9). Provide project management services

(10). Provide Intranet consulting

(11). Collect performance data about equipment sold

(12). Collect customers' feedback on sale and service.

These goals then guided the ensuing development of a plan for a Web-based customer service environment.

3. Analysis of Business Processes (Stage 2).

The total number of processes comprising the corporate value chain of SHI is around 150. Out of these processes, we identified seventeen that constitute "marketing and sales" and "service" categories of the value chain. Table 8.1 describes these processes and their purpose. The table is printed in pages 122-123.

Processes	

1.0 Customer Processes
  1.1 Manage Orders
      1.1.1 Receive Order
          Inquiry
      1.1.2 Bid Orders
      1.1.3 Book Orders
      1.1.4 Confirm Delivery
  1.2 Verify Availability
      1.2.1 Review Inventory
          Plan
      1.2.2 Decide Alternatives
      1.2.3 Propose Allocation
          Rules
	Scenario: An inquiry is received through phone/ FAX from a customer, dealer or a branch about a new product or for changing or canceling an existing order. This order is entered on an order sheet, and the order is evaluated in terms of the price that needs to be quoted for the product and delivery date. Product is checked for availability, and the delivery date promised to the customer updates the manufacturing schedule.

1.3 Prepare Daily Schedule
      1.3.1 Schedule Shipping
      1.3.2 Schedule Production for
          Manufacturing
	These processes provide the linkage between customer and manufacturing processes mentioned in the above scenario.

1.4 Track Orders
      1.4.1 Monitor Orders
          Processed
      1.4.2 Follow Sales
          Delivered
	These processes are used to analyze the gap between planned and actual order fulfillment, review alternatives to customer change requests, check product delivery status, and deal with customer claims after delivery of the product.

2.0 Customer Service Processes
  2.1 Manage Service Part
      2.1.1 Process Service Part
          Request
      2.1.2 Receive Service Part
      2.1.3 Ship Service Part
      2.1.4 Control Service Part
Inventory
      2.1.5 Return Wrong Service Part
      2.1.6 Transform Manufacturing
          Part to Service Part
	Main processes comprising after sale service are concerned with providing service part to customers on time. It might happen that, at a given time, there is a demand for a service part that is not available but can be taken out of existing new machinery without disturbing any schedules. The last process deals with such a change of part status.

Table 8.1: Marketing & Sales and Service Processes (pp. 122-123).

4. Business Process Redesign (Stage 3)

The core of the study was an effort to analyze the impact of the Internet goals on the business processes involved. We would recognize the participation of processes, prioritize their involvement, and identify their interrelationship in light of the Internet effort. The effort then leads to a redesign of the business processes. We document the effort below.

Specification of Process Linkages (Stage 3.1)

Value Chain Analysis is concerned with linkages among processes. These linkages may even extend beyond conventional organizational boundaries. For example, linkages may exist between a supplier's value chain and a firm's value chain. Information technology helps organizations focus on these linkages among processes and optimize them. In the context of this study, the Internet technology would be the tool SHI would use to accomplish the optimization. Identifying these linkages, therefore, was the target here. In the value chain of SHI considered here, linkages exist between customer processes and manufacturing processes. We describe these linkages among these processes in Table 8.2 below (pp. 123-125).

Customer & *Service* *Processes* ↓	*Material* *Processes*	*Planning Processes*	*Product* *Development* *Processes*
1.1.1 Receive Order Inquiry			Product catalog content (specification/opti on/service part) affect the order inquiry process
1.1.2 Bid Orders		Price and allocation policies affect the bidding process	
1.1.3 Reserve Orders			

1.1.4 Confirm Delivery			
1.2.1 Review Inventory Plan	Inventory in stock information affects review of inventory plan	Machinery/part allocation policy affects review of inventory plan	
1.2.2 Decide Alternatives	Delivery lead times and inventory carrying costs affect alternatives	Total cost criterion affects alternatives	
1.2.3 Propose Allocation Rules	Manufacturing constraints and production capacity affect allocation rules	Revenue and profit objectives affect alternatives	Availability of alternative products affects review of inventory plan
1.3.1 Schedule Shipping	Product inventory and loading capacity affect shipping schedule	Shipping plan gets affected by shipping schedule	
1.3.2 Schedule Manufacturing	Manufacturing schedule affects shop floor control	Manufacturing schedule affects next iterative planning	Product specs and manufacturing constraints affect manufacturing schedules
1.4.1 Monitor Orders Processed	Manufacturing and shipping problems affect order processing		
1.4.2 Follow Sales Delivered	Sales delivered affect inventory status	Sales delivered affect revenue, profit, review, and update	Sales delivered affect discovery of fault in products and quality of production
2.1.1 Process Service Part Request			Service part catalog affects the service part request process
2.1.2 Receive Service Part	Purchase order affects the receipt of service part from suppliers		Quality specs affect the receipt of service part from suppliers
2.1.3 Ship Service Part			
2.1.4 Control Service Part Inventory	Service part inventory control process affects the warehouse operations		

2.1.5 Return Wrong Service Part	Returning of wrong service part by a customer is linked to taking up claim with the supplier if supplier is responsible for the wrong service part		
2.1.6 Transform Manufacturing Part to Service Part	Transformation of a manufacturing part to a service part affects warehouse operations (parts inventory is updated)	Production plan affects the process of transforming manufacturing part to service part	Parts catalog affects transformation of manufacturing part to service part

Table 8.2: Process Linkages Matrix (pp.123-125).

4.2 Impact of Goals On Processes (Stage 3.2).

An important constituent of process redesign stage is the impact analysis matrix that specifies the impact of Internet goals on processes. As described in Section 3 of Chapter 5, the impact of a goal could be that it needs to create new processes, modifies some processes, or deletes some processes. It could use existing processes as they are, too. In the case under study, we have shown this impact in the matrices of Tables 8.3 to 8.6. The four matrices are actually four parts of one large matrix that has been partitioned vertically to fit printing (pp. 125-129). The horizontal dimension shows processes (see Table 8.1) and the vertical the Internet goals (see Stage 1). The four tables have the same vertical dimension; thus, their horizontal dimensions should be concatenated to show all processes and recover the entirety of the matrix. The first part, Table 8.3, is printed in pages 125-126.

Internet Goal	Receive Order Inquiry	Bid Orders	Book Orders	Confirm Delivery	Review Inventory
Provide information about orders	M		U	M	U
Fulfill S/Part order					
Provide information about new products	M				
Provide info about product modification					

Provide geological information						
Provide project management tool						
Create Intranet for customer project						
Sell geological data						
Provide project management services						
Provide Intranet consulting						
Collect performance data on equipment sold						
Collect customers' feedback						

Table 8.3: Impact Matrix (I).

The second part, Table **8.4,** is printed below and continues in page 127. It contains the next six processes shown in Table 8.1.

Internet Goal	Decide Alternative	Propose Allocation Rules	Schedule Shipping	Schedule Production	Monitor Orders Processed	Follow Sales Delivered
Provide info about orders	U	U	U	U	U	U
Fulfill S/Part order						
Provide info about new products						
Provide info about product modification						
Provide geological information						

126

Provide project management tool						
Create Intranet for customer project						
Sell geological data						
Provide project management services						
Provide Intranet consulting						
Collect performance data on equipment sold						
Collect customers' feedback						

Table 8.4: Impact Matrix (II).

The third part, Table **8.5,** is printed below and continues in page 128. It shows six more processes relating to the same set of Internet goals.

Internet Goal	Process S/Part Request	Receive S/Part	Ship S/Part	Control S/Part Inventory	Return Wrong S/Part	Transform Manufacturing Part to Service Part
Provide info about orders						
Fulfill S/Part order	M	M	M	M	M	M
Provide info about new products						
Provide info about product modification						
Provide geological information						
Provide project management tool						
Create Intranet for customer project						

127

Sell geological data					
Provide project management services					
Provide Intranet consulting					
Collect performance data on equipment sold					
Collect customers' feedback					

Table 8.5: Impact Matrix (III).

The fourth and last part of the Impact Matrix, Table **8.6,** is printed below in pages 128-129. It concludes the Impact Matrix with the last five processes studied. Again, all processes are summarized in Table 8.1 and the Internet goals are listed in Section 2, or the first stage of the planning.

Internet Goal	Provide Product Information	Provide Geological Data	Provide Project Mgmt Tool	Create Intranet For Customer Project	Obtain F/B From Customers
Provide info about orders					
Fulfill S/Part order					
Provide info about new products	C				
Provide info about product modification	C				
Provide geological information		C			
Provide project management tool			C		
Create Intranet for customer project				C	
Sell geological data		C			

Provide project management services			C		
Provide Intranet consulting				C	
Collect performance data on equipment sold					C
Collect customers' feedback					C

Table 8.6: Impact Matrix (IV).

In summary, the application of the Internet for the chosen goals would require five new processes, modify eight, and use the rest as they are. A description of the new and modified processes is given in the next section.

4.3 Description of New and Modified Processes (Stage 3.3).

Five processes would need to be created and eight modified. These processes are described in the following Table 8.7. The purpose of this description is to provide a working definition for these processes such that the ensuing, more detailed system development effort can follow. This stage also helps in the task of designing Web-based information systems (stages 4 and 5). The table is printed in pages 129-132 below.

Process	Modified/ Created	Old Process Description	New Process Description
Receive Order Inquiry	Modified	Inquiry about orders is received from customers and dealers. Domestic customers use phone/FAX to inquire about order status while dealers use the existing VAN.	Order inquiry is received through an interactive web page. Customers and dealers use their PIN and order # to inquire about the status of their order.
Confirm Delivery	Modified	After verifying availability of the product ordered by the customer/dealer, contract specifying the price, terms, and conditions of delivery and delivery date are advised to the customer/dealer by FAX or letter.	After verifying availability of the product ordered by the customer/dealer, contract specifying the price, terms, and conditions of delivery and delivery date are advised to the customer/dealer by a dynamic web page and/or secured e-mail.

Process Service Part Request	Modified	As in respect of an order for new equipment, domestic customers use phone/FAX and dealers use VAN to request a service part.	This process, too, will be enabled through an interactive web page. Customers and dealers will use their PIN number to access the SHI's order entry system and place their orders on-line.
Receive Service Part	Modified	This process receives the service part from the material process. As the process works now, the service part, after being received in the warehouse, is manually entered in the warehouse database before being shipped to the customer/dealer.	In the modified process the manufacturing, warehouse and customer order databases will be integrated. Manufacturing will shift the service part to the warehouse, which will automatically update their database. The part will be shipped to the customer and the customer advised of the shipment by a dynamic web page and/or secured e-mail. The order status will be integrated with a web page that the customer/dealer will be able to access using their PIN and order #.
Ship Service Part	Modified	Right now, the part is shipped after it is received in the warehouse and entered in their database.	In the modified process, shipping will take place without any additional delay. The process of intimating customers/dealers about details of shipment will also be modified as above.
Control Service Part Inventory	Modified	This process controls the warehouse operations.	The modification will integrate warehouse database with manufacturing and order databases.

Return Wrong Service Part	Modified	The way in which this process works right now is that a customer returns a wrong or a defective service part to the company, and the process comes into effect after the service part has been received. The process returns the service part to the inventory.	The modified process will work similar to the ordering process. Customers will be able to use a web page to fill in their complain about a defective part. The web page will also help as an on-line help to customers. If customer's problems cannot be resolved by offering help to them and the customer must return the part, then this process will automatically link to Process Service Part Request process – customers' request to return the part will automatically become their request for a replacement part. This will reduce the time to service customers and will also make it easier for them to get a replacement.
Transform From Manufacturing Part To Service Part	Modified	This process handles parts that were originally made for new equipment but cannot be used there. Instead those parts are used as service parts requested by customers. The process links to material processes.	The modified process will call for integration of manufacturing, service part, and warehouse databases.
Provide Product Information	New	-	This process is used to provide information to customers about the company's existing, forthcoming, and modified products. A non-web-based counterpart of this process is to print catalogs and newsletters and mail them to customers and potential customers.

Provide Geological Data	New	-	Since the products of the company are used mainly in construction (earth moving) activities, the company might consider providing geological data to its customers, either free of charge or for a fee. This can be accomplished through either general web pages or through web pages created specifically for a customer.
Provide Project Mgmt Tool	New	-	This process focuses on providing some project management tool(s) to SHI customers to enable them to better manage their projects. Such a tool can either be distributed for free through the firm's web site or can even be sold as a separate product.
Create Intranet For Customer Project	New	-	The purpose of this process is to provide something useful to customers - an Intranet to manage their project and, at the same time, reduce transaction costs for SHI by enabling their interaction with customers and their project through the Internet.
Obtain F/B From Customers	New	-	After connecting its customers and dealers through the Internet and the world wide web, SHI can conveniently collect feedback from customers and dealers about their products and service.

Table 8.7: Process Description (pp. 129-132).

4.4 Prioritization of Processes (Stage 3.4).

Now, we can endeavor to prioritize the business processes of the preceding stages with reference to the Internet goals of stage 1. This prioritization helps in setting up system implementation milestones and allocation of resources. In this study, a value on a scale of 1 to 10 was assigned to each goal chosen at stage 1 with 1 denoting the lowest priority to SHI and 10 the highest. A correlation coefficient on a scale of 0 to 4 was used to denote the relevance of a process in attaining a goal: 0 denoting no relevance and 4 the maximum relevance. Summations of total process weights decide the overall priorities of processes. The results are shown in Tables 8.8 (pp. 133-134) and Table 8.9 (pp. 134-135). Similar to the situation with the Impact Matrix (Tables 8.3-8.6), these two tables are two parts of the large Prioritization Matrix that has been broken up into two. They should be concatenated vertically (sharing the same vertical dimension) to recover the original matrix (pp. 133-135).

Process ↓	Total Process Value	Provide info about orders	Fulfill S/Part order	Provide info about new products	Provide info about product modification	Provide geological information	Provide project management tool
Goal Value ->		4	4	8	7	3	4
Receive Order Inquiry	61	(2) 8		(4) 32	(3) 21		
Bid Orders	12	(3) 12					
Book Orders	12	(3) 12					
Confirm Delivery	16	(4) 16					
Review Inventory	8	(2) 8					
Decide Alternative	34	(1) 4		(2) 16	(2) 14		
Propose Allocation Rules	4	(1) 4					
Schedule Shipping	4	(1) 4					
Schedule Production	12	(3) 12					
Monitor Orders Processed	56						
Follow Sales Delivered	72	(4) 16					
Process S/Part Request	28	(3) 12	(4) 16				
Receive S/Part	16		(4) 16				
Ship S/Part	8		(2) 8				
Control S/Part Inventory	16		(4) 16				
Return Wrong S/Part	24	(3) 12	(3) 12				

Transform Manufacturing Part to S/Part	16		(4) 16				
Provide Product Information	76	(4) 16		(4) 32	(4) 28		
Provide Geological Data	16					(4) 12	
Provide Project Mgmt Tool	16					(4) 12	
Create Intranet For Customer Project	12						
Obtain F/B From Customers	56						

Table 8.8: Prioritization Matrix (I).

The second part of the matrix, Table 8.9, is printed below and continues in page 135. It contains the remaining Internet goal values.

Process ↓	Create Intranet for customer project	Sell geological data	Provide project management services	Provide Intranet consulting	Collect performance data on equipment sold	Collect customers' feedback
Goal Value ->	2	1	5	1	7	7
Receive Order Inquiry						
Bid Orders						
Book Orders						
Confirm Delivery						
Review Inventory						
Review Re-make						
Decide Alternative						
Propose Allocation Rules						
Schedule Shipping						
Schedule Production						

Monitor Orders Processed						(4) 28	(4) 28
Follow Sales Delivered						(4) 28	(4) 28
Process S/Part Request							
Receive S/Part							
Ship S/Part							
Control S/Part Inventory							
Return Wrong S/Part							
Transform Manufacturing Part to S/Part							
Provide Product Information							
Provide Geological Data		(4) 4					
Provide Project Mgmt Tool					(4) 4		
Create Intranet For Customer Project	(4) 8				(4) 4		
Obtain F/B From Customers						(4) 28	(4) 28

Table 8.9: Prioritization Matrix (II).

5. Technology Requirement Analysis (Stage 4).

The technology requirement analysis matrix shows the classes of the Internet technology that SHI would need to acquire to implement the goals. We mapped the business processes on to the Internet goals and then indicated the highest class of technology required for each cell, representing the involvement of the corresponding process for the corresponding goal. We consider five classes of Internet technology, as defined in Section 4 of Chapter 5. These categories are progressive in capability and a higher capability includes all capabilities in lower classes. For example, enterprise connectivity, class 5, assumes database connectivity (4), application connectivity (3), document connectivity (2) and communications connectivity (1). Table 8.10 and Table 8.11 together document the matrix. Again, they represent two vertical partitions of the Technology Requirement Analysis

Matrix (pp. 136-138). The first part, Table 8.10, shows the required processes (the vertical dimension) assessed against the first six Internet goals for their technological requirements. The table is printed below in pages 136-137.

Internet Goal -> *Process* ↓	Provide info about orders	Fulfill S/Part order	Provide info about new products	Provide info about product modification	Provide geological information	Provide project management tool
Receive Order Inquiry	4		4	4		
Bid Orders	4					
Book Orders	4					
Confirm Delivery	4					
Review Inventory	4					
Decide Alternative	4		4	4		
Propose Allocation Rules	4					
Schedule Shipping	4					
Schedule Manufacturing	4					
Monitor Orders Processed						
Follow Sales Delivered	5					
Process S/Part Request	4	4				
Receive S/Part		5				
Ship S/Part		4				
Control S/Part Inventory		4				
Return Wrong S/Part	5	5				
Transform Manufacturing Part to S/Part		4				

Process						
Provide Product Information	4		4	4		
Provide Geological Data					4	
Provide Project Mgmt Tool					2	
Create Intranet For Customer Project						
Obtain F/B From Customers						

Table 8.10: Technology Requirement Analysis Matrix (I).

The second part of the matrix is shown in Table 8.11 in pages 137-138. It contains the remaining six Internet goals.

Internet Goal -> / Process	Create Intranet for customer project	Sell geologic data	Provide project mgmt services	Provide Intranet consulting	Collect performance data on equipment sold	Collect customers' feedback
Receive Order Inquiry						
Bid Orders						
Book Orders						
Confirm Delivery						
Review Inventory						
Review Re-make						
Decide Alternative						
Propose Allocation Rules						
Schedule Shipping						
Schedule Manufacturing						
Monitor Orders Processed					4	4

Follow Sales Delivered					4	4
Process S/Part Request						
Receive S/Part						
Ship S/Part						
Control S/Part Inventory						
Return Wrong S/Part						
Transform Manufacturing Part to S/Part						
Provide Product Information						
Provide Geological Data		4				
Provide Project Mgmt Tool			4			
Create Intranet For Customer Project	5			5		
Obtain F/B From Customers					4	4

Table 8.11: Technology Requirement Analysis Matrix (II).

The above matrix indicates that SHI needs to develop a full suite of Internet capabilities, up to multiple databases for enterprise integration, in order to implement their limited Internet goals. This fact is interesting. The analysis for process redesign at stage 3 has also shown an implication on the enterprise that is not as limited as first thought. Therefore, a simple question to ponder would be whether or not additional strategic goals ought to be considered as well. Either the limited goals might not deliver enough bang for the investment, or the company might have missed many other significant benefits that the same investment and effort could have delivered.

6. Design of Internet-Based Information Systems (Stage 5).

The last stage of the planning process was to develop a high level information requirement model for the Web-based information system that implements the Internet goals for Customer and Customer Service Processes of SHI. We used data flow diagrams to assist our analysis. We describe below, as examples, some details pertaining to the redesigned "manage orders" sub-process of the

138

customer processes and the modified processes for providing after sales service (service part) to customers.

The manage order process accepts customer's inquiry through an interactive Web page. The Web page presents the product catalog to the potential customer. The potential customer can assemble the machinery that he desires by selecting different parts. He is guided by a Java applet to configure his order correctly. The potential customer fills in the city and country of the destination of delivery as well as the date by which the machinery is required. This information feeds to the bidding process along with a system-generated customer ID number. Based on the customer input, the Web site presents a price and delivery date for the requested product to the customer through a dynamically generated page. If the customer accepts the offer, the Web page then starts a credit check and authentication process to verify the customer's affiliation, the buying organization, and so on. At the end, the Web page generates a formal order and sends a confirmation (or even an invoice) to the customer through a secured e-mail. The customer could choose from a number of payment methods, depending on the type of machinery and the history of his organization's relationship with SHI. The order could involve financing and deposit. This process will use some embedded algorithms or agents to assist the decision and customize the choices. The customer, in some cases, has the option of paying on-line through the secured server of SHI or through an Internet bank. After the order is confirmed, by virtue of an initial payment or some other means, the order is released to sales and the shipment # is returned to the customer. At the same time, the customer order is entered in the database of the local dealer for the customer.

The above analysis accepted a premise that SHI itself is an integrated enterprise capable either of an efficient make-to-stock operation or of an effective assemble-to-order manufacturing. The online confirmation of product availability, price, and delivery as well as the confirmation for customer is a very involved practice. The study went on to examine a few specific design issues.

- The product catalog needs to have rich graphics and possess some simulation or animation capabilities. The reason is simple - heavy machinery is complex, and SHI has over 100 models with numerous features. The customer needs an option to configure the machinery they require. Performance would be a critical technical issue here. Mirror sites, therefore, should be an option to the overall system design.

- The order database is a big and active database that must inter-operate seamlessly with the Web pages. In addition, the confirmation and payment processes could require significant computing. The algorithms and application software must run together with the database, too. In SHI, the order database is implemented using an Oracle database management system, running on UNIX machines. Oracle Web server and application server are a possible solution here. Depending on the technical sophistication wanted and the complexity of the online processes, such as confirmation, the system architecture could vary significantly.

- Security issues are crucial. The bidding of orders involves a secured server. The invoice, payment, and confirmation processes all require extensive security mechanisms, too. In the case where SHI decides to opt for payment through Internet banking, it needs to create additional processes to inter-operate with the banking processes (see Chapter 7). One possible implementation of such ideas is shown in Figure.8.2.

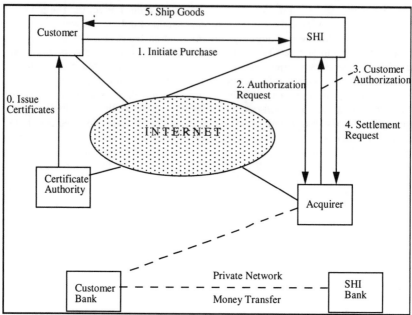

Figure 8.2: On-line Sales System.

7. Remarks.

The Samsung Heavy Industries case illustrates the application of the planning methodology suggested in Chapter 5. It focused on a few basic but common processes of customer service to allow for a realistic examination of these processes. The planning methodology was then thoroughly applied. This significant study has illustrated a few interesting points.

- The planning methodology seems to work as intended. However, the case also reveals that the efficiency of the planning depends as much on the nature of the application as on the professional knowledge of the planner. The reference model itself could be too generic to inspire concrete ideas of e-commerce application, especially when the information technology is new and beyond the expertise of the planner. In this sense, the e-commerce version (see Chapter 5) is an improvement over the generic model. The e-commerce planning model includes specific guidelines and possibilities to serve as some benchmarks and, thereby, stimulate inspiration. In a converse way, the analysis matrices (stage 3) could be unnecessary for rather straightforward applications. The priority matrix, for instance, would be useful only when there are significant conflicts or competition among goals for processes. This would be the case for serious e-commerce, and serious e-commerce only. However, another deciding factor is the planner's appreciation of the goals and his/her insight into the complementary nature vs. competing nature of processes. If the potential complexities are not understood or sufficiently exposed, then the matrices cannot serve their purposes.

- The study, again, shows that enterprise integration is the key. Even some seemingly simple applications of the Internet could require significant integration of enterprise processes and activities. The customer ordering Web page discussed in Section 6 is a perfect example. When the customer service functions become online and real time, the interactive processes become an interaction of the customer with the enterprise as a whole, rather than with the "customer service representative" only. The real time connection of the Internet forces the issue of integration on the enterprise. The company, i.e., SHI, does not have to offer the online services prescribed in the example, of course. It could opt to use the Web site only as a front desk to the real, regular enterprise, as many e-commerce sites are doing. The front desk would not have to offer real time, online workflow with the real processes. However, this choice would prevent many of the more powerful applications from serving the company. Thus, Principle 2 (2.1-2.3) is vividly present in the above examples.

- Furthermore, even simple applications of the Internet could lead to serious review of the business processes and, consequently, serious investment and effort. Conversely, the investment and effort required for simple applications could actually support quite sophisticated e-commerce practices. All Internet applications work in two ways: they serve some immediate functions (the applications), and they lay in some information infrastructure. The second part is an extremely powerful fact, but many companies and professionals often overlook it. The point here is, again, a holistic approach pays. The new information technology is pervasive and so is its application. The application is not amenable to limited and restrictive visions. E-commerce is an integrated business. Internet enterprise is an integrated enterprise. The effort could be gradual, but the planning might as well be comprehensive. One only needs to recall the CFAR case to appreciate this point. There is nothing to stop the SHI from pursuing the CFAR style supply chain integration once its customer service information infrastructure is in place. Conversely, there is every reason to believe that the company could tap into its investment on customer services and extend the benefit to the domain of supply chain.

- We have also indicated that the conglomerate is large enough to be able to run its own financial operations. In other words, it could put its financial weight to work in a manner similar to providing Internet banking for its customers. In fact, many large U.S. manufacturers operate significant financial businesses that rival major banks in the areas of, at least, customer loans. General Electric and General Motors are two well-known examples. The Samsung Corporation is large enough to consider running similar financial services or joining with some banks towards the same end. With this thought in mind, the previous case of the Asian Bank becomes pertinent to the corporation. However, the intriguing thought does not stop here. Once the initial vision is opened up for including other possibilities, all principles of e-commerce planning would become useful for the

SHI enterprise. We would emphasize extended enterprises and e-commerce style of information services and products. We would also, of course, reiterate the principle of enterprise integration. The previous two cases, the CFAR (supply chain integration) project and the Asian bank (Internet banking), offer good clues for the manufacturing conglomerate. It would be thoroughly fascinating to contemplate the possibilities of joining some of the processes of SHI with those of the Asian bank and the CFAR enterprise. At least, the manufacturer could apply to itself what Warner Lambert has done for its demand or supply chain.

9

A FEW MORE THOUGHTS

We discussed some visions for e-commerce. We presented a planning model for e-commerce. We analyzed a number of cases of e-commerce. We also developed a few plans for some industrial enterprises to start e-commerce. What more do we want to say at the end of the book? There are several interesting points that we covered in the above discussions; maybe they deserve a little more attention.

1. The promises of e-commerce stem from the global connection of persons and organizations, not from the Internet per se.

The Internet had been in existence long before the Web for connecting organizations. However, the Internet was not a business tool, even for most organizations connected by it, until it became the connection for *persons*. The perception and use for personal connection gave the Internet life as we know today. The personal connection breeds the Web community and then e-commerce, including e-commerce for organizations that had long had the Internet right under their nose. Nonetheless, we want to stress that e-commerce is not just business use of the Internet. The Internet is, without a doubt, *the* platform of conducting business for e-commerce, up to now. This will not be the case forever. Wireless communications and mobile computing are already available, and they are fast becoming viable tools for e-commerce. The difference these new technologies make is the broadening of the personal connection and, hence, the vision of e-commerce. The Internet-based vision is associated with the Web community. This association confines e-commerce strategies to Web sites; thus, it confines innovative ideas of e-commerce to only what the Web did, does, and can do. Wireless communications and mobile computing allow persons and organizations to be connected without using the Internet, at least the Internet today. E-commerce, therefore, does not have to be exclusively relying on Web sites. The magic of the universal user interface needs not to be equated to Web *sites* (in the sense of a business server on the Internet). The Web-style user interface does not have to premise on the existence of "traditional" Web sites. The argument here is not an advocate for abandoning the Internet; to the contrary, it is an urge to liberate the Internet. The new information technology would still have the Internet (or Internet 2 and other successors) there as a backbone of the global connection that e-commerce relies. The main point is mentality; our mentality determines how we perceive the technology and the rest follows. There is beautiful life outside Web sites for e-commerce. There could be a personal portal residing in a place none other than the person, who connects wirelessly to all kinds of e-commerce business. The wireless connection, such as some extended applications of today's geographical positioning systems, *would still be* a part of the overall environment including the Internet. It, however, does not limit the business to the Web site model. It is too often in today's e-commerce that the business vision stops with Web sites per se. Thinking what else the new information technology could do is a powerful way to break away with this spell. This book assumes the Internet for the most part of its discussion, too. We would like to redeem ourselves in the conclusion.

2. E-commerce thrives on reduction of transaction cost, which requires information products in both the information and transaction sides of the house.

Any enterprise can practice e-commerce but might not benefit from its practice. An e-commerce enterprise can be extremely successful in sales and popularity but might not make any (positive) money. A traditional firm might put any part of its business on the Internet; its Internet-based business might not bring in any strategic advantage or make any difference. The key to innovative planning for e-commerce is to look beyond the obvious or the "usual suspects," is to deliberately - and systematically - look into the non-obvious. To transactional firms, the information side is non-obvious, and to information firms, the transaction is non-obvious. However, an e-commerce must strive for both in order to thrive. The practice of e-commerce is not a mere use of some Web sites to enhance the previous business activities that can work on the Internet. A mere benchmarking mentality of planning would not be sufficient for creating strategic visions. An enterprise must understand the strategic value of e-commerce before even embracing it. The practice cannot just be a copy of what the competitors are doing or what the trade magazines are preaching. Instead, an enterprise must realize that e-commerce alters the traditional paradigm, changes the business model, and renews the value chain. Any practice of e-commerce, regardless how small or how limited the immediate plan is, is bound to impact fundamentally on the enterprise processes. Therefore, the enterprise might as well do it right, to think and plan beyond the initial practice. This means the development of *new* information services and products that the traditional enterprise would never consider, but its new e-enterprise self could attempt. The essence of the new thinking would be to extend its capabilities and connections to help the customers reducing transaction cost in as many aspects of their business as possible and make money in the process. An enterprise could regard its customer ordering process, for example, just as an obvious practice to put on the Internet, without also preparing to exploit the new promises of e-commerce. Alternatively, it could treat the Internet-based ordering as a strategic marketing weapon and look for all possibilities around it. The technical requirements might be similar either way, but the richness of the practice could differ dramatically. The latter would definitely award the enterprise with much more aggressive and effective use of the practice. Powerful new information products could come only from the non-obvious mentality. With the right mentality, businesses that sell material goods would discover information services (free or for sale) and those selling information services would discover transactional products.

3. E-commerce always forces changes beyond the immediate processes of their original practices; thus, an enterprise might as well go for the big picture.

This observation follows immediately the previous comment. It could sound self-righteous; therefore, we provide here some basic reason as to why this must be the case. The root cause of the change is expectation. Take the traditional ordering process. The process is off-line, meaning that there is a sequential procedure the customer must follow, and the procedure involves some steps that take hours, days, weeks, or even longer time to finish. The assumption here is, therefore, the customer

144

should not expect an immediate response to his/her order, let alone any confirmation of any of the transactions required. It might even take a few iterations between the customer and the seller before the ordering process is completed. The customer is willing to expect less than real time response from the company because the delivery of the order itself is not real time, anyway. This is why the practice of ordering through the telephone changed the catalog sales industry. Once the customer can place an order real time, s/he started to expect more: real time response, real time confirmation, and real time promise of delivery date, and more. Catalog retailers who initially just wanted merely to put the transaction of receiving orders online discovered in no time that they must also tighten up their inventory, accounts receivable/payable, and delivery processes, and much more. The e-commerce, as plainly as the broad daylight, has raised the customer's expectation a few notches. Everything in e-commerce communications is real time or, at least, as the expectation goes. The customer sees more and does more at an e-commerce site, far more than direct sales used to handle. The ante is raised far higher. Thus, putting only the paper work of the ordering process on the Internet is far from enough. Doing merely that would simply expose the non-compatibility (or inefficiency) of other parts of the process. Customer would expect, in a competitive marketing sense, more services, functions, and transactions. However, to do more is to require involving more internal processes, to reengineer and connect them to the Internet processes. In other words, simple e-commerce practice could force the issue of integration on the enterprise. The technological investment needed for doing small e-commerce could be similar to that of going for bigger. Even the organizational effort, such as business process redesign, could be similar, too. We see this situation in both the Asian banking case and the Samsung case. The moral is that there is no turning back when an enterprise enters e-commerce; thus, it should consider all nine principles of the planning model.

4. E-commerce always cascades and always diffuses itself; it would eventually erase the distinctions among businesses and blur boundaries among organizations.

One recurring theme we have observed in all the cases we discussed in the book is the fact that every e-commerce enterprise can create any kind of information products that other e-commerce enterprises are "traditionally" selling. They arguably can do this through extended enterprises. A company-owned retailing site can become a domain portal site and even a business marketplace site. A producer can become a retailer, and a retailer can become a producer of information products. Internet banking can evolve to give rise to virtual banks and become certain clearing houses for e-commerce transactions between buyers and sellers. A manufacturer could join force with banks to offer financial services and products to customers and other e-commerce enterprises. These ventures become easier to develop when every party involved is practicing e-commerce while only industrial giants could enjoy this kind of possibility in the past. The issue of regulation is not as prohibitive in e-commerce as in traditional business either. Enterprises can readily create numerous innovative information products in the finance area that face less than formidable hurdles in regulation. If an enterprise does not want to get involved in any of the diffusion, it is fine. Just be aware that its competitors might be thinking differently - or more to the point, the traditional non-competitors might be eyeing its business. The hospitality industry is a prime case in point. The airliners and travel reservation businesses are busy selling hospitality industry's products to their customers who, otherwise, would go to the hospitality providers to make the first contact. First contacts matter greatly in marketing.

5. E-commerce renders all middle layers of the traditional societal value chain obsolete; thus, it promises to create new businesses and eliminate a whole lot of old ones.

Textbook publishers have started to advertise directly in student newspapers and sell directly to them. These examples are becoming too numerous to follow. The CFAR case and the success story of Amazon.com both show the rapid evolution of the value chain in their respective industry. Both industries traditionally call for many middle layers between the producer and the end consumer. The CFAR project eliminated the need for some third party vendors of EDI or some facilitators and service bureaus to manage supply chain. The Internet bookstore erased the need for local bookstore chains. However, the larger societal value chain is also changing their very own industries. Their present positions in the societal value chain could be vanishing, too. The continuing success of the CFAR could render itself unnecessary. The model of Amazon.com could point the way for publishers to do the same by themselves. They are not alone, of course. Ultimately, when the new mentality sets in and both the persons and producers realize that they are connected, all facilitators making money in the middle would have to do much better to justify their existence. The Person-Centered Commerce model is an example of what drastic changes there could be in a highly connected society. E-commerce promises to change more than just the traditional boundaries - and protection - among businesses; it redefines the societal value chain. The winners will be, of course, enterprises that take full advantage of the new model using the new capabilities.

6. E-commerce brings global competition to every enterprise; the question is only to thrive with the competition or demise for it so others can thrive.

All the above observations are consistent with the common theme articulated in Chapter 1. In the end, a simple fact stands: e-commerce is a mentality of global village and perfect competition. Of course, the world is not truly global, and the competition is far from perfect. Enterprises, however, do not have to wait until the ideal situations have proven themselves to face the consequences of heightened competition. Even the above statement is only half-true; the half-truth is already enough to change the world of business. E-commerce enterprises should not inherit the traditional confines. Neither should they be content to stay within the cultural and physical boundaries of their home countries. "The Russians are coming." Cannot beat them, join them.

The planning model (Chapter 2) is consistent with these views. It is justified in Chapters 3 and 4 vis-a-vis the literature in order to give it some objectivity and accountability. The CFAR case illustrates how the planning model could be applied to generate strategic goals for e-commerce practices. A methodology is suggested in Chapter 5 to assist the process. The methodology also includes suggestions for business process analysis and redesign. These ideas are shown in the two industrial studies we conducted with professionals from each company. The Internet banking study explores some obvious possibilities of e-commerce for a bank. Chapter 7 provides an in-depth discussion of these possibilities. The second industrial study is concerned with customer service, including ordering, for a heavy industry conglomerate. The full methodology guides the study. Chapter 8 reports a comprehensive documentation of the results. All three cases, including CFAR, show two levels of thinking: immediate applications and full-fledged e-commerce. They each show the e-commerce possibilities for their respective industry, but together, they also demonstrate certain commonality that other industries can use as well. We would like to consider these three cases, in their generic sense, as three aspects of a generic enterprise: supply chain, financial transaction, and customer service. This way, they collectively constitute a benchmark for detailed planning for e-commerce. Therefore, the planning model serves as the high lever planner, supported by the benchmark to assist in developing concrete ideas for specific applications - or elaboration of the high level goals.

APPENDIX:
Information-Integrated Enterprises

Reprinted from
Cheng Hsu, *Enterprise Integration and Modeling,* 1996.

INFORMATION-INTEGRATED ENTERPRISES

1.1 INFORMATION ENTERPRISES AND NEW ENTERPRISES

The Berlin Wall didn't fall as a direct result of information technology, but the fall of organizational walls certainly have. **Information Technologies** (IT) such as telecommunications, distributed computing, and databases have afforded people a phenomenal degree of freedom to form working relationships with others from anywhere in the world, and rearrange those working relationships with great alacrity as missions and conditions change, expand, or otherwise evolve. People and organizations have a growing potential to distribute throughout the world while remaining in dynamic alignment with other economic partners and valuable resources. IT has freed the enterprise from its history of geographical and physical constraints that allowed only for fixed and static alignment of resources, processes, and organizations with missions. As a result, the past decades have witnessed a parade of new business strategies focusing on the potential of the new enterprise. In the late 1970s and 1980s, we strove to create Computer-Integrated Manufacturing and Concurrent Engineering. Since then, we have seen a continuous stream of new visions each promoting a new enterprise model that claims to improve productivity, quality, and market timing. These models have included Agile Manufacturing, Virtual Corporation, Total Quality Management, Enterprise Re-engineering, Horizontal Corporation, Electronic Commerce, Global Information Enterprises, and many more models adopted within particular contexts, such as the Adaptive Integrated Manufacturing Enterprises developed at Rensselaer Polytechnic Institute.

All enterprise models have one thing in common: they build a vision of how IT will affect the future of dynamic alignment within an enterprise. Within this vision, each model predicts which new modes of production or products will enable an enterprise to pull ahead of its competitors. Defined as such, they are all examples of how the technological innovation called IT *extends new core competencies to a firm through dynamic alignments that create new competitive advantages*. Enterprise models also hold in common the fact that they are each but transient models in the fast moving age of information. As long as IT continues to remove old constraints and open up new possibilities for innovative enterprises, one can count on the proliferation of new models that explore the theme of dynamic alignment and predict the fall of some physical or logical block to perfect dynamic alignment. To be sure, there are many walls that restrict free exchange among and across the customer, the producer, and the supplier.

We refer to the removal of walls as **enterprise integration** and the preparation for new alignments, **modeling**. There are ways to foresee to where this wave of integration is leading. We explore what knowledge and tools will be required to envision, develop, and realize the enterprise of the future. The vision elaborated within this book is predicated on five enablers of IT:

- Consideration Of The Extended Enterprise
- Integration Of Information, Integration Through Information
- Planning For Strategic Goals
- Implementing IT Using Organic Architecture
- Managing With Ubiquitous Enterprise Metadata

One can best forecast the future by understanding the limitations of the present. Any new vision for building and deploying IT structures needs to consider the five enablers presented here. For example, Enterprise Re-engineering is a celebrated case of dynamic alignment. Yet, it is constrained by not considering the extended enterprise nor information integration using organic architecture and ubiquitous metadata.

1.1.1 Consideration of the Extended Enterprise

No company is too small to conduct business at a global scale. Many family restaurants or small retailers order ethnic foods or deliver purchased clothes in small packages via international shipments. An enterprise is considered global when it considers its customers/prime contractors and suppliers/vendors, yet is never so large to be able to ignore its extended constituencies. By its very nature, an enterprise is extended beyond the boundaries of the immediate organizations involved; it is an endeavor spanning the customers (and to some extent the customers' customers), suppliers, vendors, dealers, distributors, creditors, shareholders, as well as the product producer and service provider of the enterprise. When modeling for integration, it is natural to consider all of these extended economic members of an enterprise. The sole reason for not considering the extended enterprise would be the difficulty of doing so. Due to the growth and development of more powerful IT, management has more options to develop creative solutions to integrating and modeling the extended enterprise than ever before. The examples of integration and modeling given below demonstrate recent capabilities, yet they are merely the prelude to mind-boggling new visions that will arise along with newer and more powerful IT. The examples below are success stories of firms that have applied the traditional notion of systems integration. Systems integration is concerned with automating the intra-organizational flow of information across functional systems to similar functional systems distributed inter-organizationally when all organizations belong to the same extended enterprise.

Electronic Data Interchange (EDI). EDI models automate routine order processing and billing functions of an extended enterprise. Rather than circulating papers, organizations send electronic files or forms through networks to other organizations. Applications of EDI typically include aligning the order-origination at the producer side with the order-entry at the supplier side, or similar alignments involving billing procedures between the producer and the customer. The mechanism EDI uses to align is an electronic linkage using protocols (that usually include bar coding systems and other standards of automation) and a dedicated application system which can be a third-party value-added network (VAN) that processes the orders. EDI has been employed for intra-organizational order processing such as work orders across shops. However, the inter-organizational order processing illustrates the power of the concept of an extended enterprise. The health care industry and other distributed systems overwhelmed with paperwork are emerging as the dominant domains of EDI applications.

Just-in-Time (JIT). The original concept of JIT was practiced in Japan to streamline production planning and control functions across the producer and the supplier of the extended enterprise. In essence, the supplier must deliver parts at the point in production when the producer needs them. Therefore, the supplier is in fact considered as another shop or factory in the producer's production planning and control, effectively eliminating "in-process" stock, that is, the producer's inventory. JIT is fundamentally an alignment of the extended enterprise's production resources. Transportation systems are used in addition to conveyor systems to move materials while global scheduling systems are developed to move information. The concept and technology of JIT is and has been scalable to intra- and inter-organizational applications. This scalability is a testimony to the "natural logic" of an extended enterprise.

Concurrent Engineering (CE). Promoted by the U.S. Department of Defense, the original concept of CE required that the voluminous design information such as engineering drawings and product design files be electronically sharable among all contractor and sub-contractor design engineers working on the same weapon system. Such a network of shared resources would most certainly represent an extended enterprise. However, we would better understand the past, present, and future of CE as the alignment of design resources within and across organizations within an extended enterprise. While JIT involves the flow of materials as well as information, CE and EDI are primarily information technologies that integrate the enterprise through the flow and management of information resources.

These three examples are all based on the logic of aligning producers with providers to achieve a global savings and optimization of effort. Understanding the logic of aligning producers with providers, one can easily generalize the concept and apply it across the entire enterprise for inter-organizational integration and modeling. Practically, we must work out more logical than physical means when using IT to align such massive enterprises.

1.1.2 Integration Of Information, integration through information

The examples of extended enterprises given above demonstrate a salient principle of **Information Integration**. CE and JIT have demonstrated that IT is the logical alignment of resources that hinge foremost on the integration of information resources and systems, such as illustrated by connecting the design databases or production planning with control information across organizations. In turn, this integration creates synergism with other resources that affect the physical production. In this sense, *enterprise integration is about using IT to achieve dynamic alignment of resources through information and information systems*. This focus is especially

153

important when the physical scale of the enterprise is larger than what a typical local-area network (LAN) can sufficiently cover. For instance, in the case of EDI, there is no mechanism nor need to place the order processing functions of different organizations under the perpetual control of a single fixed configuration that requires dedicated personnel organization, office, computer, and telecommunications structures. The relationships in an EDI enterprise change frequently from one contract to another; thus, the configurations must remain logical. Using a third-party VAN is one way to achieve a kind of logical integration for the enterprise. The VAN provides physical configurations without the order processing functions of each (direct partner) organization can be logical and remain flexible, distributed, and autonomous. But the same function can also be achieved internally through proper use of information integration. In general, when it is feasible to integrate all resources into a single physical structure to achieve internal dynamic alignments, one would choose this simple design over the logical alternative. However, when it is not feasible to choose integration through a single physical structure, the case of all non-trivial enterprises, logical integration by virtue of information would be the only way to proceed. As IT has progressed technologically and enterprises have become global, information integration has flourished in virtually all of the visions mentioned above. Some recent achievements are discussed below from this perspective.

Computer-Integrated Manufacturing (CIM). The U.S. Air Force's Integrated Computer-Aided Manufacturing (ICAM) Program initiated the worldwide race to integrate manufacturing with computers in the late 1970s and early 1980s. In essence, the ICAM vision extended the previous efforts of CAD/CAM (Computer-Aided Design/Manufacturing), a physical integration approach, into an approach that focused on the logical synergism among CADs, CAMs and eventually all other major functions of integrated manufacturing. It became clear to all involved that there was no way and no need to unite CADs and CAMs in the same physical configuration with, for example, Manufacturing Resources Planning (MRP II) and administration systems. Thus, CIM established the principle since operative that information integration is the best means to achieve overall synergistic control of physical resources and operations in large-scale systems.

Agile Manufacturing (AM). Initiated by an effort at Lehigh University and supported by the Advanced Research Programs Agency (ARPA) of U.S. Department of Defense, Agile Manufacturing is concerned with adding flexibility to CIM to better respond to the market's changing demands (e.g., rapid new product development and flexible small batch production at mass production efficiency). In addition to IT, a new organizational mode—the team approach—is also featured in the definitive model of AM. Teams, however, are not to be confined to physical configurations. Virtual teams, whose members are not necessarily co-located in the same building or site but rather physically distributed and logically grouped through the use of IT, are the real backbone of AM in significant enterprises. These virtual teams and the processes that enable them to exist are all results of dynamic alignments through information integration.

Virtual Corporation (VC) and More. When the concept of virtual teams is generalized to encompass all aspects of a corporation, a VC results. Employees of a

VC perform their assigned activities from anywhere, either within an independent consultant arrangement or under the virtual auspices of organizations that participate within the VC. As such, employees have a project-oriented association that precludes committing themselves to a fixed, traditional organization characterized by physical configurations. In fact, a VC is concerned primarily with forming external, flexible missions derived from multiple organizations.

When an organization forms flexible missions internally across its multiple divisions, the concept of a VC becomes that of **Enterprise Re-engineering (ERE)** and the **Horizontal Corporation (HC)**. ERE is focused on the internal business processes of an organization. Its goal is to promote optimal resource alignments that result in leaner running business processes that add net value to the enterprise. An HC features an organizational model centered around flexible internal processes that give rise to a lateral and flexible structure different from the traditional organizational hierarchy. Middle managers are either becoming entrepreneurs of such processes or eliminated altogether. The dynamic nature of alignments and processes revealed in these models illustrate once again the pivotal role of information integration.

The above visions employ information as the agent of integration and deploy IT to remove physical constraints within the enterprise. In a similar but more visible manner, other visions also exhibit a reliance on information integration. They include **Total Quality Management (TQM)** which uses the team approach to improve customer satisfaction by installing and managing quality and quality information processes throughout the enterprise; **Electronic Commerce** which renders the Internet and other emerging global networks a marketplace for conducting all aspects of commerce, ranging from transaction to production and organization; and **Global Information Enterprises** which combine information repositories and merge various information industries such as publications, news media, entertainment, education, software, and various information services into information conglomerates such as cyberspace. To the extent that IT has enabled these visions, information integration has been and will continue to be a strategic weapon for an enterprise to compete in the global marketplace.

1.1.3 Planning for Strategic Goals

The full promise of IT can only be revealed in strategic thinking and yet this level of thinking would not necessarily present itself without a proactive review of IT in light of *yet developing* competitive opportunities. Enterprise integration and modeling share many system development tasks with mundane operations of an organization; hence, they can often be cut to incremental projects that do not change the status-quo. However, the significance of enterprise integration lies precisely in its promise to effect new regimes and paradigms and to lift organizational performance beyond the status quo. In particular, IT's promise of dynamic alignment has served to remove organizational constraints and allow extended enterprises to develop, while information integration has suppressed physical barriers. Both have opened up new fundamental, strategic opportunities for enterprises. We derive several heuristics from past examples and theoretical analyses in order to facilitate new developments in IT planning and begin a concerted search for strategic IT opportunities.

Managing External Environments. The following heuristics focus on the direct, external application of IT on the market as a strategic weapon to gain competitive advantages. The principle is to manage uncertainty in the enterprise environment.

• *Provide Information Services to Customers.* The idea is to lure and lock customers in to the enterprise by investing in IT that provides unique and crucial services to them. The added value is in external orientation. For example, an organization develops IT primarily for facilitating its customers' business rather than for its own internal use. Classical cases include the American Airline's Sabre system for travel agencies and Citibank's Automatic Teller Machine (ATM) for individual customers. Although both technologies have now become mundane operations holding little strategic value, initially they were conceived as strategic marketing weapons in order to leapfrog their competitors. They accomplished just that. There are numerous obvious opportunities for an organization to develop new generations of information services for customers and reap the same in strategic benefits, especially given extended enterprise and information integration. Generalizing the ATM to an on-line, free-of-charge banking and other services network for customers would be a natural potential. Healthcare Management Organizations have begun to explore the unlimited possibilities following along this line of thinking. Being the first innovator and possessing core IT competencies in terms of know-how, models, techniques, and systems are key factors for success.

• *Turning Information Services into Products.* We can extend the above notion of customer service to information products or information service profit centers. The Sabre system has become a major source of revenues for American Airlines since travel agencies pay significant fees for its extended services. As a matter of fact, the company later spun off the operation and expanded it into a significant travel information services company of its own. In a similar way, proprietary information technology and services that an enterprise develops can be turned into dedicated information service providers or spin-offs in the market. Electronic commerce and global information enterprises seem to be especially ripe for this type of opportunity.

• *Monitor the Market and Customer Behaviors.* Marketing databases have proven to be a potent weapon for gathering marketing intelligence and assisting in new product development. Their key is to exploit ubiquitous interfaces with customers (coupons, purchases, repairs, surveys, and the like) and turn them into intelligent information for strategic uses. Every organization by definition has numerous contacts with its customers throughout the life-cycle of a product. The question is only whether or not the contact is used to benefit the organization's marketing intelligence. Background data repositories such as the census database complement direct contact data. Between these two sources, organizations have unlimited possibilities for marketing research to create innovative strategies.

A broader implementation of managing external environments would include not only the customer but also the supplier and other constituencies of the extended enterprise including external users of the IT. Analyzing the information needs of these external users within the context of their respective enterprises and employing IT to satisfy their needs will work to the organization's benefit. Basic strategic gains result when an organization is able to do more in the way of extended

156

contact and use the feedback gained to improve internal and external business processes.

Maximizing the Internal Networking of Processes and Resources. The second set of heuristics is oriented towards improving the production function of an enterprise, thereby enhancing its productivity (measured through cost and quality). Linkages will be created across an enterprise to connect all stages of cycles, including: differing levels of granularity (product, production, and part); flows (information vs. materials); and businesses (administration vs. production). By connecting all stages of the business cycle, maximum channels of communications can be created to minimize the internal uncertainties facing an enterprise, and resources can be pooled and utilized throughout the extended enterprise. Globally optimized performance can result.

• *Employ and Deploy IT to the Core Production Processes.* A production system that delivers higher quality at lower cost than competitors is the most fundamental strategic advantage for any enterprise. IT is proven to be a key element in achieving this goal within manufacturing enterprises and many other operations-oriented enterprises (e.g., the mail and parcel delivery industry). However, this previous utilization of IT is merely the tip of the iceberg. In manufacturing, the vast majority of robotic systems and workstations are "hard-coded" with control programs that cannot be easily changed. At this basic level of production, there is scarcely any use of rulebase and database technologies that can perform in real time. These technologies would allow a manufacturing plant to acquire a logical layer that can define the (re-)configuration of their systems in terms that would connect the part processing jobs directly to work order control, materials handling, in-process inspection, production scheduling, order entry, warehousing, processing planning, and product design. Even more promising is the direct application of IT to the very production systems that are not traditionally considered production tasks, such as the medical functions of a hospital (e.g., diagnosis, surgery, treatment, and pharmacy) and the educating function of a university (e.g., lectures, assignments, and laboratories). Although IT has been increasingly employed in these functions—with examples ranging from CATSCAN/MRI in medicine to studio style classrooms and World Wide Web-based virtual classes in education—the majority of them are still isolated within a traditional paradigm where IT is sequestered to administration jobs. Deepening the role of IT in manufacturing and broadening it to more traditional enterprises promises to provide new and endless strategic opportunities for IT use.

• *Create Forward and Feedback Linkages for All Cycles.* An enterprise has three basic cycles: part, production, and product. The product cycle includes everything from marketing and product planning to recycling used materials; the production cycle satisfies the customer's orders and demands; and the part cycle processes the individual elements involved in producing a product. Previous visions of integration tend to focus only on a single cycle apart and aside of the other two, primarily integrating the forward stages into a connected sequence in the cycle, but without closing the cycle through feedback. Forward linkage allows some jobs in the later stages to be performed simultaneously with earlier jobs; or, at least, the requirements of the later stages can be explicitly considered early in the product cycle. For example, Concurrent Engineering (CE) is primarily concerned with creating some forward linkage by overlapping the stages of new product development, product design, and process planning. The feedback aspects are largely overlooked. Thus,

157

CE would incorporate a static set of assembly requirements into design (Design-for-Assembly), but not concern itself with on-line feedback of in-process inspection, nor shop floor control systems. Both forward and feedback linkages are needed to complete a cycle. Furthermore, all three cycles are interwoven in a truly agile enterprise. Therefore, new strategic opportunities for IT will arise from creating feedbacks to complete a cycle and from connecting all cycles through forward and feedback linkages. Both forward and feedback set the stage for dynamic alignment in its fullest potential.

• *Connecting Administration Systems with Production Systems.* IT has been historically applied to business administration functions of an enterprise first. Then, when it is also employed within production, the two sides are kept separate functions. Information Integration allows and asks that the walls separating administration from production come down, just as IT bridges information flow with material flow. An interesting example showing the significance of this connection is activity-based costing and management, in which the classical administrative function of accounting is conducted on the basis of monitoring the alignments of resources around activities. This monitoring certainly can be and should be made on-line and in real time. Total Quality Management (TQM) is also based on performance information cutting across administration and production. Calibrating and aligning administration with production on an on-line, real time basis produces the ultimate decision-making information within an agile, lean, and productive enterprise.

Transforming into a Three-Dimensional Enterprise. The following three sets of heuristics provide some proactive guidelines for high-level IT planning towards enterprise integration and modeling. They expand the scope of enterprise from the traditional view into both extended enterprises and information enterprises.

• *Think Extended Enterprise.* All the discussions pertaining to the internal production systems and administration of an enterprise are applicable to the virtual systems of an extended enterprise. As mentioned in Section 1.1.1, the strategic opportunities for streamlining operations across organizations to gain synergism and efficiency are practically unlimited. The fact that there are tremendous constraints and difficulties against fully applying IT to an extended enterprise is also the reason for its tremendous significance. The health care industry is arguably the most fertile ground for this concept. The opportunities implicit in connecting insurers, hospitals, physicians, patients, government agencies, and research institutes through information integration is mind boggling. Other industries have, of course, similar opportunities.

• *Establish/Expand to Information Enterprises.* Traditional business thinking focuses only on the material enterprises of products, resources, and the marketplace. Running parallel to the material enterprise is an equally large world of information enterprises in cyberspace that can utilize the same enterprise thinking. A virtual medical center could be constructed by using personal medical instruments located in patients' homes and linking them with doctors and researchers through multimedia telecommunication systems. A third-party information server/clearing house could provide pooled inventories and other resources to its client organizations through information integration in an extended enterprise manner. An Army/Defense logistics system could be integrated in cyberspace with visualization, simulation, and global information management capabilities. A studio-style virtual classroom could result from combining virtual laboratories, multimedia courseware, and the World Wide Web to enable distance learning. This kind of electronic commerce and global information enterprise opportunities are often hidden just under one's nose. When planning these new information enterprises, one could retain familiar paradigms by only transforming the perspective.

• *Evaluate IT on Micro-Economic Bases.* Mundane applications of IT are usually motivated by and justified on the basis of cost/expenditure savings. To move beyond this rationale looking for strategic opportunities, the valuation criteria must change. An enterprise can evaluate IT on three micro-economic criteria: transaction cost reduction, utility improvement (value/benefit added), and organizational design. In theory, the best representation of the role of IT is its impact on the basic production function of the enterprise. One could formulate information to be the fourth basic factor of production in addition to labor, land, and capital. In reality, however, such a function is impractical for any enterprise. Thus, these criteria become useful surrogates for the production function theory. They may not be specific enough to quantify the value of IT in operational terms, nonetheless; they are sufficiently substantive to shed light on qualitative investigations for IT planning.

All of the above ideas develop strategic opportunities for using IT and call for enterprises to build core competencies in IT concerning, in particular, dynamic alignment. Since the driving force of IT stems from its capacity to bring about dynamic alignment within and without an enterprise, the information architecture of the enterprise needs to be organic in order to allow it to fully exploit the potentials of IT.

1.1.4 Implementing it using Organic Architecture

The strategic plans of IT must be mapped out to implement an enterprise information architecture for implementation. One thing is known about this architecture: there cannot be only one, single physical system that fits all requirements and yet supports dynamic alignment. Even for small enterprises that consider linking with external constituencies along with its own internal needs, there is no need nor way to satisfy all functions with the same uniform software and hardware environment. Multiple system environments all using different software (for example, Fox Pro, Lotus 1-2-3, Excel, Access, Oracle, Objectivity, C, C++, Pascal, FORTRAN, dedicated EDI systems, CAD/CAM systems, MRP II and other application systems) and hardware environments (e.g., IBM PC, Mac, Digital, VAX, IBM mainframes, and other computing and telecommunications systems) are bound to be the norm. Efforts to define standards that enable data exchange between diverse systems will not change the multiple-systems nature of enterprise integration. The reality of IT enterprise environments exhibit several characteristics that continue to make IT distributed, heterogeneous, and hard to control.

The Complexity of Reality. Consider a traditional organization. The introduction of information systems into such an enterprise is often ad hoc and "bottoms-up." This tendency to rely on customized and compartmentalized technology is due to technical necessity as well as the need of the organization to control. Technically, the most successful environments for automation are those in which well defined business requirements can be isolated and solutions customized to meet the specific user requirements. Such specialized systems are not designed to meet information access requirements from other enterprise users. Once specialized systems are in place; however, they must interact with other systems and software across local, wide, or even global area networks to support many different enterprise activities. In other words, an enterprise cyberspace environment must be created to accommodate interaction. It is difficult to implement information exchanges among independently designed systems in contexts that were not fully known or understood by their very designers. To enable the system access to multiple databases through decision support applications, procedural rules and data semantics that have been designed into the systems must be understood and often extended. Finally, systems must continually evolve if they are to respond to changes in technology and business requirements. Unfortunately, the need to understand complex integrated systems that serve many application systems and user communities in order to modify them often increases rather than reduces the expense and time required to adapt them to changing requirements. The integration of systems to meet enterprise needs rather than the requirements of their primary users can be perceived as an inhibitor to local autonomy, flexibility and performance. When finally this extended enterprise endeavors to integrate its processes, the complexity involved is clearly compounded many times over.

The Characteristics of Organism. The architecture that supports enterprise information integration must be able to grow, change, and adapt like an organic entity. The following working definitions list certain key requirements of such an architecture in multiple system environments distributed over wide-area or even global networks.

• *Scalability.* The total enterprise information integration environment must allow incremental development and expandability, such that the integration can start with a small part of the enterprise and gradually extend to the rest (even to other organizations) over time, without losing operational continuity and structural integrity.

• *Adaptability.* Systems that use either standard or non-standard technologies as well as new and legacy systems, can be incorporated into the integrated environment in a seamless way without causing any disruption to any existing systems.

• *Parallelism.* Multiple systems must be able to operate concurrently while achieving synergism for the enterprise and without imposing on any instance-level transaction a global serialization requirement or similar synchronization mechanism.

• *Autonomy.* Local systems need to have the flexibility to be designed, constructed, and administered independently by the local management, without having to conform, nor later convert, to a global schema.

• *Visualization.* The enterprise information should be represented and presented through intuitive visualization and virtual interface environments that avail the end

160

users of an accessible cyberspace. This interface is essential in order for the system solution to be accepted and utilized by all employees.

An organic architecture clearly needs to be intelligent. Technically speaking, at the very least it needs to possess on-line knowledge enabling it to be dynamically (re-)configured to monitor the underlying processes and adjust itself to respond. With a system using internal knowledge, distributed and synergistic management of the enterprise information environments becomes feasible.

1.1.5 Managing with Ubiquitous Enterprise Metadata

Enterprise information architecture cannot rely on a global controller to manage the widely-distributed, multiple systems it supports. For performance reasons and many other practical as well as theoretical reasons, the architecture must have enough knowledge to sustain and manage itself, with only occasional instructions from distributed enterprise information managers who operate on a management-by-exception basis. The knowledge itself needs to be distributed wherever needed and embedded into the architecture without the users having to know nor to deal with them explicitly. Global information management, processes support, and a cyberspace user interface can utilize this ubiquitous knowledge. On-line knowledge is in essence to what we refer as *enterprise metadata*.

Categories of Enterprise Metadata. The traditional notion of metadata is simply "data about data," or a dictionary and summary for data. This notion is extended to include four categories of knowledge:

- Global Data Models,
- Contextual Knowledge and Processes Models,
- Software, Hardware, and Network Resources Models, and
- Information Users and Organizations Models.

The first two models, Global Data and Contextual Knowledge and Processes, represent the logical contents of enterprise information that characterize dynamic alignments. The last two models, Software, Hardware, and Network Resources and Information Users and Organizations, describe how to physically implement the first two models within an organization.

- *Global Data Models* provide an enterprise-wide, consolidated representation of information resources. They define the basic building blocks of the enterprise information which includes unit data items, the entities and relationships manifested by these data items, and application subjects that encompass these entities and relationships. Examples of Global Data within a factory environment would include part identification (an item), the part itself (an entity), and inventory control (a subject).

- *Contextual Knowledge and Processes Models* abstract the dynamism of alignments, such as work flows, process configurations, information management requirements, operating rules, and mission-critical events. The models also define the semantic and activity contexts of data, software, and users that are not

161

sufficiently represented by the other three categories of models. For example, Contextual Knowledge and Processes within a manufacturing facility would provide an invaluable service: an alert would be triggered for shop floor operators if a part manufacture is at the point when the machining processes need to be changed, another alerts when the inventory of the part is depleted to a certain definable level, and yet another alert would re-route a part design file to design engineers in distant factories.

• *Software and Network Resources Models* define stand-alone and re-usable application programs such as formal conversion routines, applications management systems such as databases, and distributed computing and interface environments such as LANs and virtual reality systems.

• *Information, Users and Organizations Models* distribute enterprise information to its users, application systems, and throughout its organizational contexts. It includes user profiles, the clustering of enterprise information environments or managers, and boundary conditions for individual domains of the extended enterprise. This information architecture is able to support customized use, management and even appearance for differing constituencies and functions. For example, it allows users to tailor their information security, and even give access privileges to teams.

Unified Metadata Model. To support the ubiquitous applications envisioned above, enterprise metadata needs to be represented, processed, and managed in an integrated way. Metadata includes the following characteristics and requirements: (1) the representation method combines data and knowledge models, both of which are present in enterprise metadata; (2) the processing method, coupled with the representation of data, must allow enterprise information architecture to exhibit intelligence, such as that implicit within rule-based configurations and knowledge-based user interfaces; and (3) the management method should satisfy the organic requirements of the architecture (discussed in Section 1.1.4) by supporting, for example, the maintenance of a *logical enterprise layer* independent of its physical systems. This logical layer would span from the shop floor which uses real time control processes to high-level, executive support systems. The logical layer would be implemented and managed through the enterprise metadata.

Basic Applications. The enterprise metadata should be embedded into all key elements of the information architecture. It would be used within all key activities. A partial list of generic, basic applications for information architecture includes:

• *User Interface.* The enterprise metadata, specifically user profiles and contextual knowledge, is a potent source of on-line knowledge to support information visualization for the end users. Cyberspace cannot deliver on its full promise and be beneficial to enterprise users unless it possesses on-line knowledge used to interpret underlying systems and information for users dynamically.

• *Flows Configuration.* Paths and conditions for transferring files and charting work flow within an enterprise need to be "programmable," such as in a rule-based

162

manner. Flow configuration would include a logical layer to network computing environments and application systems. Metadata would help to define the paths and conditions that constitute a logical layer.

• *Global Query.* Enterprise users need specific assistance from system intelligence to surf in cyberspace and retrieve or assemble information residing at single or multiple sources anywhere across the enterprise. Enterprise metadata needs to support the articulation, processing, and presentation of "location" queries for the system to be efficient, effective, and accurate for users.

• *Data Management.* Global data management traditionally required a global synchronizer that was fixed— hard-coded—into its control logic. This design is not amenable to the principle of organic architecture discussed in Section 1.1.4. In lieu of hard-coding a synchronizer, enterprise metadata should be used to provide flexible and distributed control logic.

• *Process Management.* The operating rules, events, and applications or users that define a process can themselves be defined in enterprise metadata terms. As such, it is possible to have a knowledge-based approach dynamically align and manage these management processes, including operation (real-time control) processes and higher level business processes. Data Management logic applies here as well.

• *Network Management.* Similar to Flows Configuration, a logical layer, parallel to the physically networked environments, will allow "virtual networks" to be developed using the same foundational facilities. Enterprise metadata define the logic and establish the parameters and scope of the virtual networks.

• *Global Transactions.* The functions of Global Query and Process Management also support Global Transactions. The same principles can also provide additional support to the complex problems facing global transactions, such as distributed control logic for coordination across multiple systems and recourse rules (back-up, roll-back, security, and the like) that occur under certain dynamic events.

• *System Development.* System planning, analysis, design, implementation, and control are traditionally conducted in a sequential manner and do not involve nor require enterprise information architecture. The development is typically based on information requirements that are determined at a fixed point in time with little regard to continuing evolution. In an information-integrated enterprise, however, distinct boundaries between these stages would no longer exist. The system development function would embody cycles that would require forward and feedback linkages across stages with shortened and overlapping cycle times. As such, the integrated system development functions need to be anchored on-line within enterprise information architecture. With sufficient metadata support, system development can actually be performed continuously in response to the changing requirements of dynamic alignments; thereby becoming a part of the business processes of the enterprise. The walls that divide the system and the process that the system supports are also dismantled.

1.2 ENTERPRISE INFORMATION MANAGEMENT

IT-based enterprises impose additional demands on information integration and management; therefore, all new visions for IT development must be based on the requirements of enterprise IT: organic architecture, multiple systems, and integration technology. The notion of an *enterprise information manager (EIM)* helps reveal the technical challenges. The EIM is a logical global structure that coordinates enterprise IT in order to provide the necessary information integration with which the enterprise achieves synergism. Its physical implementation can, however, be deployed in almost any conceivable way. The simple prototypical EIM sits on top of the enterprise information architecture and manages the multiple, heterogeneous, distributed, and autonomous information systems of the enterprise.

Since dynamic alignment requires dynamic exchange, sharing, and controlling of information stored in files and databases at these systems. The EIM needs to provide three levels of inter-operability among multiple systems: (1) file transfer (or work flow), (2) global query ad hoc inquiry and request, and (3) information (data, knowledge, and processes) management as summarized in Figure 1-1. File transfer is widely understood, and most large-scale integration technology commercially available today is devoted to it. Examples of file transfer would include users of office or personal information systems swapping files between Fox Pro and Lotus 1-2-3, customer order files from Oracle being submitted to Sybase for accounting, and design engineers exchanging CAD files in a concurrent engineering environment. Typically, file transfer is achieved through a custom designed and created Application Protocols Interchange (API) (see Figure 1-2). An API is generally non-reusable. As well, adding a new system to a system based on file exchanges would require writing and compiling a pair of new APIs for each of the existing systems. The situation can multiply very fast, becoming unwieldy even for enterprises that use only a few information systems. A second example of file transfer are work flow management systems that a user can query to retrieve particular information in a fixed and predetermined way.

Although this class of work flow managers comes close to our second level, global query; it tends to have some or all of the following limitations:

- Intelligence of what information is to be had is limited.
- Most available information exists in a format suitable to only a few select users, or rather specific technical knowledge is required to get desired information.
- Current solutions address pre-defined needs as opposed to supporting ad hoc inquiries on a casual basis.
- Systems are not changed easily to either re-configure or support a different process.
- Redundant information exists but accuracy between them is lacking.

Remove these limitations and global query with its level two capabilities results. Commercially available IT does not fully support global query unless the scope of systems is limited to, basically, a Local-Area Networked (LAN) low-volume database system. Figure 1-3 illustrates the need for level two capabilities not satisfied presently.

Level three capabilities of information management are similar to global query in certain functions. Both global query and information management require file transfer and global query capabilities. However, information management goes well beyond retrieving information to undertake the task of managing changes made to data, knowledge, and processes. As in the case of global query, traditional IT has similar limitations for managing such changes that extend beyond LAN environments; for example, the configurations (paths, methods, and contents) of

---

A TRUE ENTERPRISE SYSTEM

Functional requirements for any globally-distributed, enterprise database are three-fold:

1 **FILE TRANSFER**
Application to application read/write compatibility without unwieldy application protocol interchanges;

2 **GLOBAL QUERY**
An enterprise-wide search by a non-technical user returns all threads related to search term;

3 **MANAGING INFORMATION & SYSTEM-LEVEL CHANGES**
Changing data, rules, control, configuration, processes, and systems without down time, inflexible or slow data exchange, or inappropriate locking of shared resources.

Fig. 1-1: Three levels of inter-operability

CURRENT TECHNOLOGY INADEQUACIES OF FILE TRANSFER

APPLICATION PROTOCOAL INTERCHANGE (API) USES COUPLED CONNECTIONS FOR FILE TRANSFER

LOTUS

SYSTEM ADMINISTRATOR
MUST PROVIDE N (N - 1)
APIS TO CONNECT USERS

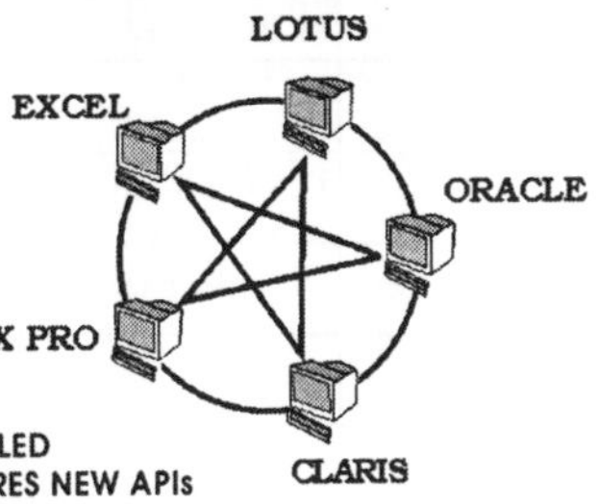

EXCEL

ORACLE

CHARACTERISTICS:

FOX PRO

• APIs CONFIGURED FOR LOCAL USE
• CANNOT BE EXCHANGED OR RECYCLED
• NEW SOFTWARE ACQUISITION REQUIRES NEW APIs

CLARIS

AMOUNT OF CONVERSION WORK IS COMPOUNDED;
FILE EXCHANGES ARE LIMITED FOR PRACTICAL REASONS TO
STABLE, SMALL GROUPS.

Fig. 1-2: Typical file transfer is achieved through APIs.

165

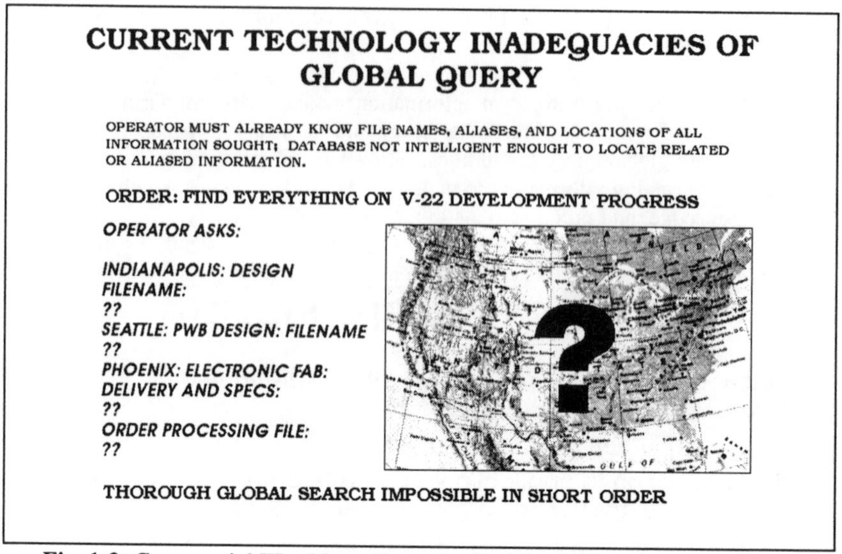

Fig. 1-3: Commercial IT seldom allows for flexible global query capabilities.

Fig. 1-4: Current IT technology cannot manage data or system changes globally.

updates must be fixed. Furthermore, it must shut down the current systems before new systems can be added on-line, or even just to overhaul some parts of the current systems. Figure 1-4 illustrates this situation.

The EIM technology available previously can be analyzed in the above context. The broad-based DAE (Distributed Application Environments) class technology deals with API and other inter-system interface tasks to provide a file transfer level of integration. A prime example is CORBA (Common Object Request Broker Architecture), which supports direct inter-operability for object-oriented systems. CORBA also provides gateway services for these systems to connect with

166

relational or other traditional systems. This class of EIM technology lacks a global model of the enterprise and typically does not include much enterprise metadata (e.g. on-line contextual knowledge) in its inter-system configuration. Methods such as intelligent interfacing agents and rule-based shells are not supported in present commercial solutions, and are left to be implemented by database-class technology. In between DAE and database classes, data warehouse-class EIM's exist, such as IBM's Information Warehouse and Hewlett-Packard's WorkManager. Some limited global query capabilities, as mentioned above, are provided in addition to file transfers. The database-class EIM technology is exemplified by various HDDBMS (Heterogeneous Distributed Database Management Systems) results. While more elegant and complete, commercial HDDBMS's are less robust than the other two classes of EIM technologies; they tend to be limited to LAN environments and cater to low volume transactions. For example, HDDBM's are not amenable to transferring large engineering drawing files across continents. They also lack the ability to dynamically change inter-system processes and intra-system structures, nor can they incrementally build or group systems in the case of adding a new system to an existing HDDBMS environment. All of these gaps in technology are required for dynamic alignment as discussed in Section 1.1.

The value of an Enterprise Information Manager (EIM) that can provide shared access to enterprise data and knowledge through an intuitive graphical visualization system and support distributed and scalable client/server systems, multiple database technologies and legacy systems, can best be illustrated by a specific industrial case. Consider a multi-billion dollar world-wide enterprise whose objective it is to be the marketplace leader through excellence in products and services and superior service to the customer at the lowest industrial cost. Its products include heavy machinery, industrial systems and service activities. This enterprise employs over 30,000, 80% domestically and the remainder overseas. With regard to the necessity for sharing information, consider that there are over 20 manufacturing facilities, over 75 apparatus shops, over 100 sales offices, almost 200 engineering offices and almost 100 business associates/licensees in over 50 countries. A recent internal study uncovered a number of suspected, but not previously known, factors associated with the manner in which information was utilized. The factors they found concerning information usage and flow are completely in agreement with the above discussions concerning EIMs. Minimally speaking, access to required information throughout the business can easily save over five million dollars per year. With 10% usage from a population of 37,000 who work 240 days per year at a savings of only 15 minutes a day, they would easily realize savings in productivity and corresponding cycle reduction of 222,000 hours per year. Additionally, a large proportion of the information access requirements involve at least one other person, thereby multiplying additional opportunities for saving. The minimum base line savings in dollar alone is significant, but still does not recognize the extent of reduced cycle time and additional opportunities created with information integration.

1.3 THE METADATABASE TECHNOLOGY

The **Metadatabase model** is inspired by the principles of organic architecture using enterprise metadata, as discussed in Sections 1.1.4 and 1.1.5. As such, it is poised to support the EIM's dynamic alignment for enterprise integration and modeling. Its structure directly represents the design goal of effecting a logical layer for the enterprise to accomplish information integration. A high level overview is provided in this section that paves the way to the details elaborated in the balance of the book.

The concept of a Metadatabase has a few basic elements. First, it employs the full range of enterprise metadata (see Section 1.1.5) and manages the metadata as an independent, full-fledged database which can be distributed, hence the term Metadatabase. Second, it deploys the inter-system operating knowledge into a concurrent (rule-based) shell system to inter-operate multiple systems at all three levels (see Section 1.2) without requiring, yet allowing for, a global synchronizer.

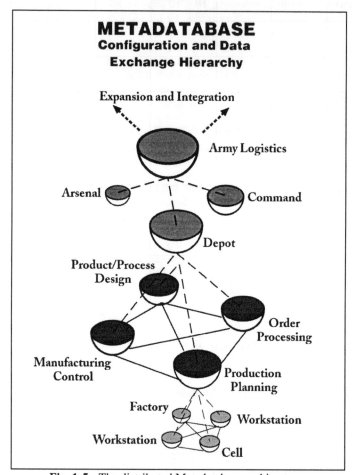

Fig. 1-5: The distributed Metadatabase architecture.

The Metadatabase acts not only as the repository of models but also as the Enterprise Information Manager (EIM), managing directly the enterprise metadata and then using the deployed metadata to indirectly coordinate the operation of local systems. In other words, the Metadatabase embeds the knowledge of all three levels of integration into local environments and allows those local systems to operate with this knowledge thereafter on their own. It intervenes only when the enterprise metadata is changed; for example, when introducing new systems or updating the previous dynamic alignments. In such a case, the Metadatabase EIM will update the peripheral metadatabase(s) and their shells which are distributed into local systems. These tasks are all accomplished on an on-line, non-disruptive, and automated basis.

An Army Logistics example is used below as a scenario to illustrate the proposed metadatabase technology. Figure 1-5 depicts an overview of the distributed Metadatabase architecture. Figures 1-6, 1-7 and 1-8 correspond to Figures 1-2, 1-3, and 1-4. These six figures suggest how the new Metadatabase EIM would improve the inter-operation of multiple systems at all three levels of integration: file transfer, global query, and information management.

Flow of information for Army logistics, which upholds the most rigorous requirements for response time, is literally a matter of life and death. The Army's intricate logistics issues are further compounded by the many kinds of Army entities (ranging from arsenals and depots to commands and bases), that are distributed across wide physical geography. These Army entities may also use a myriad of information systems that may not operate together seamlessly. Decision makers within this distributed environment would like to have access to integrated sources of information representing their own base or depot, as well as the entire distributed Army. They would further like to be able to change this data, have their changes automatically update the entire Army information network, and then have all affected Army processes instantly brought into line. This type of information management is called global query and events control. Having this control would enable a widely distributed enterprise to maneuver its entire heterogeneous operation within days in anticipation of future events, and, upon encountering adverse conditions, to change that course of action immediately. With such information control, changes made on the shop floor of an arsenal or a depot, distribution center, or command level would be registered in real time throughout the entire enterprise structure, eliminating the need for an exceptional communications effort from a central control.

Metadatabase technology would provide a comprehensive linkage between each Army locale, giving personnel the ability to search the global Army environment for particular pieces of data and to control global events. If one were, for instance, performing a search on the status of a weapon system, the search would return the information on the widget development at Arsenal A, the frame manufacture at Depot B, the subcontractor's schedule for the electronics PWB, and the schedule for assembly at Plant C. This information would be drawn in real-time from each Arsenal and Depot connected through the Metadatabase.

The strength of the proposed EIM's global query is matched by its ability to control events from a distance. Personnel may modify data on a global scale, such as would be required in changing the development schedule of the research, prototype, and manufacture of a new weapons system. Normally, changing the development of any distributed effort that involved an enterprise and multiple commercial contractors would begin a cascading effect: one Army arsenal would inform another by telephone until the chain of developers and contractors were informed. Each in turn would have to determine which of their local information systems required updating, locate the databases and implement the changes piecemeal. Finally, each would realign all local development processes to the new schedule to ensure consistency across a

---

FILE TRANSFER USING METADATABASE TECHNOLOGY

APPLICATION PROTOCOL INTERCHANGE (API) IS ALWAYS WRITTEN TO THE GLOBAL METADATABASE REPRESENTATION.

ONE API WRITTEN PER CONNECTION

IF AN API IS WRITTEN FOR FOX PRO, ANY CURRENT OR NEW USER WHO WANTS TO SWAP DATA WITH FOX PRO FROM ANY APPLICATION IN THE MDB CAN USE THE SAME FOXPRO API SIMPLY BY CHANGING THEIR LOCAL DATA EXCHANGE PREFERENCES — NO NEW CODE!

CONVERSION WORK DONE ONLY ONCE WITHIN GLOBAL MDB SYSTEM; AS MDB SYSTEM GROWS, FILE EXCHANGE GROWS MORE FLEXIBLE & SIMPLE.

Fig. 1-6: File Transfer using Metadatabase technology.

GLOBAL QUERY USING METADATABASE TECHNOLOGY

GLOBAL SEARCH STRING: V-22

[MDB RETURNS]
INDIANAPOLIS: DESIGN:
FILENAME: V22AR7.52
WANT TO SEE IT?

SEATTLE: PWB DESIGN:
FILENAME: FBW_B4.DSS

PHOENIX: ELECTRONIC FAB
DELIVERY AND SPECS: JULY 7
ORDER PROCESSING FILE:
LINE6/JULY16/ASDFO9.BO
....

OPERATOR CAN SEARCH FOR STRING IN SPECIFIED MDB REGIONS

GLOBAL SEARCH RESULTS ARE ATTAINABLE BY NON-TECHNICAL USERS

Fig. 1-7: Global Query using Metadatabase technology.

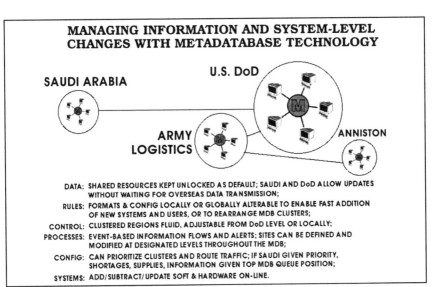

Fig. 1-8: Managing information and system-level changes with Metadatabase technology.

single arsenal or depot. In contrast, the Metadatabase would perform all of these repetitive and error-prone tasks on-line. Personnel (who were given such access privileges) would be able to change the global schedule associated with a particular weapon system in real time, thus simultaneously redirecting all Army efforts with a minimum loss of time in the transition.

Due to its rule-based structure, installation of the Metadatabase does not have to replace existing Army data structures; all depot and arsenal activity would continue undisturbed. However, the Metadatabase would add unique capability on top of current and future depot and arsenal data banks by allowing them to interact as one entity within the Metadatabase. Personnel with Metadatabase "management" access privileges could perform enterprise-wide searches, and modify the returned data to affect future events on a global scale. The Metadatabase is also expandable; its knowledge-based (using enterprise metadata) architecture and structure provides for computing growth within all arsenals and depots. All three types of networks are supported within the Metadatabase environment because of this expandabiltiy: Local Area Networks (LANs) that connect workstations to a server in a single locale, Wide Area Networks (WANs) that operate across regional distances, and single system mainframes. The above scenario represents the development goals of the Metadatabase technology. The major elements are disseminated in chpaters in 7, 8, 9, and 10.

Acknowledgment

Mr. Alan Rubenstein of Rensselaer, Mr. John Manthorp, formerly of GE, and Mr. Jay Lieserson of IBM have given input to the discussions of industrial experiences in Sections 1.1.4 and 1.2. Ms. Tara Rosenberger edited Chapter 1, wrote the Army logistics example included, and created the figures. Ms. Debra Winchell word-processed the text of Chapter 1.

REFERENCES

Alavi, M. and Carlson, P. "A review of MIS research and disciplinary development," *Journal of Management Information Systems* (8:4), 1992, pp. 45-62.

Anthony, Robert, N., *Planning And Control Systems: A Framework For Analysis*, Harvard University Press, Cambridge, Mass., 1965.

Barlow, J.F., "Putting Information Systems Planning Methodologies Into Perspective," *Journal of Systems Management*, July 1990, pp. 6-9.

Battaglia, Greg, "Strategic Information Planning: A Corporate Necessity," *Journal of Systems Management,* February 1991, pp. 23-26.

Battaglia, Greg, Strategic Information Planning: A Corporate Necessity, *Journal of Systems Management*, February 1991, pp. 23-26.

Beath, C.M., and Ives, B., "Competitive Information Systems In Support Of Pricing," *MIS Quarterly*, March 1986, pp. 85-93.

Beath, C.M., and Orlikowski, W., "The Contradictory Structure of Systems Development Methodologies: Deconstructing the IS-User Relationship in Information Engineering," *Information Systems Research*, Vol. 5, No. 4, 1994, pp. 350-377.

Belkin, L., "Computers Cross-Checking Use Of Medicines," *New York Times*, July 1, 1984.

Ben-Aaron, D., "DP Helps FedEx Get It There Overnight," *Information Week*, May 26, 1986, pp. 48-49.

Benjamin, R., and Wigand, R., "Electronic Markets and Virtual Value Chains on the Information Superhighway," *Sloan Management Review*, Winter 1995, pp. 62-72.

Bott, H.s., Passino, J.H., and Hamilton, J., "How To Make A Strategic Move With Information Systems'" *Information Week*, May 26, 1986.

Boyer, E., "Citicorp After Wriston," *Fortune*, July 9, 1984, pp. 146-152.

Bradley, S.P., Hausman, J.A. and Nolan, R.L., *Globalization, Technology and Competition*, Harvard Business School Press, 1993.

Bray, Olin H., *Computer Integrated Manufacturing: The Data Management Strategy,* Digital Press, 1988.

Buday, R., "AHSC On-Line System Ships Supplies ASAP," *Information Week*, May 26, 1986, pp. 35-38.

Buday, R., "Sabre Gives The Edge To American Airlines," *Information Week*, May 26, 1986, pp. 34-35.

Burck, C.G., "Why Merrill Lynch Wants To Sell You A House," *Fortune*, Jan 29, 1979, pp. 86-89.

Burstein, D. and Kline, D., *Road Warriors*, Dutton, USA, 1995.

Business Week, "A Food Suppliers Bigger Bite," *Business Week*, February 22, 1982, pp. 136.

Business Week, "A New Marketing Blitz In The War Of The Plastic Cards," *Business Week*, July 25, 1983, pp. 126-128.

Business Week, "American Express Expands Its Supermarket," *Business Week,* July 25, 1983, pp. 72-73.

Business Week, "Can Don Lennox Save Harvester," *Business Week*, August 15, 1983, pp. 80-84.

Business Week, "Federal Express Wants To Deliver In Space," *Business Week*, July 4, 1983, pp. 42.

Business Week, "Foremost-McKesson: The Computer Moves Distribution To Center Stage," *Business Week*, December 7, 1981, pp. 115-119.

Business Week, "The Golden Plan Of American Express," *Business Week*, April 30, 1984, pp. 118-122

Business Week, "Why Dun And Bradstreet Is Going Off The Air," *Business Week*, July 4, 1983, pp. 72-73.

Business Week, "Why Procter And Gamble Is Playing It Even Together," *Business Week*, July 18, 1983, pp. 176-186.

Business Week, "How Long Can This Last," *Business Week*, May 19, 1997, pp. 30-34.

Business Week, "Can You Make Money On The Net," *Business Week*, September 23, 1996, pp. 104-118.

Business Week, "How Long Can This Last," *Business Week*, May 19, 1997, pp. 30-81.

Business Week, "What Every CEO Needs to Know About Electronic Business: A Survival Guide," *Business Week*, March 22, 1999, pp. EB9-49.

Carter K., "Baxter, GE Develop Hospital Purchasing Network," *Modern Healthcare*, July 17, 1987, p.11.

Chung, C. and L. Krajewski, "Planning Horizons for Master Production Scheduling," *Journal of Operations Management*, August 1984, pp.389-406.

Clemons E.K., and Row, M.C., "A Case Study of Economist - A Strategic Information System," *Proceedings of the Twenty-first Hawaii International Conference on System Sciences*, 1988, pp. 141-149.

Clemons E.K., and Row, M.C., "The Merrill Lynch Cash Account Financial Service: A Case Study In Strategic Information Systems," *Proceedings of the Twenty-first Hawaii International Conference on System Sciences*, 1988, pp. 131-140.

Coase, R. 1937, "The Nature of the Firm", *Economics*, n.s. 4: 386-405. Reprinted in: Coase, R., *The Firm, the Market and the Law*, Chicago: University of Chicago Press, 1988.

Cohen, R.B., "Moving Toward a Non-U.S.-Centric International Internet," Communications of the ACM, Vol.42, No. 6, pp. 37-40.

ComputerWorld, "Sharing IS Secrets," *ComputerWorld,* September 23, 1996.

ComputerWorld, *Premier 100-Making Dollars and Sense out of the Internet*, November 16, 1998.

Cronin, M., *Doing More Business On the Internet*, Van Nostrand Reinhold, 1995. URL:http://www.novalink.com/cronin/

Datamation, "The Web: Open For Business," *Datamation*, December 1, 1995.

Davenport, T.H. & Short, J.E.. "The New Industrial Engineering: Information Technology and Business Process Redesign," *Sloan Management Review*, 1990 summer, pp. 11-27.

Dreyfuss, J., "Reach Out And Sell Something," *Fortune*, May 26, 1984, pp. 127-132.

Economist, "America's Power Plants," *Economist*, June 8, 1996, p.82.

Elden, M. and Chisholm, R.F. "Emerging Varieties of Action Research: Introduction to the Special Issue," Human Relations (46:2), 1993, pp. 121-142.

ESPRIT Consortium AMICE (eds.), *Open System Architecture For CIM*, Springer-Verlag, 1989.

Evans, E. and Rogers, D., "Using JAVA Applets and CORBA for Multi-User Distributed Applications," *IEEE Computer*, May-June 1997, pp. 43-55.

175

Fischer, A.B., "Dow Jones Is Still Better Than Average," *Fortune*, December 24,1984, 38-54.

Fischer, A.B., "The New Game In Health Care: Who Will Profit," *Fortune*, March 4, 1985, pp. 138-143.

Gates, Bill, *The Road Ahead*, New York: Viking, 1995.

Glushko, R.J., Tenenbaum, J.M. and Meltzer, B., "An XML Framework for Agent-Based E-Commerce," *Communications of the ACM*, Vol.42, No.3, 1999, pp. 106-116.

Hammer, M., Champy, J., *Reengineering The Corporation*, Harper Business, 1993.

Hardwick, M., Spooner, D.L., "STEP Mosaic - Sharing STEP Models Across the Internet" Laboratory for Industrial Information Infrastructure Rensselaer Polytechnic Institute Troy, New York 12180. http://www.rdrc.rpi.edu/niiip/NSF96.iita.html.

Harn C., "Citicorp's Interest In ATMs Paid Off," *Information Week*, May 26, 1986, pp. 41-44.

HBS Case "McGraw-Hill Book Company: Microcomputer Resource Center," *HBS Case*, 182-017, 1981.

HBS Case "United Airlines," *HBS Case*, 9-184-083, 1984.

Hoffman, T. and Nask, K.S., "Titanic tangle: Integration Thorns May Puncture Citigroup's Plans," *ComputerWorld*, April 13, 1998, pp. 1, 94-95.

Hofmann, W. and Hsu, C., "The Value of Information: An Evaluation Model for Enterprise Integration Using Transaction Cost and Information Requirements Analysis," *Selected Essays on Decision Sciences*, The Chinese University of Hong Kong Press, 1993, pp. 1-19.

Hsu, C. and Tuan, C., "An Information-Theoretic Approach to the Determination of Organization Structure: a Framework," *Business Management Review*, Vol.1, No.3, 1983, pp.129-151.

Hsu, C. and Skevington, C., "Integration of Data and Knowledge Management in Computerized Manufacturing Systems," *Journal of Manufacturing Systems*, Vol.6, No.4, 1987, pp. 277-285.

Hsu, C. and Rattner, L., "Information Modeling for Computerized Manufacturing," IEEE Transactions on Systems, Man, and Cybernetics," Vol.20, No.4, 1990, pp. 758-776.

Hsu, C., Bouziane, M., Rattner, L. and Yee, L., "Information Resources Management in Heterogeneous Distributed Environments: A Metadatabase Approach," IEEE Transactions on Software Engineering, Vol.17, No.6, 1991, pp.604-625.

Hsu, C., *Enterprise Integration and Modeling: The Metadatabase Approach*, Kluwer Academic Publishers, 1996.

Huitema, C. Cameron, J., Mouchtaris, P. and Smyk, D., "An Architecture for Residential Internet Telephone Service," *IEEE Internet Computing*, May-June, 1999, pp. 73-82.

Information Week, "Agreement Connects Mead Databases To IBM Hardware," *Information Week*, July 11, 1983.

Information Week, "Uncertainty A Thing Of The Past," *Information Week*, December 9, 1996.

Integrated Computer-Aided Manufacturing (ICAM), *Architecture PART III/Volume VI: Composite Information Model of 'Manufacture Product* (MFG1), AFWAL-TR-82-4063 Vol. VI, Wright-Patterson AFB, OH, 45433, Sept. 1983.

Kalakota, R. and Whinston, A., *A Manager's Guide*, Addison-Wesley, 1996

Kaplan, B. and Maxwell, J.A., "Qualitative Research Methods for Evaluating Computer Information Systems," in *Evaluating Health Care Information Systems: Methods and Applications*, J.G. Anderson, C.E. Aydin and S.J. Jay (eds.), Sage, Thousand Oaks, CA, 1994, pp. 45-68.

Keen, P.G.W., "Information Technology and the Measurement Difference: A Fusion Map," *IBM Systems Journal*, Vol. 32, No. 1, 1993.

Kling, A., "The Econoomic Consequences of WWW," *Electronic Proceedings of the Second World Wide Web Conference, 1994.*

Labich, K., "Toys R Us Moves In On Kiddie Couture," *Fortune*, November 26, 1984, p. 135.

Lange, L., "The Internet: Technology Analysis and Forecast," *IEEE Spectrum*, January 1999, pp. 35-40.

Lederer, A.L., and Sethi, V., "The Implementation of Strategic Information Systems Planning Methodologies," *MIS Quarterly*, Vol. 12, No. 3, September 1988, pp. 445-460.

Lewis, T., "Why the Economy Is So Good," *IEEE Computer*, May-June 1998, pp. 110-112.

Louis, A.M., "Does Gannett Pay Too Much," *Fortune*, September 15, 1986, pp. 59-64.

Lucas, H.C. Jr., *Information Technology and the Productivity paradox: Assessing the Value of Investing in IT*, Oxford University Press, 1999.

McFarlan, F.W., "Information Technology Changes the Way You Compete," *Harvard Business Review*, May-June 1984, pp. 98-105.

McFarlan, F.W., McKenney, J.L., Pyburn, P., "The Information Archiptelago - Plotting the Course'" *Harvard Business Review*, January-February, 1983.

McKinsey Global Institute, *Capital Productivity*, McKinsey Global Institute, June 1996.

McNurlin, B.C. and Sprague, R.H.Jr., *Information Systems Management in Practice*, Prentice-Hall, 1998.

Mueller, M., "Commentary: ICANN and Internet Regulation," Communications of the ACM, Vol. 42, No. 6, 1999, pp. 41-43.

Newcomb, P., Web-Based Business Process Reengineering, *IEEE Software*, November 1995, pp. 116-118.

New York Times, "High Technology for Money Management," New York Times, July 12, 1999.

O'Keefe, R., Marketing and Retail on the World Wide Web: The New Gold Rush. URL:http://www.rpi.edu/~okeefe/nikkei.html

Oliphant, M.W., "The Mobile Phone Meets the Internet," IEEE Spectrum, August 1999, pp. 20-28.

Orlikowski, W.J. & Baroudi, J.J. "Studying Information Technology in Organizations: Research Approaches and Assumptions", *Information Systems Research* (2) 1991, pp. 1-28.

Pant, S., *Internet Enterprises Planning*, unpublished doctoral dissertation, School of Management, Rensselaer Polytechnic Institute, Troy, NY 1997.

Pant, S. and Hsu, C., "Strategic Information Systems Planning: A Review," *Proceedings Information Resources Management Association International Conference*, May 21-24, 1995, Atlanta, Georgia .

Pant, S. and Hsu, C., "An Integrated Framework For Strategic Information Systems Planning And Development," *Information Resources Management Journal*, Vol.12, No.1, 1998, pp. 15-25.

Pant, S., and Ruff, L., "Issues in Economic Justification for Flexible Manufacturing Systems and Some Guidelines for Managers," *Information Resources Management Journal*, Vol. 8, No. 1, winter 1995, pp. 26-34.

Pant, S., Rattner, L., and Hsu, C., "Manufacturing Information Integration Using a Reference Model," *International Journal of Operations and Production Management,* Vol.14, No.11, 1994.

Parsons, G.L., "Information Technology: A New Competitive Weapon," *Sloan Management Review*.

Parvi, F., and Ang, J., " A Study of the Strategic Planning Practices in Singapore," *Information & Management*, Vol. 28, No.1, January 1995, pp. 33-47.

Porter, M.E. and Millar, V.E., How Information Gives You Competitive Advantage, *Harvard Business Review*, July-August, 1985.

Porter, M.E., *Competitive Advantage*, Free Press, 1984.

Rayport, J., and Svikola, J., "Exploiting the Virtual Value Chain," *Harvard Business Review*, November-December, 1995, pp. 75-85.

Rouse, W.B., and Howard, C.W., "Software Tools For Supporting Planning," *Industrial Engineering*, June 1993, pp. 51-53.

Schindler, P.E.Jr., "USAA Insures Success With Data Processing," *Information Week*, May 26, 1986, pp. 56-57.

Schlueter, C. and Shaw, M.J., "A Strategic Framework for Developing Electronic Commerce," *IEEE Internet Computing*, November-December 1997, pp. 20-28.

Siegel, J., "A Preview of CORBA 3," *IEEE Computer*, May 1999, pp. 114-116.

Sipper, M., "The Emergence of Cellular Computing," *IEEE Computer*, July 1999, pp. 18-26.

Strassman, P.A., *Information Pay-Off: The Transformation of Work in the Electronic Age*, New York: Free Press, London: Collier Macmillan, 1985.

Takahashi, K., and Liang, E., "Analysis and Design of Web-based Information Systems," *Proceedings 6th International World Wide Web Conference,* April 7-11, 1997, Santa Clara, California.

The Wall Street Journal, "Reuter Announces Sale Of 28% Of Equity To British And American Investors," *The Wall Street Journal,* May 16, 1984, p. 37.

The Wall Street Journal, "Xerox Takes New Marketing Tack To Improve Poor Customer Sales," *The Wall Street Journal,* May 9, 1984, p. 31.

Treese, G.W. and Stewart, L.C., *Designing Systems for Internet Commerce*, Addison-Wesley, 1998.

URL:http://www.ncsa.uiuc.edu/SDG/IT94/Proceedings/ComEc/kling/webeconc.html

Vernadat, F., "Modeling CIM Enterprises with CIM-OSA," *Proceedings 2nd International Conference on CIM*, IEEE Computer Society Press, 1990, pp. 236-243.

Vetter, R., "Web-Based Enterprise Computing," *IEEE Computer*, May 1999, pp. 112-113.

Vitale, M., Ives, B. and Beath, C., "Identifying Strategic Information Systems," *Proceedings. 7th Int'l Conference on Information Systems*, San Diego, December 1986, pp. 265-276.

Walsham, G. *Interpreting Information Systems in Organizations*, Wiley, Chichester, 1993.

Ward, John, Griffiths, Pat and Whitmore, Paul, *Strategic Planning for Information Systems*, John Wiley & Sons, 1990.

Westland, C. and Clark, E., *Global Electronic Commerce: Theory and Cases*, MIT Press, 1999.

Williamson, O., *The Economic Institutions of Capitalism: Firms, Markets, Relational Contracting*. New York: Free Press, 1985.

Wiseman, C, *Strategy and Computers: Information Systems As Competitive Weapons*, Dow Jones - Irwin, 1985.

Yin, R.K., *Case Study Research, Design and Methods*, 2nd ed. Newbury Park, Sage Publications, 1994.

INDEX

182